Music
Methods
for the
Elementary
School
Teacher

BRINGING MUSIC TO CHILDREN

Harper
&
Row

Lloyd H. Slind and **D. Evan Davis**

BRINGING MUSIC
TO CHILDREN

BRINGING MUSIC TO CHILDREN

Music Methods for the Elementary School Teacher

LLOYD H. SLIND
D. EVAN DAVIS

Associate Professors
University of British Columbia

HARPER & ROW, Publishers
New York, Evanston, and London

CONTENTS

PART I. Learning from the Sounds of Music Around Us

PART II. A Way of Looking at Music: The Printed Score

Preface

For those who believe that all children can be taught to understand and re-spond to music while learning the functional skills, this work is written.

It is designed to serve classroom teachers and prospective teachers in their understanding of the fundamentals of music, and to elucidate methodologies for involving children in musical discoveries and for helping their development.

D. Evan Davis
Lloyd H. Slind

Note to the Student

The student is advised to complete the Pointers and Practice questions found at the end of each chapter. These may be removed from the text and turned in for checking or marking.

PART I
Learning from the Sounds
of Music Around Us

INTRODUCTION

Most elementary classroom teachers, and teachers in training, want to see that the children entrusted to them are not denied the refreshment and growth which music can provide. These teachers believe the dicta of great personalities throughout the ages who ascribe the highest educational significance to musical pursuits because music has spoken to them in its own mystic, intangible way—as it has to all humans in all ages (and interestingly, of all the vast animal kingdom, apparently only to humans) wherever man has relaxed his frenzied pursuit of material advantage long enough to listen and to create. Yet many of these teachers labor through the required music-methods courses in a state of anxiety, even bordering on hysteria at examination time.

Among other things, music is—as the Music Educators National Conference proposed in its theme for the 1962 biennial convention—"an academic discipline," with skills and thought patterns of its own. Without an elementary mastery of these skills and thought patterns the educational and enjoyment values in music activity are but dimly experienced. The testimony of hundreds of elementary teachers across the continent is that these skills and thought patterns can be developed in even the so-called "nonmusical" adult, that the doors to life-long growth through music have been opened to them and hence to their children, and that music is an invaluable aid to daily life in the classroom. Many other elementary teachers assume that musical habits and responses are neither teachable nor learnable, and they go into the classrooms fearing music, feeling guilty and occasionally belligerent toward the subject, and withal, keeping the doors to musical enjoyment, participation, and education securely closed to the children entrusted to them.

The explanation is not in the folk superstition of a magical endowment called "talent," bestowed upon the fortunate few and withheld from the many. It has been wisely said: "A musician is not a special kind of person. Rather, every

1

person is a special kind of musician." The critical point of difference between the two types of teachers mentioned above is that one group, working constructively to build within themselves new behavior responses, has "stirred up the gift" within them as admonished by the Apostle Paul, has come alive to music in terms of the ability to think, create, and respond to rhythm, pitch, harmony; while the other group, unwilling to venture forth to develop new perceptive tools and powers, has remained inert and unresponsive. The achievement of excellence may be reserved for the few, but the ability to function is within any person of teacher caliber.

As in arithmetic numbers do not teach quantitative and comparative thinking but symbolize quantitative and comparative thought patterns previously gained by experience with counting, measuring, and computing, so in music, notation does not teach rhythmic, melodic and harmonic thinking, but symbolizes musical thought and feeling previously gained by experience with rhythmic movement, vocal expression, manipulating of instruments, and listening.*

Our concern in elementary music is first to provide varied and deliberate experiences in music-making and listening, made meaningful by concurrent attention to the fundamental patterns of sounds being experienced. The teacher must involve himself in simple but varied musical activities and through it develop the ability to recognize, respond to, and think musical patterns.

Some teachers, instinctively rebelling at the sterile "teach-them-to-read-notes" goal of music, have substituted a nondescript "sing-songs-purely-for-enjoyment" program. Between these extremes, and actually transcending both, lies the desired course. We wish to involve children in listening to and making their own music—continuing the exploration of vocal and instrumental sounds begun as babes in the cradle, cooing or crying, striking rattles or banging the crib walls. In many homes a premium is early placed on one type of vocal utterance to the exclusion of all others: that which leads to speech and language. All else in this wonderful natural world of sound is rejected, discouraged, or stoically tolerated. In school it becomes the teacher's privilege to rekindle this native desire to explore sound and movement and to express oneself through them.

The elementary teacher or trainee who studies this book must realize that no textbook can provide him with actual, essential musical-sound experiences. It is possible, however, to involve the conscientious student in simple rhythmic movement in his own study room, to teach him to think through certain tonal patterns as found in familiar songs, and through his own "inner ear" or auditory introspection to begin to develop musical thinking. Just as we can learn to perceive a mental visual image of a square, a spiral, or of a figure-eight, so can we learn to develop a mental auditory image of a running rhythm, a minor scale, or of a pulse-accent pattern of threes. The essential condition is that the student project himself into that thinking activity, and that as a teacher he help children to think about and to consider musical ideas. Indeed, is this not actually the goal in all subject teaching? Should it be less so with music? This becomes the challenge and responsibility thrown to the student of this book: to read it musically, with inner ears, and not just verbally with the eyes.

The typical elementary music education textbook emphasizes musical content, on the one hand, and teaching on the other. Years of experience in classrooms with student teachers has convinced the present authors that many students have

---

*It is regrettable that in our culture so much importance is given to notation that even the paper printed with notes on a staff is referred to as "music." Despite common practice, this has no more validity than calling the architect's blueprints a cathedral.

2

difficulty translating content and philosophy into practice. As one writer puts it, "We lift our student teachers high in the clouds of soaring thought and then give them no parachute with which to return to earth and reality." In Part I of this book you will look in on a class of children and see how a musically untrained elementary school teacher brought fundamental music experiences to herself and to her children. You will learn with them as you try out the same activities, and at the same time you will see how principles of educational psychology are applied. These basic principles are valid for any class at any grade level. Part II will help you to carry on in the upper grades when you, and they, have developed past the basic concepts of Part I and are ready to use staff notation easily.

Read each chapter of Part I at least twice: the first time to <u>do</u> the activities and gain the skills along with the children and to apply the practice materials at the end of each chapter; the second time to study the methods by which the teacher involved her class in music and to respond to the questions raised in the pointers at the end of each chapter.

One explanation needs to be made. For expediency, the first three chapters emphasize rhythm, pitch, harmony, in a mutually exclusive fashion. In Chapter 4 we begin to see the <u>preferred</u> balance of listening, moving to music, singing, and playing of instruments, all highlighting interesting features which are inherent in the song itself. After all, to paraphrase Hamlet, "The song's the thing!"

1

BECOMING AWARE OF
RHYTHM, PULSE,
AND ACCENT

Pulse and Rhythm in Language

Miss Johnson sat in the empty classroom making the final entries of the spelling tests for her class.

TIC-tok . . . TIC-tok . . . TIC-tok

The large clock on the wall sounded loud in the empty room as she mused absently over the names in the roll before her.

AN-drews . . . AN-drews . . . JIM-my . . . AN-drews

TIC-tok . . . TIC-tok . . . TIC-tok . . . TIC-tok
AN -drews   AN -drews   JIM-my   AN -drews

Casually her eye caught the next entry and she smiled:

TIC-tok . . . TIC-tok . . . TIC-tok . . . TIC-tok
AR -cher   AR -cher   HEN-ry   AR -cher

Purposefully she examined the next name:

TIC -tok . . . TIC-tok
JOHN Ber - GEN-strom

No, that didn't fit at all, but look . . .

5

```
TIC  -tok  . . .TIC  -tok  . . .TIC  -tok  . . .TIC  -tok
BUSH-man      BUSH-man      STAN-ley      BUSH-man
```

The children would enjoy this. . . .

The children _did_ enjoy their exploration of rhythm the next day. They listed on the board all the class members who belonged to that rhythm family. Bill Smithson was quite put out that he was not related to his TIC-tok pals, HEN-ry ARCH-er and STAN-ley BUSH-man—until suddenly he could hardly contain himself. Making a concession he would never ordinarily have considered, he tried out his full name, "Willis," and that's what excited him:

```
TIC   -tok  . . .TIC   -tok  . . .TIC-tok  . . . TIC   -tok
SMITH-son       SMITH-son       WIL-lis      SMITH-son
```

He fitted!

And then there was John; he just could not squeeze in even if he tried calling himself "Jack" or "Johnnie." A last name like "Bergenstrom" was too much for TIC-tok—until after recess. John came in, in excitement. "I've _got_ it. Listen!"

```
TIC-tok  . . .TIC -tok       . . .TIC-tok  . . .TIC -tok
JO -ohn      BER-gen-strom   JO -ohn      BER-gen-strom
```

"Now do I fit?"

"You bet you do, John. Maybe not a brother, but even better, a favorite cousin!"

That discovery opened the door to the other "shut-outs." And when music time came the next day all the children (with a little help from the class for Beverly Hemingway and Carroll Smith*) could fit their names against the TIC-tok TIC-tok pulse of the clock.

Within a week the children had a game they played with each other and which they found particularly suited to jumping rope and similar rhythmic movement:

```
Question:  TIC -  tok  TIC  -   tok    HEL - lo  WHAT'S your name?
Answer:    BEV-er-ly   HEM -ing-way    TIC - tok  TIC - tok.
Question:  TIC - tok   TIC  -   tok    WHEN'S your BIRTH -day?
Answer:    FEB-ru-ar-y TWEN-ty Sec-ond TIC - tok  TIC - tok.
```

With endless variations the new fad swept the school. Instead of introducing each question with TIC-tok some children would tap the TIC-tok pulse with a pencil on a book, or desk, or lunch pail, or (it must be admitted) even on the head of a friend—on the playground of course. Then one teacher brought finger castanets made from two halves of a walnut shell strung with a rubber band and worn on thumb and middle finger:

```
*TIC  -  tok . . .  TIC  -   tok   TIC - tok . . .  TIC-tok
  BEV-er-ly         HEM-ing-way    CAR-roll         SMI-ith
```

6

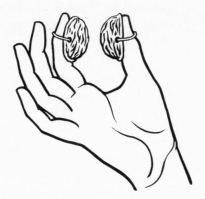

This gave the game a new dimension; <u>instruments</u> were added:

In Miss Johnson's room the class would divide, with perhaps the "shakers" playing the steady <u>TIC-tok</u> pulse, the "strikers" playing the word rhythms. It was inevitable that in geography class somebody would spot the <u>TIC-tok</u> in LON-don, ENG-land. Then, writing on the chalkboard all the countries and cities the children could name, they explored them rhythmically, one group keeping the steady pulse, the other ticking the word rhythms:

London, England   Rome, Italy
Paris, France   Hamburg, Germany

So that "eye could help ear" for the slower learner, they would indicate the <u>TIC-toks</u> with check marks:

Lon-don, Eng-land   Rome,   It-a-ly
√   √   √   √   √   √   √   √
Par-is,   France   Ham-burg, Ger-man-y
√   √   √   √   √   √   √   √

Thus "France" took two pulses: TIC - tok / FRA - ance', and with "Italy" two syllables came on one pulse: $\begin{matrix}\text{TIC-tok}\\\text{IT-a-ly}\end{matrix}$. Therefore these latter were circled to show "two-on-a-pulse":

LON . . . don	ENG . . . land
PAR . . . is	FRA . . . ance
RO . . . ome	IT -a -ly
HAM . . . burg	GER-man-y*

By this time the music supervisor for the school could no longer ignore the "facts of music life." So he pointed out that in most music the steady TIC-tok pulse the children now felt so well was symbolized by the quarter note ♩: two-on-a-pulse was shown by the eighth-note ♫ ; two-pulse sounds like FRA-ance were shown by the half note ♩, or as played by rhythm instruments incapable of sustaining pitch (tap-wait) by a quarter note plus a quarter rest ♩ ♩. He challenged them to rewrite the geography rhythms and their own names (secret rhythm signatures) in regular rhythm notation:

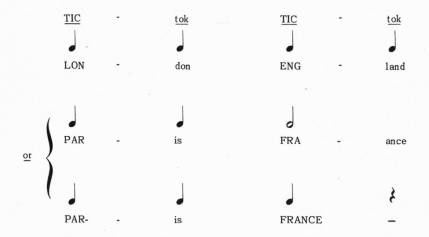

---

*FRA-ance and RO-ome caused a problem in that when they were divided into two syllables some children wanted to tap them twice on instruments instead of tapping once and then waiting the second pulse:

FRA - ance	RO - ome
TAP wait	TAP wait

To overcome this the word was written with a dash to show it needed two pulses:

France —	Rome —
TAP wait	TAP wait

even though in saying it we sustain the chant for two pulses:

FRA-ance and Ro-ome.

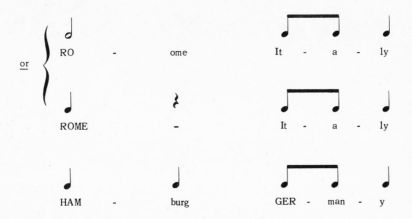

As an added surprise for the music supervisor's next visit, Miss Johnson helped them to get at the rhythmic meaning of a new song from notation. The supervisor was so pleased with their mastery of rhythm that he promised to help them learn to understand tune notation too. How proud JO-ohn BER-gen-strom was to discover that he had the only music code signature using all three kinds of notes:

He also began to be a self-appointed expert in anything the class studied about:

Drum Talk and Movement

One day when the class had assembled in the gym for physical education, Miss Johnson held up her hand for silence. Then, reaching behind the piano, she drew forth—a drum, a real Indian tom-tom!

"Who would like to play the drum?"

Miss Johnson noticed that Ralph de Groot, the retiring immigrant boy who had joined the class just after Christmas, raised his hand with the others, and she gave the tom-tom to him. He accepted questioningly as though wanting directions.

"There's no 'right' or 'wrong' in this, Ralph; just strike it any way you wish."

Softly, timidly, the sound began, Thup, thup, thup, thup. Obvious disappointment showed in some children's faces, and Ralph was ready to quit, for he had not made the kind of drum sound both he and the class expected.

"Can you make it do that again, Ralph, while we try to decide what it sounds like?"

Ralph took heart. He could surely do that again. Marie said it sounded like water dripping on a sponge. Could we make it sound like water dripping on an upside-down saucepan? The drops would bounce, someone suggested. Ralph knew he could bounce his drumstick, so he tried that.

DUM . . . dum . . . DUM . . . dum . . . the somber, mysterious tone reverberated. All the children wanted to play.

"Marie, will you walk around the court? . . . Who can play walking sounds to match Marie's footsteps?" continued Miss Johnson. Several children tried while Marie walked.

"Music can tell us WALK-walk WALK-walk just as the clock tells us TIC-tok TIC-tok, can't it? Everybody make the clock noise and listen to what I play on the drum."

Voices: TIC - tok   TIC - tok
Drum: Dum-da Dum-da Dum-da Dum-da

Four children tried. Shirley's beat seemed to fit best with an even

TIC - tok   TIC - tok
run-run run-run run-run run-run

All the girls tried it; then all the boys tried. Many were able the first time to match their running steps to the drumbeats.

"Well! Our drum has told us to WALK walk, WALK walk and to RUN-run, Run-run. What does this tell your feet to do?"

TIC - tok   TIC - tok
Drum: TUM - ta TUM - ta TUM - ta TUM - ta

Bernie said it went Walk-run, Walk-run. Five other children agreed with him. Miss Johnson let them try it to the drumbeat, but they found it awkward and had trouble keeping balance. Milton said he could skip to it. Others nodded, so Miss Johnson let them try skipping. It worked easily:

TIC - tok   TIC - tok
SKIP-ty SKIP-ty SKIP-ty SKIP-ty

Everyone tried making his feet match the drumbeat with free, easy skipping. To end the period, Miss Johnson mixed the patterns, about thirty seconds each for Walk, walk, walk, walk, for run-run, run-run, run-run, run-run, and for Skip-ty, skip-ty, skip-ty, skip-ty, and she promised more movement rhythm on Thursday.

Associating Rhythm Symbols with Movement

Behind the scenes Miss Johnson and the music supervisor were working together so that when the supervisor—or more appropriately now, the music consultant—came again he had a set of flash cards and a visual rhythm board.*

---

* The visual rhythm board is available commercially under the registered trade name "Rhyth-o-meter" from: Peripole, Inc., 51-17 Rockaway Beach Blvd., Far Rockaway 91, L.I., N.Y.; Empire Music Company, 934 12th St., New Westminster, B.C., Canada.

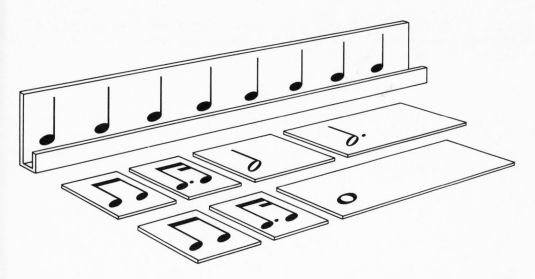

Under student leadership the children demonstrated to him the rhythms they had learned. The consultant in turn showed them, by displaying the flash cards from the visual rhythm board, that each movement has a corresponding symbol in music notation. In fact the children were able to identify walking, running, and skipping notation correctly merely because, as one child observed, "They look the way they sound and feel." Then they practiced chanting the rhythms and stepping them out and playing them on instruments as Miss Johnson held up the symbols on the Rhyth-o-meter flash cards.

Games were invented where one child would tap a pattern repeatedly while another would step out the pattern he was hearing and then go forward and point to the appropriate flash-card symbol which represented that movement. Later, spell-downs were popular. A student would build a rhythm pattern on the Rhyth-o-meter by placing a skip-ty, a run-run, a slo-ow, a slo-o-ow, or a slo-o-o-ow flash card over appropriate walk note pulses. Then he would tap the pattern, for example:

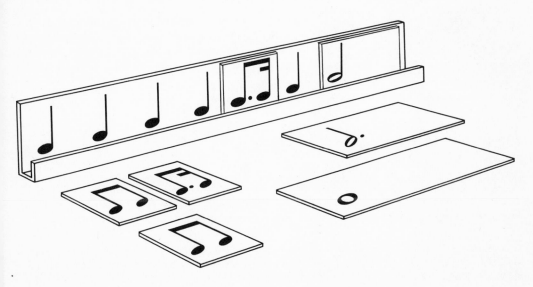

A child in Team One would answer by:

1. Tapping the same pattern.
2. Saying the pattern in rhythm on "tah."
3. Chanting it with the proper movement values, as for example:

<u>Walk</u> walk walk walk <u>skip-ty</u> walk <u>slo-ow</u>

If he missed, he had a chance to step it out in the aisle, and this activity would usually help him to discover the movement. By this time a child in Team Two would have the pattern correctly written at the chalkboard, comparing it with the pattern built previously on the Rhyth-o-meter.

Pulse Accent and Its Notation

One time when the children were reading poetry in their silent reading lesson, Miss Johnson noticed several people tapping lightly to the rhythm and she smiled with satisfaction. Then she noticed Carroll Smith. Carroll not only was tapping, but was alternating a gentle slap of his hand with a tap of his forefinger. "He is finding the accent of the meter," she thought.

When Miss Johnson told them what she had observed, they all wanted to try Carroll's way of <u>slap-tap</u>. After a moment of experimenting, they read aloud Longfellow's "The Song of Life." Miss Johnson wrote the first two lines on the board:

> Tell me not in mournful numbers
> Life is but an empty dream.

To differentiate the strong and weak pulses she had them clap their hands, palms down, on the desk for the strong beat, then snap their fingers in the air for the weak pulse as they read. Someone immediately asked if they could use rhythm instruments. Soon the louder instruments were playing the strong pulse and the softer instruments were playing the weak pulse as the children chanted. Then Miss Johnson underlined on the board the places where the strong instruments were playing:

> <u>Tell</u> me not in <u>mournful</u> numbers
> <u>Life</u> is but an <u>empty</u> dream.

When the music consultant heard of these latest activities, he showed them that music does the same thing. Instead of underlining the strong pulse, however, the children discovered by singing, moving to, and observing the notation to familiar songs that music notation puts a vertical bar-line before the accented syllables:

> |Tell me not in|mournful numbers
> |Life is but an|empty dream.

They found that a composer helps them to understand his musical idea by giving a preparatory instruction in the meter signature at the start of the piece. In

12

Longfellow's poem above a composer would advise the music reader that the song he was about to read moves in twos (i.e., strong-weak). Two what? Two walk pulses! And since the walk is being represented by a quarter note he writes "two quarters": $\frac{2}{4}$.

"Doesn't all music move in 'strong-weak' pulse patterns?" Meredith wanted to know.

"That's a fair question. Let's see if we can find out. Name one of your favorite songs."

"Clementine," was the suggestion.

The class tapped the desk in a walk pulse. The consultant hummed up and down the tonic chord and they began to sing: "In a cavern, in a canyon, excavating for a mine . . ." Gradually a strong, regularly recurring pulse accent began to emerge from the steady pulse tapping. The children followed the consultant's lead into a slap-snap-snap pattern, and he began sketching the pattern on the chalkboard:

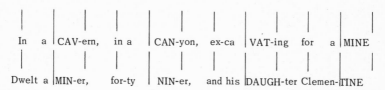

"Now, do all songs move in twos, Meredith? Right! This one at least swings in threes. Notice the pattern?" he asked. " 'Mine' gets two pulses, doesn't it? And 'In a' both come on the one pulse, don't they? What kind of notes will represent two-on-a-pulse?"

Together the class worked out the pattern:

Three-on-a-Pulse and Compound Meter

The consultant left the remainder of the activity in the hands of Miss Johnson. Together teacher and class discovered the pulse-accent pattern of: "Alouette, Gentille Alouette," "Swing Low, Sweet Chariot," "God Save Our Gracious Queen" ("My Country, 'Tis of Thee").

John Bergenstrom, being early an expert on SLO-ow run-run walk patterns, was always finding new rhythms to dissect. Then came that day when the class was singing "Row, Row, Row Your Boat" and John's hand shot up:

"Miss Johnson, I've got that song figured out all except the mer-ri-lys."

"Write it on the board, John, as far as you've worked it out."

<pre>
WALK Walk SKIP-ty   Walk SKIP-ty Skip - ty SLO-ow
ROW   Row   ROW your Boat GENT-ly Down the   STRE-eam

                                   SKIP-ty Skip-ty SLO-ow
MER-ri-ly Mer-ri-ly MER-ri-ly Mer-ri-ly LIFE is But a DRE-eam
</pre>

The class tried it over several times. Miss Johnson noted that the ta-ta-tas felt as though they happened three-on-a-pulse.

<pre>
TA -ta-ta Ta -ta-ta TA -ta-ta Ta -ta-ta SKIP-ty Skip-ty SLO-ow
MER-ri-ly Mer-ri-ly MER-ri-ly Mer-ri-ly LIFE is But a   DRE-eam
</pre>

Some children tried to "step out" the troublesome spot. Henry Archer decided it went:

<pre>
RUN-run-run Run-run-run RUN-run-run Run-run-run SKIP-ty Skip-ty SLO-ow
MER-ri -ly   Mer-ri -ly   MER-ri -ly   Mer-ri -ly   LIFE is But a   DRE-eam
</pre>

"That's certainly the way it sounds, looks, and feels, Henry, but I really don't know. Let's ask the music supervisor what he'd call it," said Miss Johnson, candidly acknowledging her need for help.

The following day the children reviewed the problem with him.

"Well," he said, after thinking it over, "there are no rules to cover this the way you folks are approaching it, but from a notational point of view Henry's answer is about the best. We know that a walk ordinarily breaks down into two-on-a-beat (run-run). And in music 'merrily' is written with three eighth-notes

♪ ♪ ♪ but since we're crowding three-on-a-pulse where only two belong, we need special permission to put three. Hence under these three eighth-notes you'll

find a special figure '3' and a curve joining them on one pulse ♪ ♪ ♪. That being the case, our song would look like":

MER - ri - ly Mer - ri - ly | MER - ri - ly Mer - ri - ly | LIFE is But   a   DRE-eam

"Now, about a name for it," the supervisor continued. "I think we ought to save run-run for what it is—'even-Steven' partners, two-on-a-pulse:

PART - ner   Part - ner   EV - en   Stev - en

Among musicians the three-on-a-pulse is called a triplet rhythm."

"Why don't they call it tri-ple-it?" asked Marie. "Then it would sound like ta-ta-ta when you say it."

"Fine idea, Marie. Let's try it that way ourselves."
The children then sang the song with their new understanding of the rhythm:

```
WALK Walk |SKIP-ty    Walk |SKIP -ty Skip -ty |SLO -ow
ROW  Row  |ROW your Boat |GENT-ly Down the |STRE-eam
```

```
|TRI -ple-it  Tri-ple-it |TRI -ple-it  Tri-ple-it |SKIP-ty Skip-ty |SLO-ow
|MER-ri -ly Mer-ri -ly |MER-ri -ly Mer-ri -ly |LIFE is But a |DRE-eam
```

"By the way, you young folks are right on the border of a new discovery. I can't stay longer today, but Miss Johnson can be your guide in this new exploration."

Since there was a movie, Rhythm Is Everywhere,* scheduled for the following day, Miss Johnson had to delay the new work. The day after that, however, the class would be put off no longer.

"All right, you rhythm explorers, here we go into a new land of discovery. As we sing 'Little Tom Tinker' I want all of you to notice, as John did in the rowing song, just what kind of rhythms there are."

The class sang, and before they had finished the whole group had noticed the many tri-ple-its it contained:

```
|TRI-ple-it    Tri-ple-it |TRI -     ple-it Tri- ple-it
|LIT-tle  Tom  Tin-ker got|BURNED by a Clin-ker and
```

```
|SKIP-ty  Skip-ty |SLO -ow
|HE    be-Gan -to |CRY-y
```

```
|WALK walk|WALK walk|TRI- ple-it  Tri-ple-it |SLO-ow ||
|MA - a!  |MA - a!  |POOR lit -tle In-no-cent|GUY-uy ||
```

"If we wrote that song in notes, almost every phrase would have to have that 'special-permission' three-on-a-pulse, wouldn't it?"

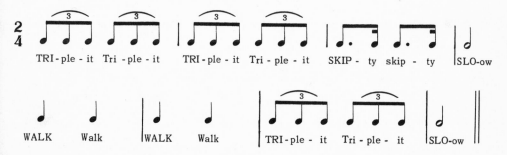

"Look at the notation to the song in your books and see if you can find something at the very start of the song which warns us that our pulse notes will break into three-on-a-pulse in this song."

_____

*Rhythm Is Everywhere, Carl F. Mahnke Productions, 215 E. Third St., Des Moines, Iowa. This film is mentioned especially to bring to mind that many fine film aids for classroom music are generally available through film rental services.

Lit - tle Tom Tink - er got burned by a clink - er and

he be - gan to cry. Ma - a

Ma - a Poor lit - tle in - no - cent guy.

Shirley asked if it were the $\frac{6}{8}$ sign, because most of their other songs were "4s"—$\frac{2}{4}$, $\frac{3}{4}$, $\frac{4}{4}$, etc.

"Yes, Shirley, that's what our consultant told me. He said this $\frac{6}{8}$ is their way of saying that instead of a plain quarter note to represent the <u>walk</u> pulse, in these $\frac{6}{8}$ songs a <u>dotted</u> quarter note will represent the <u>walk</u> pulse. On 'Ma-a, Ma-a' where the rhythm feels like <u>WALK Walk WALK Walk</u> there are dotted quarter notes in the notation to show it.

"That dot gives the quarter note just enough added value," continued Miss Johnson, "to let <u>three</u> eighth-notes ♪♪♪ spill out instead of the usual two ♪♪ when it is broken open. We can all feel how 'Little Tom Tinker' swings in a STRONG-Weak pulse pattern, can't we? This means that we have $\frac{2}{\text{walk}}$ meter. In all our other music the <u>walk</u> note has been a quarter note, so this song should be written $\frac{2}{4}$ meter. But here a dotted quarter note, not just a plain quarter note, represents the <u>walk</u> pulse. Wouldn't it look odd if they tried to write $\frac{2}{\text{dotted } 4}$ meter for this song? So they do the next best thing. Instead of telling us there are two dotted quarters in the pulse-accent grouping, they tell us what these <u>walk</u> notes contain: $\frac{6}{8}$ means six eighth-notes, <u>tri-ple-it, tri-ple-it</u>. The consultant says it's very important to remember, though, that $\frac{6}{8}$ feels like <u>STRONG-Weak</u> $\left(\frac{2}{\text{walk}}\right)$ time, and not <u>STRONG-weak-weak-Weak-weak-weak</u> $\left(\frac{6}{\text{walk}}\right)$ time."

When this new idea seemed to be readily and correctly used by the children Miss Johnson continued with other things the consultant had explained to her.

"He said," she told the class, "that the way to decide whether to write a song in $\frac{6}{8}$ $\left(\frac{2}{\text{dotted }4}\right)$ time or in $\frac{2}{4}$ time is to listen to the pulses when they break

16

up. If they break into <u>run-run</u> we know we want plain quarter notes for the <u>walk</u> pulse, $\frac{2}{4}$ meter. If we hear the pulses subdivide into <u>tri-ple-it</u> we know we need dotted quarters for the <u>walk</u> pulse, or $\frac{6}{8}$ meter. And lastly, the music consultant said if the song has only <u>walk</u> and <u>skip-ty</u> and <u>wa-alk</u> rhythms it can be written in either $\frac{2}{4}$ or $\frac{6}{8}$.

"By the way, where does 'Little Tinker' go <u>SKIP-ty</u> <u>Skip-ty</u> <u>SLO-ow</u>? Right, Jimmy! On the words 'HE be-Gan to CRY-y.' Look again and see how <u>skip-ty</u> notes are written in $\frac{6}{8}$ meter (see p. 16). Maybe it would be well to show on the board our familiar rhythm movements as they appear in simple meters where the quarter note represents the walk pulse and as they appear in compound meters where the dotted quarter note represents the walk note."

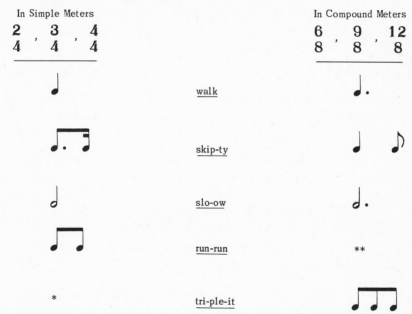

In Simple Meters		In Compound Meters
$\frac{2}{4} , \frac{3}{4} , \frac{4}{4}$		$\frac{6}{8} , \frac{9}{8} , \frac{12}{8}$

walk

skip-ty

slo-ow

run-run **

* tri-ple-it

Miss Johnson closed the lesson by suggesting that on the way home they could explore two songs as they walked by thinking the words against the walking pulse:

Hump-ty Dump-ty sat on a wall
Hump-ty Dump-ty had a great fall,
All the king's hors-es and all the king's men
Could-n't put Hump-ty to-geth-er a-gain.

Old King Cole was a mer-ry old soul
And a mer-ry old soul was he.
He called for his pipe and he called for his bowl
And he called for his fid-dlers three.

"Is either song in $\frac{6}{8}$ (three-on-a-pulse) meter? Is either song in $\frac{2}{4}$ or $\frac{3}{4}$ (two-on-a-pulse) meter? Which song has no <u>skip-ty</u>s in it?"

*Since <u>two-on-a-pulse</u> is the normal breakdown of a quarter note, <u>tri-ple-it</u> may appear in $\frac{2}{4}$ $\frac{3}{4}$ $\frac{4}{4}$ meters only by special permission: .

**Since <u>three-on-a-pulse</u> is the normal breakdown of a <u>dotted</u> quarter note used as the pulse note, <u>run-run</u> may appear in $\frac{6}{8}$ $\frac{9}{8}$ $\frac{12}{8}$ meters only by special permission: .

POINTERS AND PRACTICE–
CHAPTER 1

PRACTICE

I. To secure your understanding of the relationship between simple and compound meters, write the $\frac{2}{4}$ and $\frac{6}{8}$ alternate notations to the song below using the rhythm-movement help given. Refer to pages 14-17 as needed.

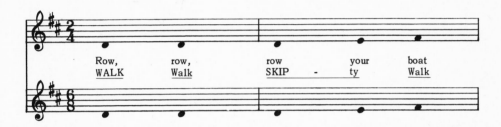

Row,   row,   row   your   boat
WALK   Walk   SKIP - ty   Walk

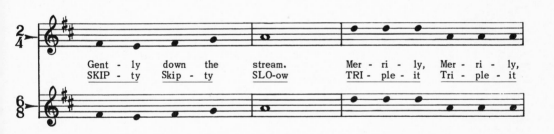

Gent - ly down the stream.   Mer - ri - ly, Mer - ri - ly,
SKIP - ty Skip - ty SLO-ow   TRI - ple - it Tri - ple - it

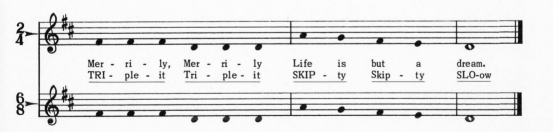

Mer - ri - ly, Mer - ri - ly Life is but a dream.
TRI - ple - it Tri - ple - it SKIP - ty Skip - ty SLO-ow

II. Against the TIC-tok pulses think through the following word chants using one word-syllable per pulse and using each name twice. Chant the patterns over and over against a steady pulse until they flow smoothly. Try walking steadily and thinking the various word patterns against the pulse of your steps if you find it difficult to maintain a steady pulse feeling while seated. Make this an active rhythmic experience rather than a pencil-and-paper exercise.

In the "A" line write the words themselves, syllabicated to fit the pulse.
In the "B" line write the rhythm-movement words.
In the "C" line write the actual music-rhythm notation.

	TIC	tok	TIC	tok	TIC	tok	TIC	tok
1. Wolfgang Mozart (example)								
A.	WOLF-	gang	MOZ-	art	WOLF-	gang	MOZ-	art
B.	WALK	walk	WALK	walk	WALK	walk	WALK	walk
C.	♩	♩	♩	♩	♩	♩	♩	♩
2. Fred'ric Chopin								
A.								
B.								
C.								
3. Robert Schumann								
A.								
B.								
C.								

The following word rhythms will require slo-ow or run-run patterns as well.

	TIC	tok	TIC	tok	TIC	tok	TIC	tok
4. J. S. Bach (example)								
A.	J.	S.	Ba-	ach	J.	S.	Ba-	ach
B.	WALK	walk	SLO-	ow	WALK	walk	SLO-	ow
C.	♩	♩	♩		♩	♩	♩	
5. Robert Franz								
A.								
B.								
C.								
6. Edvard Grieg								
A.								
B.								
C.								
7. Franz Schubert (not the same rhythm as 4, 5, and 6)								
A.								
B.								
C.								

	TIC	tok	TIC	tok	TIC	tok	TIC	tok
8. George Fredrick Handel (example)								
A.	GEORGE	Fredrick	HAN-	del	GEORGE	Fredrick	HAN-	del
B.	WALK	run-run	WALK	walk	WALK	run-run	WALK	walk
C.	♩	♫	♩	♩	♩	♫	♩	♩
9. Artur Rubinstein								
A.								
B.								
C.								
10. Montreal, Canada								
A.								
B.								
C.								
11. Boston, Massachusetts								
A.								
B.								
C.								
12. Winnipeg, Manitoba								
A.								
B.								
C.								
13. Franz Liszt								
A.								
B.								
C.								
14. Richard Wagner								
A.								
B.								
C.								
15. Marian Anderson								
A.								
B.								
C.								
16. Valley Forge, Pennsylvania								
A.								
B.								
C.								
17. Your own name; use initials, middle name, if you get into trouble								
A.								
B.								
C.								

III. The phrase rhythm notation at left is a good notation for the first phrase of which choices suggested on the right? Indicate your choice by writing "a," "b," "c," or "d" before each rhythm notation. Try to step out the rhythms.

a. "Twinkle, Twinkle Little Star."
b. "Jingle Bells."
c. "London Bridge Is Falling Down."
d. "Old King Cole Was a Merry Old Soul."

a. "Jingle Bells."
b. "Merrily We Roll Along."
c. "The Farmer in the Dell."
d. "Are You Sleeping?"

a. "Oh Give Me a Home Where the Buffalo Roam."
b. "London Bridge Is Falling Down."
c. "The Farmer in the Dell."
d. "Oh Come, All Ye Faithful."

a. "London Bridge Is Falling Down."
b. "Are You Sleeping?"
c. "Jingle Bells."
d. "The Farmer in the Dell."

a. "Twinkle, Twinkle Little Star."
b. "Are You Sleeping?"
c. "Old King Cole."
d. "Jingle Bells."

IV. While we introduce <u>run-run</u> and <u>skip-ty</u> patterns with a shared beam ♫ and ♩. ♪ because visually it helps children to get the two-on-a-pulse concept, these may also be written with individual flags, as ♪ ♪ and ♪. ♪. Music notes may also be inverted without changing their meaning. Here are several ways the same movement may be written:

Movement:	walk	skip-ty	run-run	slo-ow
A (<u>original</u>).	♩	♩. ♪	♫	♩
B (<u>inverted</u>).	♩	♩. ♪	♫	♩
C (<u>separate flags</u>).	♩	♪. ♪	♪ ♪	♩

22

Movement:	walk	skip-ty	run-run	slo-ow	
D (separate and inverted).					(walk-"tie")

Write this rhythm movement four ways as shown above:

walk slo-ow walk skip-ty skip-ty walk run-run run-run slo-o-ow

A.

B.

C.

D.

POINTERS

Discuss each point briefly in the space provided.

1. Poets and composers have always pointed out that music and musical stimuli lie all around us. How was this true in Miss Johnson's case? List other examples of "informal music stimuli" in a child's environment.

2. Much is said about "individual differences" in learning. Cite two examples of Miss Johnson's awareness of these.

3. Music education recommends that music be used to enrich the school day and other subjects as well as being a study for its own sake. Is there evidence of this in Miss Johnson's class? What are other ways in which music might enrich the entire school day?

4. It seems reasonable that a music specialist knows more about how music should be presented than the general classroom teacher. Was Miss Johnson's supervisor derelict in his duty by not insisting that his approach be followed rather than the approaches Miss Johnson developed?

5. It is advocated that children "learn by doing." How was this honored or disregarded in Miss Johnson's teaching?

6. Children learn earliest through large body muscles and slowly refine their co-ordination to smaller skills. How may this principle be applied in music education?

7. Educational psychology recommends that children be taught "the thing before its symbol." Discuss this in terms of rhythm movement and rhythm notation.

8. We learn best through successful participation. Which child did Miss Johnson help to gain success from an initially disappointing experience? How? Are children always to be protected from failure? Discuss.

9. The rhythms the children learned (run-run, walk, skip-ty, etc.) are often called the fundamental, natural rhythms because they are fundamental to simple musical expression and are movements which are natural to children. In what order were these movements presented? How many were introduced the first day?

10. It is highly recommended by the authors, and indeed by most music educators today, that the elementary classroom provide balanced activity for all children in the areas of:

Singing.
Playing instruments.
Listening (to classroom music as well as to phonograph records).
Moving to music.

Notice that Miss Johnson's class has been involved in all four, even though the rhythmic aspect has been overemphasized both to illustrate a teacher following up those aspects of music in which he or she feels personally secure (Chap. 2, p. 27 shows predilection for physical education), and to begin somewhat systematically to acquaint the reader with the raw materials of music—rhythm, pitch, and harmony—as these pertain to the elementary school. We will see later how Miss Johnson's own confidence and security have grown to the point that she is able to involve her children in a wide variety of activities using all four of the above areas very substantially and in balance.

2

BECOMING AWARE OF PITCH AND MELODIC TENDENCY

Tuned Water Glasses

In each of her six years of teaching Miss Johnson had attended sessions of the teachers' In-Service Training weekend—always knowing that she should slip into the music section, from which she would benefit most; always going, instead, to the art or physical education sections. But the recent successes of her rhythm activities had given her added confidence, and the next In-Service Training weekend found her seated inconspicuously at the back of the room for the music workshop session. The spirit of enjoyment and good-natured participation by those assembled drew her inevitably into the fun, and soon she was playing a rhythm figure on the maracas, then moving through phrase patterns with the group, and singing simple descant patterns as she played the tones on three tone bells. . . . Autoharps, Harmolins, simple piano chords, movement, melody instruments, rhythm makers, singing, phonograph enrichments—Miss Johnson felt like a child turned loose in a candy shop.

So this was music! And she had been withholding it from her children because she felt she "wasn't musical." It would take time to equip her classroom with a complete music corner, but it was not too late to start. She might still be able to make a request from this year's budget—the principal kept a fund for emergency needs. And hadn't she seen an autoharp gathering dust on the shelf in a neighboring classroom? Surely the music consultant could tune it for her.

Miss Johnson returned home in a glow of anticipation. That evening while washing the dishes, she found herself tapping one of the water glasses.

"I'm getting as bad as the children about tapping out——." She stopped short. Here was just the answer: tuned water glasses! They would provide a simple bridge from purely rhythmic instruments and activities toward tonal recognition and skill, and what fun the children would have, too. A little searching and tapping among the dishes in the cupboard revealed a set of inexpensive glasses delicate enough to give a pleasing tone and tunable when water was added.

Monday morning when the children came in from recess Miss Johnson was ready. She showed them a single glass, and several experiments were made to discover its tonal resources. It was held in hand, set on the desktop, turned upside down and on its side, tapped with fingernails, pencils, a large iron nail, a wooden mallet, a rubber mallet. It was struck gently on the rim, at the top, the bottom, and in the middle. All the time the children listened, criticized, and expressed their choice. Most of the children agreed that the sweetest tone sounded when the glass, set right end up on a folded paper towel, was struck lightly with a wooden mallet or with a large nail. Then Miss Johnson had them compare the sound of the glass with the sound of a rhythm stick. To focus their attention she asked them to sing the pitch of the rhythm stick—an impossible request, of course. Then she asked them to sing the pitch of the water glass. After a short period of adjusting the high pitch of the glass downward into their own voice ranges the children found that the glass had a singable pitch.

"Using this pitch as a starting tone, let's sing 'Old MacDonald Had a Farm,'" said Miss Johnson.*

"Now," she continued after they had sung the song, "can anyone suggest a rhythm pattern from this song for us to chant or play?"

The suggestions were many.

"Who would like to play a rhythm from the song on the glass, then step it out, then go to the board and write its notation?"

Stanley tapped and chanted:

‖: Old   Mac   Don- ald :‖

He stepped out its movement:

Walk walk walk walk

Then he wrote on the board:

♩ ♩ ♩ ♩

Curtis suggested:

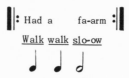

---

* The notation to this song is on p. 58.

Britton offered:

Dawn came up with:

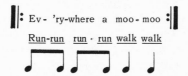

Miss Johnson commented that the last pattern gave the impression of a very busy farm with lots of activity, and this brought Henry Archer's hand up:

"I think if we use that pattern we should sing the verse about the chicks, because the glass sounds more like 'Ev'rywhere a <u>chick-chick</u>' than it does 'Ev'rywhere a <u>moo-moo</u>'!"

This brought a ripple of laughter, but as the children listened they quickly agreed that the glass sounded much more like the <u>staccato</u> (the Italian musical term for detached tones) pecking of a chick than the <u>legato</u> (connected) bellow of a cow. Miss Johnson was delighted with Henry's "aesthetic discrimination" and took a moment to recognize it and to tell the class that this ability to choose the more satisfying and appropriate of two forms of artistic expression was a trait worth developing. It would help to enrich one's daily enjoyment in life.

"Now see what we can do with this rhythm instrument because of its singable pitch," said Miss Johnson, drawing the class back to the water glass. "While Henry plays his rhythm on this pitch, let's start our song on the same tone and see how it fits the song from beginning to end."

John Bergenstrom's hand was up.

"I think our song ends on the same pitch as the glass, too," he observed.

A quick singing of the last phrase of the song and the starting note verified John's words: "Old MacDonald" starts and ends on the same tone.

"Do <u>all</u> songs start and end on the same pitch?" Janet wanted to know.

A little exploration of familiar songs revealed that this was not always so, although the children noticed with interest that if they were careful it was fairly easy to pitch any one of their songs so that it would end on the same tone as the water glass.

"I brought a set of glasses with the idea of tuning them," Miss Johnson said. "Shall we go on and tune two or three, or wait until another day?"

The children were still attentive and interested, so Janet got the pitcher of water and Dawn brought some paper towels in case of a spill. Miss Johnson let Dawn tap the glass with a wooden mallet while Janet poured quite rapidly, and the class heard the pitch change. They sang the pitch of an empty glass and then the pitch of the full glass. By holding their hands out in front of them horizontally, they showed how they heard the high pitch of the empty glass; and by dropping their hands, they indicated the low pitch of the full glass.

"If we listen well and pour carefully," said the teacher, "we should be able to start with the empty glass and tune the others so that we can play on them the 'Ee-i-ee-i-oh' from 'Old MacDonald.'"

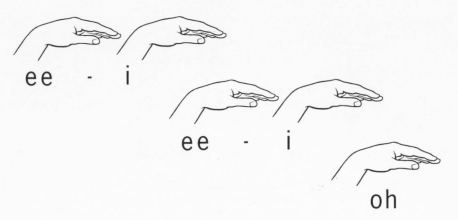

ee - i

ee - i

oh

They listened to the sound of the empty glass and then, starting on that pitch sang "Ee-i-ee-i-oh." By moving their hands, the children showed how the sounds ranged.

When they were in reasonable agreement, the teacher showed the pitch contour in dash notation on the chalkboard. They found that there were three pitch levels, so they would need three glasses, each with a different water level:

$$ee \text{-} i$$
$$ee \text{-} i$$
$$oh$$

"We have the high 'ee-i' on the empty glass. Dawn, you tap the second glass while Janet pours water slowly, and she'll stop when that glass is giving the right pitch for the second 'ee-i.' . . . Good! Now the third glass, until it sounds like 'oh.' . . . There! Now we can play it as well as sing it."

Bill Smithson had an idea.

"Since the empty glass sounds highest, why don't we set it on a book so it will look highest?"

"Put it on two books," Judy added. "The middle glass has to be on one book because it's higher than the fullest glass."

"Yes," added Ralph, "and put the empty glass on the right because that's the way a piano is—low sounds on the left; high sounds on the right."

Some discussion ensued. Several children said the high pitched empty glass should be on the left because it was the first to be played. It was finally decided that, since each song might require the glasses to be played in a different order, the piano arrangement would be best. Then the player could always count on finding high sounds to the right, low sounds to the left.

"So that we can talk about these sounds from our seats, class, why don't we also number them, letting the highest note have the highest number," suggested Miss Johnson.

1   2   3

After some experimenting, the children discovered a song which could be played entirely on the three notes, and they wrote it on the board:

3   2   1   3   2   1
Hot cross buns Hot cross buns

1 1 1 1   2 2 2 2
One a pen-ny two a pen-ny

3   2   1
Hot cross buns

"I like the way we have written the pitches," said Miss Johnson, "but I wonder about the rhythm."

The children stepped out the rhythm and the strong-weak accent, and found it to be:

Walk walk slo-ow |Walk walk slo-ow
3   2   1   3   2   1
Hot cross buns |Hot cross buns

Run-run run-run run-run run-run
1 1   1   1   2 2   2 2
One a pen-ny two a   pen-ny

Walk walk slo-ow
3   2   1
Hot cross buns

"If we used music notes we could show the rhythm more easily than by writing out the movement," said Janet.

Miss Johnson asked her to write them on the board, and the class voiced approval.*

3   2   1   3   2   1
Hot cross buns Hot cross buns

1 1 1 1 2 2 2 2
One a pen-ny two a pen-ny

3   2   1
Hot cross buns

---

* For a discussion of the use of number notation to show both pitch and rhythm, see p. 45.

Miss Johnson set the glasses in the music corner of her room and individuals who finished their seat work early were allowed to try them out softly through the day. The books were somewhat of a nuisance, though; they might get water-spotted. Yet the idea of seeing the high-pitched glass up and the low-pitched glass down lower was pedagogically desirable.

"I was wondering," Miss Johnson asked as the session concluded, "whether one of you boys would like to make a stair-step stand for our glasses? . . . Like this."

She sketched on the board:

"I have five glasses in all, so how many steps will we need? 'Four' is right. Well, Jimmy, why don't you and Henry work together on it at home? Do you have some paint around the house to make it look attractive?"

Britton was the first child to finish his seat work the next day, and asked if he could go to the music corner and try out the glasses on the new red-and-blue stand the boys had made. In a moment he was back at Miss Johnson's desk.

"They don't sound right today," he complained.

"No, I noticed that," said Miss Johnson. "We were careful to pour just the right amount of water in them yesterday, but today they're off! While I help you retune them, can you think what might have caused them to be out of pitch?"

When the science period started, Miss Johnson had Britton report on what he had discovered and how they had found it necessary to add a little water to each glass to retune it. Could anyone in the class offer an explanation? Marie quickly pointed toward the correct answer by reminding them that they had put salt water in a dish on the window ledge last week and that the water had evaporated, leaving only the salt crystals. They decided, under Miss Johnson's guidance, to mark the correct water level on each glass with red fingernail polish and to have the room monitor responsible for filling to the proper level each day.

Making Up Original Songs

There was no general music period planned this day because they had had such a long session with the glasses the day before. However, Miss Johnson gave the following lines to the children and suggested that they go to the music corner individually during the day and work out tunes for them:

Say hel-lo to the sun when a-way you run
From home to school in the morn-ing.

If anyone wanted to make up his own words, that was encouraged, too. So that their
tunes wouldn't "evaporate" overnight it was suggested that the number of the
glass struck for each syllable be written right over the words, and the following
day they would each play and write their versions, and the class would sing them.

The next day there was time to hear the new songs. First the children together
worked out the rhythms to the words on rhythm instruments. The sticks tapped
the pulse and Miss Johnson marked the syllables they sounded with an "X" to
indicate the crossed rhythm sticks:

Say hel-lo to the sun when a-way you run
X   X X   X X   X X X

From home to school in the mo-orn-ing
X   X   X X   X   X X X

This was repeated several times with the drum playing on the strong pulses, and
the bar-line accent was marked:

Say hel -|lo to the | sun when a -|way you | run
X |X X |X X |X X |X

From | home to | school in the | morn - |ing ‖
X |X   X |X   X |X   X|X ‖

It was found that the pulses moved in twos. Then the shakers played the rhythm
of the words, and they were marked:

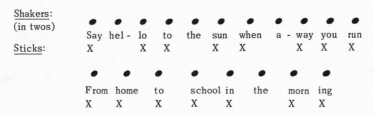

Shakers:
(in twos)
Say hel - lo to the sun when a - way you run
Sticks:
X   X X   X X   X X X

From home to   school in   the   morn ing
X   X   X   X   X   X X

Various children stepped out the words until the class was agreed on the word
rhythm:

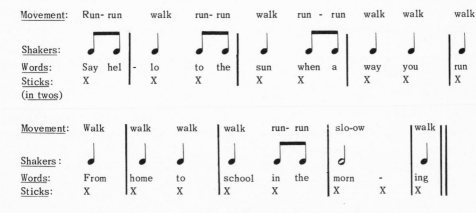

Movement: Run- run   walk   run- run   walk   run - run   walk   walk   walk

Shakers:
Words: Say hel - lo   to the   sun   when a   way   you   run
Sticks: X   X   X   X   X   X   X   X
(in twos)

Movement: Walk walk walk walk run- run slo-ow walk

Shakers:
Words: From home to school in the morn - ing
Sticks: X   X   X   X   X   X   X   X

33

The proper note values were recorded by adding stems, as shown above, to the shaker notes.

As each child played his version the class listened until each one could sing it individually when called upon. Then the young composer would write it on the board in numbers, with any necessary help from the class.

Henry Archer created his song from three tones played over and over:

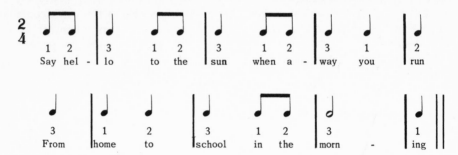

Curtis used the upper three notes of the glasses to start his tune:

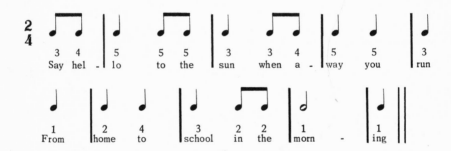

Janet started hers on sound 5 and skipped about:

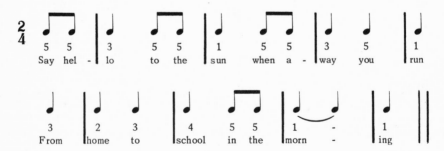

There were other variations, and each composer received a round of applause.

"Many of you seemed to like Curtis' song especially well. Can we sing it again and show with our hands how it goes up and down?"

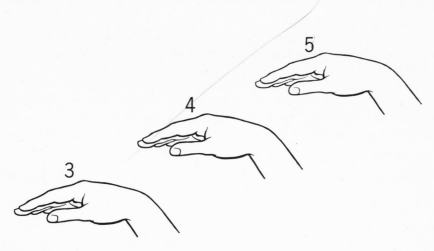

Introducing Staff Notation

At this point Miss Johnson produced the music flannelboard she had constructed, patterned after one that had been demonstrated at the music education workshop, with black India-ink staff lines and an assortment of <u>walk</u>, <u>run-run</u>, and <u>slo-ow</u> notes.* Placing a variety of notes along the top of the flannelboard she carefully set a "1-3-5" indicator (3 whole notes labeled $\begin{smallmatrix}⑤\\③\\①\end{smallmatrix}$) in place, which showed that the bottom space represented sound 1. Various children tried placing the proper rhythm notes on the correct lines and spaces to make the staff picture of Curtis' song until the "staff picture" was complete, even to the adding of bar lines to show the strong accents.**

---

*The flannelboard is made by stretching a piece of flannel approximately 2" × 24" over a piece of plywood. Notes may be cut from cardboard, with a small patch of flannel glued to the back of the note head. The large sheet is lined with India ink into two staves of five lines each. The flannel patch will cling to the large flannel, holding notes wherever they are placed. Such flannelboards are available commercially through: Educational Music Bureau, 434 So. Wabash Ave., Chicago 5, Ill.

**Observe that no clef sign (𝄞 or 𝄢) is used here; therefore, the lines and spaces have no letter names so that flats (♭), sharps (♯), and key signatures are not needed. At this stage it is immaterial whether notes are placed "stem up" or "stem down." Sometime later children should notice that a flagged eighth note ♪ will not be correct upside down: ↾. Observing printed music will reveal its proper appearance: ♪.

For the next two weeks Miss Johnson encouraged the children to invent "Good morning," "Good afternoon," and "Goodbye" sentence songs, to create melodies on the water glasses, and to make the "staff picture" for their songs on the flannelboard. Each day a new "Good morning" song appeared on the flannelboard; and after lunch there would be a new "Good afternoon" or "Goodbye" song, which the composer had put on the flannelboard during lunch hour. At first they would go individually to the glasses to find out how the songs should sound. Soon the children realized that they <u>knew</u> the five scale-sounds so well that they could "read" the songs directly from the flannelboard! No longer did they first have to try them on the glasses. They would read and sing the notation the way they thought it sounded, and then Miss Johnson would let a less skillful child go to the glasses and play it, to check if the class had read it properly.

Occasionally a child's song would end on sound 2 or 4, and Miss Johnson would help the class to find a more satisfying and conclusive ending, usually a final sound 1. They also learned to arrange the notes into the proper word picture when sound 1 was shifted to another line or space, as:

Melody Bells

One day Henry Archer brought in five pieces of metal tubing. He had been going through the scrap box in which his father, an electrician, kept odd lengths of conduit. Following his new habit of listening to the sounds of things Henry had discovered two lengths of tubing which sounded like "3" and "2." When a thorough search had failed to produce a piece that sounded like "1," Henry went to his father. Mr. Archer told him to measure the difference between the pipe that sounded like "3" and the pipe that sounded like "2"—which proved to be seven-eighths of an inch. Mr. Archer then cut a third pipe seven-eighths of an inch longer than sound 2 and Henry showed his father how they played "3 2 1" patterns from certain familiar songs at school. When Mr. Archer learned that the children were playing five-note songs on the water glasses, he cut another piece seven-eighths of an inch shorter than the shortest of the three pipes, to use for sound 4. Then he cut a fifth piece seven-eighths of an inch shorter than the fourth.

When Henry and his father played these they found that tubes 4 and 5 didn't sound right; they were a little too high. So Mr. Archer cut a piece measuring between the lengths of pipe 3 and his faulty pipe 4. This worked perfectly. A true sound 5 was produced with a piece seven-eighths of an inch shorter than the new, accurate sound 4 pipe.

The children took turns, in groups of five, playing the tubes—each holding a tube in one hand and, in the other, a pencil with which to tap it. Henry taught his friends what he had learned by experimenting: that the pieces of conduit would ring better if held at a point one-fourth of their length from the end.

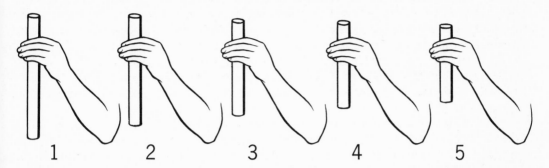

1   2   3   4   5

In this way they would play patterns of familiar songs*—tunes the teacher or a child would write on the chalkboard or put in place on the flannelboard—or sometimes a "director" would point to the pipes he wanted sounded, and the class would try to guess the tune he had in mind.

When the children discovered that they needed only one more high note in order to play the complete mer-ri-ly part of "Row, Row, Row Your Boat" Henry could hardly wait to go home and find a shorter piece to provide the missing high note:

Row, Row, Row your boat, gent-ly down the stream

Mer-ri-ly, mer-ri-ly, mer-ri-ly, mer-ri-ly, life is but a dream

By singing with the conduit "bells," the children found that there were two tones missing between note 5 and the new high tone Henry had brought. It was most noticeable when they sang and played "The First Noel," which begins with a "3 2 1" pattern:

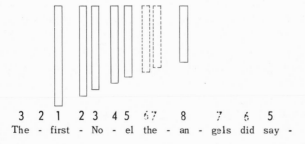

3   2   1   2 3   4 5   6 7   8   7   6   5
The - first - No - el the - an - gels did say -

---

* For familiar five-note songs see Pointers and Practice, Chap. 2, pp. 48 and 49.

With this tune and the scale to guide them, Henry and his father cut the two lengths needed to complete the scale, and dozens of songs could now be played on the "bells." The children made their own songbooks as they experimented with the pipe bells; some songs were written by hand—often in number notation for convenience, sometimes in staff notation—and some were prepared by Miss Johnson on the duplicating machine.* Original songs using all eight tones were composed and notated. Songs about—or from—countries and cultures the children were studying in Social Studies units were especially popular. (It should be noted that the rhythmic skills which had intrigued the children a few months earlier were not being neglected.)

At this juncture, the first of Miss Johnson's "budget requests" arrived: two sets of melody bells.

Ralph, who insisted that highs and lows be placed right and left but seemed reluctant to play melody instruments, had been chosen to open the box while the class excitedly waited to see its contents.

"These are melody bells," said Miss Johnson, drawing them forth. "On them we can play even more tones and songs than on Henry's fine set."

"They look like piano keys," said Ralph.

"That's right, Ralph," said Miss Johnson, "so where will the high sounds be when we play it?"

"To the right, and low sounds to the left," said Ralph, as the class laughed good-naturedly.

"Can you guess, by looking, which end has the high sounds?" asked the teacher.

"The little end," said Britton, "because on Henry's pipes the littlest bells had the highest sounds."

Ralph, tapping the melody bells with the mallet, proved that Britton was right. Soon the children found that if the white keys only were used, sound 1 was just to the left of the two black keys. To orient doubtful children Miss Johnson penciled the numbers "1," "3," and "5" on the white keys:

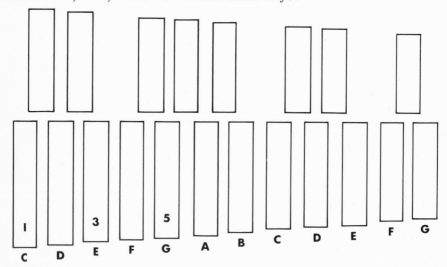

*The songs used in Part I, Chaps. 1-5, are all "in the public domain," i.e., they may be reproduced freely without violating copyright. Existing copyright law as it pertains to the reproduction of published music for school use prohibits teachers from reproducing commercially copyrighted publications. A revision of this law which thus discriminates against classroom use is to be hoped for.

Discovering the Major Scale

Many interesting music sessions centered around the melody bells, and individual class members experimented with them in the music corner at other times of day. The class had long since discovered that some songs could not be played on the commercial melody bells or on Henry's homemade set because the tune went below sound 1. At this point the music consultant made some helpful suggestions.

"After playing all the white keys, you found that a certain key seems to be sound 1. Which key is that?" he asked.

"The one just left of two black keys," said Dawn, "and it's called 'C.' I learned that from piano lessons."

"Besides, the letter names are stamped right on the keys," added John.

"Good for you both," laughed the music teacher. "When sound 1 turns out to be C, we say we are playing in the key of C. Henry, when you made your set of bells did you notice that two pieces of tubing had less difference of length between them than the others had? Look at Henry's instrument, class, and you will see a place where two pipes are nearer to each other in length than to the other pieces."

"Sure!" exclaimed Henry. "I remember when we cut pipe 4 we found it had to be only half as much shorter than pipe 3. Each of the others had seven-eighths of an inch difference."

"Good, Henry. From sound 3 to sound 4 was only half as far as between the other sounds," said the consultant. "Now if you will look closely at Henry's instrument you'll find another place that is only half as far from its neighbor."

"I see, it's between 7 and 8," said Curtis.

"Yes. Now I'll hold up your new melody bells while we all sing up the scale by numbers. Watch the bells while we sing and be ready to tell me what you see between 3 and 4 and between 7 and 8."

All hands were up as they finished singing the scale.

"There's no black key between 3 and 4 or 7 and 8," explained John Bergenstrom.

"Yes, John. We don't have to step past a black key from 3 to 4 or from 7 to 8. They are only half as far apart as the other tones, so we say these tones are a half step apart. The other tones are twice as far, so how far are they? . . . Correct! A whole step. We could describe our <u>major</u> scale, then, as having all its tones a whole step apart except the half steps from 3 to 4 and from 7 to 8."

(do)	(re)	(mi)	(fa)	(sol)	(la)	(ti)	(do)
tone	tone	tone	tone	tone	tone	tone	tone
1	2	3	4	5	6	7	8

half step   half step

"Miss Johnson told me of your trouble in trying to play some songs which go lower than sound 1. 'Skip to My Lou' was one of those songs, wasn't it?"

The music consultant helped them to work out the number notation to the song, and they played it—all but the lowest note—on the bells.

39

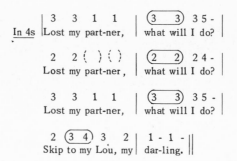

	3 3 1 1	③ ③ 3 5 -
In 4s	Lost my part-ner,	what will I do?

2 2 ( ) ( )	② ② 2 4 -
Lost my part-ner,	what will I do?

3 3 1 1	③ ③ 3 5 -
Lost my part-ner,	what will I do?

2 ③ ④ 3 2	1 - 1 - ‖
Skip to my Lou, my	dar-ling. ‖

"Could we move note 1 up to another key and play?" asked Milton.

The music teacher rubbed off the old numbering and called the second key (D) number 1 and played "Skip to My Lou":

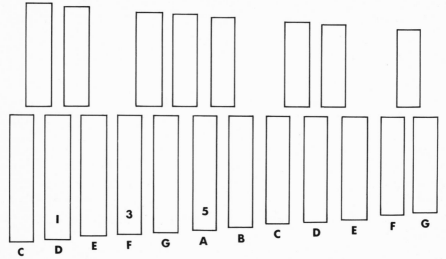

The children were amused at the strange "Skip to My Lou" they heard, but they agreed it did not sound right.

"These tones 1 2 3 4 5 don't sound like a major scale because now the half step isn't between 3 and 4 where it belongs, but between 2 and 3."

Then the consultant moved number 1 up another key (E) and played again:

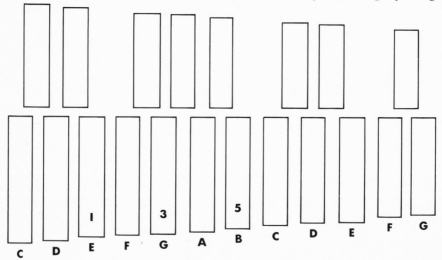

40

Once more the children laughed at the unusual sound and rejected that key.

"This time 'Skip to My Lou' doesn't sound as though it came from a major scale because the half step was . . . yes, between 1 and 2 instead of between 3 and 4."

When he moved note 1 up one more place (F) and began to play, the children nodded approval . . .

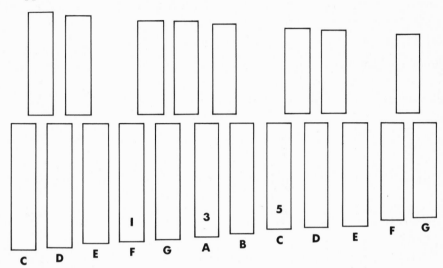

2   2   2 4-

. . . until the second phrase, "What will I do?" Note 4 was not right. Too high. The consultant tapped the black key just below the white 4, then played the whole phrase, and then the whole song, using this black, lowered sound 4. The children approved. They sang with the bells and noticed how much brighter and more dancelike their voices sounded in this key—as long as he used the lowered note 4. The teacher had them count up the alphabet from C to discover the name of this new note 1.

"If note 1 is here now, what key have we been playing in? . . . That's right, the key of F. And what do we have to do to make F really sound like note 1? Yes! We must lower white note 4 to black note 4."

The music consultant showed them how to count up the short musical alphabet from C to find the name of note 4 (B-flat) in this key of F:

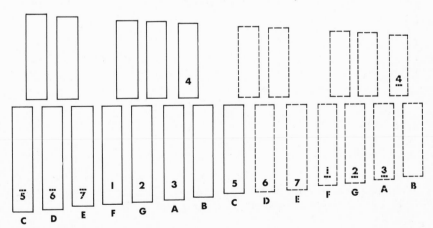

"Since number 4 could be anywhere, depending on what key we played in, we should use this note's real name—B. Because we lowered, or 'flatted,' the B in order to play in the key of F, we would say that if you want F to sound like note 1 you'll have to make all note 4s B-flat (B♭) instead of plain B in order to get the half step between note 3 and note 4."

"One more question: What number shall we call the note lower than 1? Let's look at our musical alphabet. After it goes up seven letters, A B C D E F G, what happens? . . . Right! It starts over. Then what should our numbers do after 1 2 3 4 5 6 7? . . . They should start over: 1 2 3 4 5 6 7 1 2 3. . . . What number comes just below 1? . . . Yes, Milton, it is 7. To keep from confusing it with regular 7 and to show that we went <u>down</u> to get it, we might put it under a reference line and call it 'subseven': 7̅, seven underneath."

The consultant asked Henry to complete the number notation to "Skip to My Lou":

3 3   1 1 | (3 3) 3 5 -

2 2   7̅ 7̅ | (2 2) 2 4 -

3 3   1 1 | (3 3) 3 5 -

2 (3 4) 3 2 | 1 - 1 -

"You've been excellent music detectives today. Before I leave, let me write on the board the notation to "The Paw-Paw Patch" in the key of F, and notice how the key of F always puts his 'brand' or signature on his songs. Does this song go below note 1? If so, how far?"

Where, oh, where's a   friend   to   play   with?   Where, oh, where's

a   friend   to   play   with?   Where, oh, where's a   friend   to   play

with?   'Way   down   yon - der   in   the   paw - paw   patch.

Finding Melodies at the Piano

Later the music consultant showed Miss Johnson how to find tones using G as note 1, and he suggested that the school piano be used so children could discover these same tonal patterns on the piano keyboard:

42

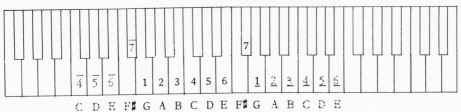

Since Miss Johnson understood so readily and was able to pick out many tunes in G either by numbers or directly from staff notation, the music specialist went on to help her learn to construct the major scale beginning on any white key by using the four fingers of each hand to play the eight tones—each tone a whole step from the next except 3 to 4 and 7 to 1.*

In forty-five minutes Miss Johnson was confident she could guide the children over the next few weeks to use scales in all keys to play familiar tunes by number and eventually to play directly from the staff notation without first rewriting in number notation. To help her gain this skill the music consultant selected several songs with simple instrumental additions that were easier to play than the tune melody itself, and which the children thoroughly enjoyed.**

*Finger and hand patterns for understanding the scales are illustrated on pp. 49-54.
**See Chap. 9 for examples, pp. 207, 211, 212, 216, 219, 221.

POINTERS AND PRACTICE — CHAPTER 2

PRACTICE

I. Footnote reference, p. 31: Miss Johnson felt that her class could move smoothly through introductory experiences with pitch number notation into traditional staff notation. However, many teachers use number notation exclusively in Primary grades and devise a way of showing rhythm notation such as:

Walk:	3	3	3	3
Run-run:	(3 3)	(3 3)	(3 3)	(3 3)
Skip-ty:	(3 · 3)	(3 · 3)	(3 · 3)	(3 · 3)
Tri-ple-it:	(3 3 3)	(3 3 3)	(3 3 3)	(3 3 3)
Slo-ow:	3	-	3	-
Slo-o-ow:	3	-	-	
Slo-o-o-ow:	3	-	-	-

In such a notation "Hot Cross Buns" would be written:

```
    3    2    1 - 3    2    1 -
    Hot Cross Buns  Hot Cross Buns
   (1 1)(1 1)  (2 2)(2 2)  3    2    1 -
    One a pen-ny  two a pen-ny  Hot Cross Buns
```

II. Find or purchase five matching water glasses of good clear tone. Tune them by adding water, and strike with a long wooden pencil. Alternative: procure five prescription bottles, each about five inches high, from a pharmacist. Tune the bottles with water and suspend them from a pole:

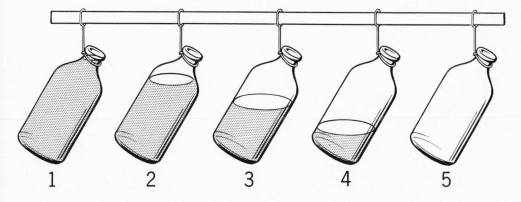

III. Construct conduit bells. Pieces of standard 1/2-inch diameter thin-wall electrical conduit from the hardware store, cut to the following lengths, give the sounds of the major scale of C:

$$12\tfrac{1}{2}'' \quad 11\tfrac{3}{4}'' \quad 11\tfrac{1}{16}'' \quad 10\tfrac{5}{8}'' \quad 10\tfrac{1}{8}'' \quad 9\tfrac{7}{16}'' \quad 8\tfrac{29}{32}'' \quad 8\tfrac{5}{8}''$$
$$\text{C} \qquad \text{D} \qquad \text{E} \qquad \text{F} \qquad \text{G} \qquad \text{A} \qquad \text{B} \qquad \text{C}$$

IV. Play the following tunes on the instruments you have constructed above, observing the rhythm indications.*

In 4s: 3 2 1 -| 3 2 1 -| (1 1) (1 1) (2 2) (2 2) |3 2 1 -‖
In 4s: (1 2)| 3 3 3 (2 3)|4 4 4 (3 4) |5 4 3 2 | 1 - -‖
In 4s: 1 1 2 2 | 3 (3 2) 1 -| 2 2 3 2 | 1 - 1 -‖
In 3s: 1 - 1 | 2 - 2| 3 - (3 2)|1 - -| 2 - -| 3 - 2 | 1 - -| - - -‖
In 3s: 5 - -| 4 - -| 3 4 5| 2 - -| 3 - 4 | 5 4 3| 2 - -| 1 - -‖
In 2s: (5·5) 3| (5·5) 3| 4 3| 2 -| (4·4) 2| (4·4) 2| 3 2| 1 -‖

V. Play by ear one of the following five-tone songs familiar to you, and notate in number notation. (Also, remember these tunes when you are searching for five-tone songs for your children to play): "Jingle Bells"; "Oats, Peas, Beans, and Barley Grow"; "Sweetly Sings the Donkey"; "Merrily We Roll Along"; "Lightly Row"; "Go Tell Aunt Rhodie."

VI. Write the number notation under the following tunes. Can you recognize what tunes they are before you play them? Play the tunes on your water glasses. Play them on the piano using <u>Middle C</u> as sound 1.

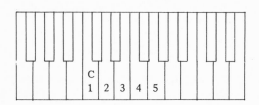

Play again using <u>G</u> as sound 1. Write the names of the tunes you recognize.

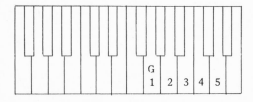

*Robert Schumann once said: "At the sight of a new score the amateur begins to play; the artist begins to think." Make it a practice first to think through the rhythm movement until you feel it securely before you begin to play.

American Song

1 1 (1 · 2) 3

(Walk   walk   skip - ty walk)

(Did you remember the rhythm movement symbols of compound meters— $\frac{6}{8}$ $\frac{9}{8}$ $\frac{12}{8}$ —Chap. 1, pp. 15-18?)

American Song

German Folk Song

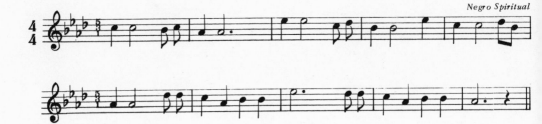

Negro Spiritual

VII. Match original words of your own to the tunes in Practice Section IV on p. 46. A familiar song like "Hot Cross Buns" might have new words such as:

In 4s: 3   2 1 - | 3   2 1 - |
       Come a-long | Come a-long |

(1 1)(1 1)(2 2) (2   2) |
Ev'ry-one is sing-ing, won't you |

     3   2 1 - ‖
     Come a-long ‖

The second tune on p. 46 might have words like:

In 4s: (1 2) | 3   3   3 (2 3) | 4   4   4
Hear the | birds so high sing-ing | in the sky

(3 4) | 5   4   3   2 | 1 - - ‖
As they | greet this joy-ful | day ‖

The third tune might take on a Christmas significance:

In 4s: 1   1 2   2 | 3 (3 2)1 - |
     Christ is born in | Beth-le -hem |

     2   2   3   2 | 1 - 1 - ‖
     Where yon star is | shin-ing ‖

VIII. Some familiar tunes using only five scale tones: see p. 46 and check your own number notation against that given here. Learn to play these tunes fluently and rhythmically correct on bells, keyboard, water glasses, flutes,* etc.

Lightly Row

5 3 3 - | 4 2 2 - | 1 2 3 4 | 5 5 5 - |
5 3 3 - | 4 2 2 - | 1 3 5 5 | 3 - - - |
2 2 2 2 | 2 3 4 - | 3 3 3 3 | 3 4 5 - |
5 3 3 - | 4 2 2 - | 1 3 5 5 | 1 - - - ‖

Jingle Bells

3 3 3 - | 3 3 3   - | 3 5 1 2 | 3 - - - |
4 4 4 4 | 4 3 3 (3 3)| 3 2 2 3 | 2 - 5 - |
3 3 3 - | 3 3 3   - | 3 5 1 2 | 3 - - - |
4 4 4 4 | 4 3 3 (3 3)| 5 5 4 2 | 1 - - - ‖

*See Appendix, p. 331.

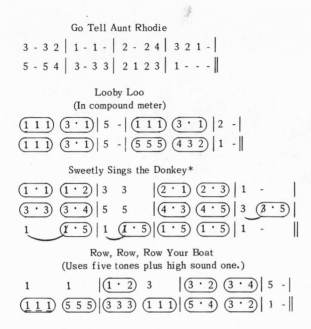

Go Tell Aunt Rhodie

3 - 3 2 | 1 - 1 - | 2 - 2 4 | 3 2 1 - |
5 - 5 4 | 3 - 3 3 | 2 1 2 3 | 1 - - - ‖

Looby Loo
(In compound meter)

(1 1 1) (3 · 1) | 5 - | (1 1 1) (3 · 1) | 2 - |
(1 1 1) (3 · 1) | 5 - | (5 5 5) (4 3 2) | 1 - ‖

Sweetly Sings the Donkey*

(1 · 1) (1 · 2) | 3 3 |(2 · 1) (2 · 3) | 1 - |
(3 · 3) (3 · 4) | 5 5 |(4 · 3) (4 · 5) | 3 (3 · 5) |
1 ⌣(1 · 5) | 1 (1 · 5) | (1 · 5) (1 · 5) | 1 -   ‖

Row, Row, Row Your Boat
(Uses five tones plus high sound one.)

1   1 |(1 · 2) 3 |(3 · 2) (3 · 4) | 5 - |
(1 1 1) (5 5 5) | (3 3 3) (1 1 1) | (5 · 4) (3 · 2) | 1 - ‖

POINTERS ON SCALES AND KEYS

When we tune water glasses or make other instruments, we tune them "by ear" so they will give us sounds 1 2 3 4 5 6 7 1 of the major scale. We don't know or particularly care whether sound 1 turns out to be F or E-flat or C or something else. We use the "no-clef" staff (p. 35) merely to picture the relative distances (intervals) of the melody, much as European musicians did in the Middle Ages. If, however, we wanted to play several homemade instruments together, all would have to have the same pitch for each tone of the scale. Calling pitches by letter-names and standardizing the pitches—each letter-name having a specified number of vibrations per second—was the way mankind solved the problem so that instruments from different manufacturers could play together.

For two or more instruments to play together not only must we have the relative sounds of 1 2 3 4 5 6 7 1, but we must say specifically in the music that sound one is to be C, or A-flat, or G, etc., with various other tones of the letter scale sharped or flatted so they will indeed function as sounds 1 2 3, etc., in relation to each other. Specifically, we must select the tones so they are everywhere a whole step apart except for the half-step intervals 3 to 4 and 7 to 1. Take a scale built upon D for example:

---

*The tie ⌣ in 1 (1 · 5) (♩ ⌣ ♩. ♪) indicates the first note of the skip-ty pattern is not to be sounded; rather let the walk note be prolonged to use the additional time represented by the skip-.

For practice, try: walk skip - ty walk skip - ty walk walk slo - ow

then: walk⌣skip - ty walk⌣skip - ty walk walk slo - ow

then: wa - alk - ty wa - alk - ty walk walk slo - ow

1 ⌣ (1 · 1) 1 (1 · 1) 1   1   1   -

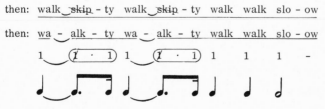

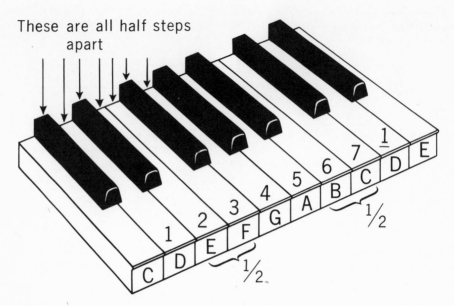

These are all half steps apart

The natural tones of the keyboard (white keys) give us half-steps from E to F and from B to C, but these are not <u>sounds</u> 3 to 4 and 7 to <u>1</u> in the D scale—the places where the half steps belong. To get the true sounds of a major scale we must raise note 3 to F-sharp, a whole step from sound 2 and a half step from sound 4. Likewise with note 7, which must become C-sharp.

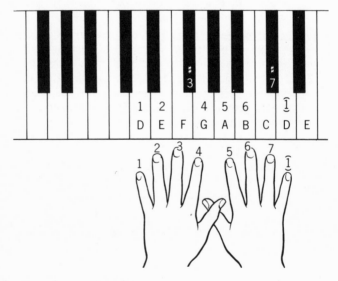

The tones of a D scale are therefore:

$$\begin{array}{ccccccc} D & E & F\sharp & G & A & B & C\sharp & D \\ 1 & 2 & 3 & & 4 & 5 & 6 & 7 & \underline{1} \end{array}$$

$\frac{1}{2}$ $\frac{1}{2}$

These tones must also be shown as sharps (or flats, in the case of some keys) when written. A D scale on the treble clef staff appears as:*

D E F♯ G A B C♯ D

Notice that when we write letters we indicate alterations exactly as we say them: "D-sharp" is written "D♯." But in music notation for a performer we warn him before he strikes the tone that it will be sharped; literally, "Sharp F."

A convenient way to learn the staff letter-names is to find *FACE* in three places: in the low spaces of the bass staff, on the middle lines, and in the high spaces of the treble staff:**

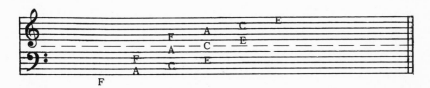

The intermediate letter-names are easily determined from the musical alphabet, the degree between A and C being B, between C and E being D, and between F and A being G.

Indicate the scale tones on the keyboard, by numbers and by letter-names, and on the staff for the sharp and flat keys. Circle the half steps between 3 and 4 and between 7 and 1. The key of G is done for you as a model:

Positioning of sharps and flats in key signatures:

G   D   A   E   B   F♯   F   B♭   E♭   A♭   D♭   G♭

* indicates that the encircled line represents the pitch of G (𝄞).

** indicates that the designated line represents F (𝄢 𝄢 𝄢:).

51

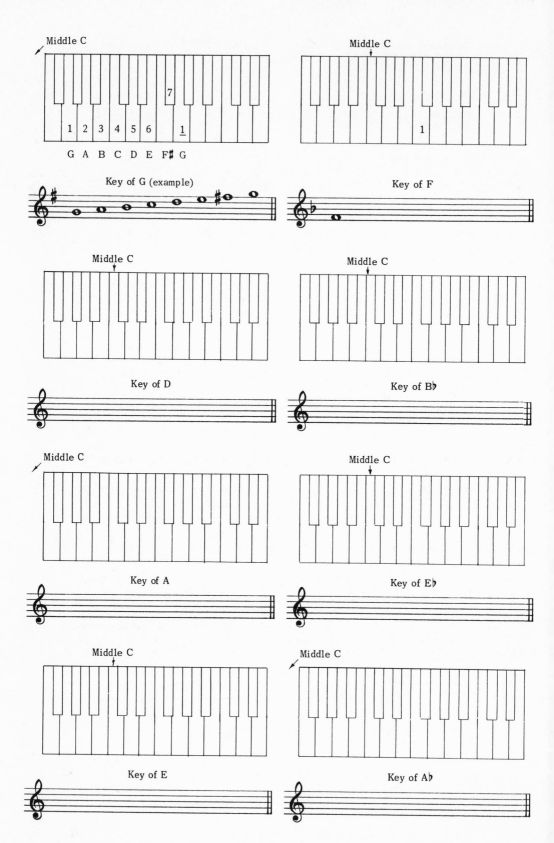

52

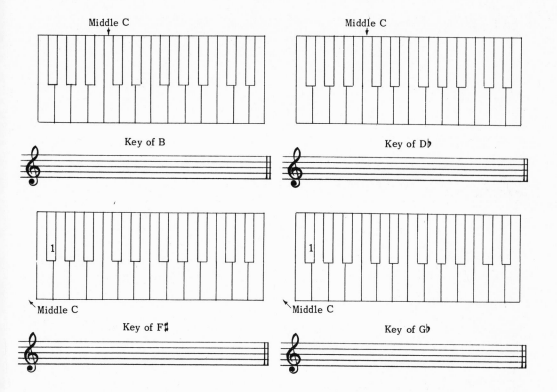

Key of B   Key of D♭

Key of F♯   Key of G♭

Notice in the sharp key scales you have done that the upper four notes (tetra-chord) in G become the lower four notes (tetrachord) in D—the starting note of G's upper tetrachord. The upper tetrachord in D becomes the lower tetrachord in A. The upper tetrachord in A becomes the lower tetrachord in _____?

Notice that the sharps in a key signature are placed exactly as they were added in each new scale: first F♯, then C♯, then G♯, then D♯, etc.

Notice in the flat key scales you have done that the lower tetrachord in F becomes the upper tetrachord in B-flat. The lower tetrachord in B-flat becomes the upper tetrachord in E-flat. The lower tetrachord in E-flat becomes the upper tetrachord in _____?

Notice that the flats in a key signature are placed exactly as they were added in each new scale: first B-flat, then E-flat, then A-flat, then _____?

Rule-of-Thumb. Because the sharps or flats of a key signature always appear in the same pattern it is possible to use a rule-of-thumb to determine from the key signature which note is acting as sound 1, or, in other words, what key the song is in.

Sharp Seven. In sharp keys, the last sharp (farthest to the right) of the signature is sound 7. From this we can easily locate the chord tones 1 3 5.

Flat Four. In flat keys the last flat of the signature is sound 4. From this we can easily locate the chord tones 1 3 5.

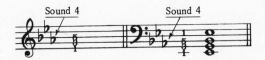

While most of the simple songs encountered in the elementary classroom end on sound 1 and one can determine the key merely by looking at the last note, some songs do not, and it is better practice to verify sound 1 by consulting the key signature as above.

POINTERS ON PEDAGOGY

Some textbooks make use of tonic sol-fa syllables to call the reader's attention to the various scale degrees of a tune. While not as helpful as numbers when instruments are being played, they are widely used in purely vocal reading and are easily learned:

1   2   3   4   5   6 7   1
do re mi fa sol la ti do

Miss Johnson found the elementary teachers' workshop helpful. What groups offer elementary music education workshops in your area? What time of year? Can you arrange to attend?* List the workshops you have found out about:

Pointers and Practice has presented all of the major scales and key signatures at the close of Chapter 2. If you are of limited formal musical background you may still be reeling from the encounter, but by referring to it frequently as you continue to explore music you will gain facility, and eventually mastery.

These theoretical matters, overemphasized, have killed many a child's in-

*Usual sponsors: College and university extension services, teacher training colleges and universities, national-state-provincial music education associations, city school systems' in-service training.

stinctive interest in music participation, to the extent that several distinguished educators have recommended that music reading and notation should not even be a part of the elementary classroom music program.

How much of this should children encounter, and at what stages of development?

How much did Miss Johnson lead her children into in her class, and for what purpose?

When and how were these learnings drawn from the musical activities?

3
BECOMING AWARE OF HARMONY

Miss Johnson had been able to secure an autoharp for the class, but she had delayed introducing them to it until they were at ease and competent in rhythmic and melodic skills, both in listening and performing. However, she continued experimenting with the instrument herself, receiving occasional help from the music consultant. She was delighted to notice how the steady rhythmic strumming of the autoharp increased her own rhythmic perception and how hearing the chordal background of a song gave support and confidence to her singing voice.

Remembering how Ralph's interest had grown after he had been asked to open the box of melody bells and be the first to experiment with them, Miss Johnson planned her approach in introducing the autoharp. Stanley Bushman had been good in the initial rhythmic experiences but somehow could not seem to concentrate sufficiently to master the complex of rhythmic, pitch, notational, and small-muscle co-ordination skills requisite to playing tunes on the melody bells with facility. Wouldn't this chording instrument with its steady rhythmic strumming and less demanding precision have a natural appeal for Stanley?

The Autoharp*

One day as the class was leaving for recess Miss Johnson asked Stanley to remain a moment. She went to the closet and brought out the autoharp.

"Stanley, we have this new instrument to use in our classroom. Would you like to sing 'The Paw-Paw Patch' with me and hear how it sounds?"

Miss Johnson played the autoharp as they sang.

"I think I see," said Stanley. "You just play on the strong pulses."

"That's right, Stanley, although there are lots of ways to use it. Here, you take the pick and strum while I push the chord buttons."

---

*See Appendix B for tuning suggestions.

Together they sang and played, and by the second phrase Stanley was strumming freely and confidently.

"Stanley, I have here a list of songs that can be chorded with just one chord.* Pick one, and try both the button-pressing and the strumming by yourself."

Stanley chose "Old MacDonald," pressed the F-button at Miss Johnson's suggestion, and played while they sang it together.

"Would you like to take the autoharp home in its case and work out the chording to a few of these one-chord songs? Let's keep it a secret and when you're ready you can introduce this new instrument to the class."

Stanley was ready the next day! Miss Johnson introduced him by saying Stanley had a surprise for the class, and then she turned the time over to him, and was pleased to observe the confidence with which Stanley got them started on a one-chord song:**

---

* For a list of one-chord songs see Pointers and Practice, Chap. 3, p. 71.
**See Chap. 6, p. 149, for different chordal applications.

It was rewarding to see the delight which they took in the autoharp, the co-operation and confidence they showed in group singing with this new instrument for accompaniment.

When they tried a second song, "Row, Row, Row Your Boat," using only the F-chord button, a few of the children laughed at the high pitch of "merrily." Miss Johnson, reminding them how they had learned to transpose melodies to a new key on their melody bells, suggested they try it again using the C-chord button. Stanley strummed on the C-chord and they began to sing, finally developing into a four-part round:

Introduction, C-chord

Row, Row, Row your boat

Gent - ly down the stream. Mer - ri - ly, mer - ri - ly

mer - ri - ly mer - ri - ly Life is but a dream.

That afternoon when time could be spared, Miss Johnson allowed Stanley and two or three other children to go to the back of the room, and under Stanley's guidance learn to play the autoharp, using one chord and singing softly. These people in turn coached other small groups and by the end of the week all who cared to learn were able to chord any of the one-chord songs on the autoharp.

Chording on Tone Bells

When the music consultant came to class that week he introduced vocal chording and harmony chants. The children listened as he drew the pick (plec-trum) across the autoharp strings one by one very deliberately—about one string per second. They noticed how certain strings were damped out and only tones 1, 3, and 5 in each octave were allowed to sound.

"Now that we've discovered that sounds 1 3 5 make the I-chord,* who could tell us how to build a I-chord in C on the melody bells?"

Counting from C, six children played on two sets of bells together. At each set of bells the first child tapped note 1, the second child note 3, the third child note 5. At first they just tapped the steady pulse rhythm as the class sang "Row, Row, Row Your Boat" and the autoharp played. Then they took a rhythmic chant from the song, as they had done weeks before on the water glass with "Old MacDonald," and enjoyed the new sound. Each player tapped out on his own tone the rhythm:

| Skip | - | ty | skip | - | ty | slo-ow |
| Life | | is | but | | a | dre-eam. |

The composite chord effect was thus:

Sound 5 (G), two players:
Sound 3 (E), two players:
Sound 1 (C), two players:

Then the consultant asked two players to go to the piano which had been rolled into the classroom, and each child played all three chord tones himself, but each one played in a different octave:

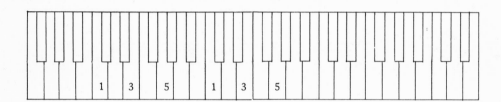

Vocal Chord Chants

With this instrumental support the music consultant was able to add vocal chording. The two pianists played their chords in this rhythm, the bell players added their chord, and the autoharpist strummed on the heavy pulses. Row One sang "Life is but a dream" on sound 1—over and over. Row Two joined in with the same chant, but on sound 3. Row Three completed the chord chant on sound 5:

---

* The I-chord (or tonic chord) is so named because this three-tone chord (triad) is formed by starting on note 1 and taking every other scale tone (notes 3 and 5).

Row, Row, Row Your Boat

Rows Four and Five entered with the melody, lustily singing it through twice, and all ended with a grand final chord on "dream"! The children laughed and applauded themselves in delight.

Following another after-school session with the music specialist, Miss Johnson was able to carry out this vocal, keyboard, and autoharp chording with other I-chord songs. By this time some of the children could play the whole tunes on bells or on the piano while various chording accompaniments were carried out.

The V⁷ Chord

The rapid progress of the children indicated that they were ready for the V^7-chord, which the music consultant introduced on his next visit to the class. Again he approached the new learning by first recognizing it in sound and then exploring its uses and symbols.

"Do you recall 'Skip to My Lou' and 'The Paw-Paw Patch'?" he inquired. "How would you like to add chords to them? Let's begin with the autoharp. Janet, will you strum for 'Skip to My Lou' on the I-chord in C?"

Janet began to strum and the class sang:

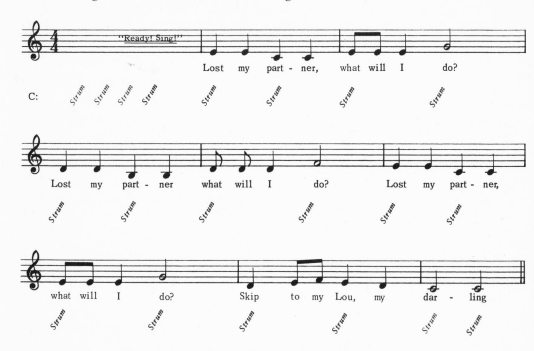

Several hands were up, and the children were excited. The consultant smiled.

"Yes, I know. I saw you squirming in the second and fourth phrases. I didn't like the I-chord sound there either. We must find another chord."

By experimenting with nearby chords, and under the teacher's indirect guidance, Janet found the G^7-chord worked well in the second and fourth phrases.

"If we count C as note 1, what number will the G-chord be?"

The specialist wrote on the board:

$$
\begin{array}{ccccccc}
1 & 2 & 3 & 4\ 5 & 6 & 7 & \underline{1} \\
\text{A} & \text{B} & \text{C} & \text{D}\ \text{E}\ \text{F} & \text{G} & \text{A} & \text{B}\ \underline{\text{C}}\ \text{D etc.} \\
 & & \text{I} & & \text{V} & &
\end{array}
$$

"Yes! So a chord built on G will be the V-chord, won't it? The autoharp tells us that this G-chord has a 'seventh' (G^7) added to it, so we really have a V^7-chord if we are to use its true label."

He then wrote on the board, under the words, the proper chording for the song:

62

Lost my part-ner, what will I do?
  I   I   I   I

Lost my part-ner, what will I do?
V^7 V^7 V^7 V^7

Lost my part-ner, what will I do?
  I   I   I   I

Skip to my Lou, my dar-ling.
V^7 V^7 I I

"Now let's try 'The Paw-Paw Patch.' Janet, will you choose someone to take over the autoharp? Fine . . . Judy, will you strum the C-chord to get us started?"

They sang in somewhat subdued voice so they could listen for the autoharp. Again they all noticed how the I-chord clashed in the second phrase, but without stopping the song Judy pressed the proper G^7 (V^7) button and finished the song, changing back to C for the third phrase and G^7 (V^7) to C (I) on the last phrase.

"This song has the chord changes in the same places that 'Skip to My Lou' does," Judy announced.

"Good detective work, Judy!" complimented the consultant. "When a musician finds two songs with the same harmonies occurring at the same places, it tells him that these two songs can be sung at the same time. Would you like to try?"

The class was divided, with the back half of the room under Miss Johnson's leadership singing "Skip to My Lou," and the front half, led by the music specialist, singing "The Paw-Paw Patch." The children enjoyed the novelty, but the music teacher noticed the singing quality was harsh and forced and he discussed this with them. After a brief TIO (trying-it-out) Session it was decided that the key of C was too low for The Paw-Paw Patch to sound gay and they would try F as the I-chord.

"Here's a problem for us then," said the man. "If we let F be the I-chord, what chord will be the V^7-chord in this new key?"

They proved their answer on the board:*

            1 2 3 4 5 6 7 <u>1</u>
A B C D E F G A B C^7 D E F G A
          I V^7

"And by the way, if we are going to let the key of F have this song, how will he put his 'brand' or 'mark' on it? . . . Yes, his signature is 'B-flat.' So even in writing the letter-names I should flat all the B's to show that this scale belongs to F":

A B♭C D E F G A B♭C D E F G A
     I V^7

Several children chorded songs in this new key using I- and V^7-chords.**

"Before we stop today, I'd like you to begin to notice the special 'flavors' of

---

*Note that the V^7-chord sound is needed, not just a V-chord. Therefore on the autoharp a C^7-chord is used, not just a C-chord.

**For a list of I and V^7 chord songs see Pointers and Practice, Chap. 3, pp. 72–73.

the I- and V^7-chords. Listen while I strum some I-chords.... And now some V^7-chords. Who could walk to these chords and show us how each makes you feel?''

Five children were chosen. Three children noticeably stiffened and increased bodily tension as they heard the V^7-chord. All noticeably relaxed as the V^7 moved back to I.

''Yes, that's the way these chords make me feel, too—more tense, and restless, for the V^7-chord, and more natural and relaxed for the I-chord. I guess musicians in olden times felt that way, too; they recognized the V-chord's dominant and demanding personality and named it the <u>dominant</u> chord. The I-chord, being the peaceful key-tone chord, is called the <u>tonic</u> (tone-center) chord. I like to think of the tonic (I) chord as being like the calm surface of the ocean and the <u>dominant</u> (V^7) chord like a big, restless wave full of power and ready to break'':

''Remember how our marchers stiffened when they heard the V^7 or dominant chord? Suppose you were sitting with your arms comfortably folded while the I-chord plays ... like this. How could you show the change and tension when the V^7-chord sounds? . . . Yes!''

The children experimented with several positions of tension and finally settled on this:

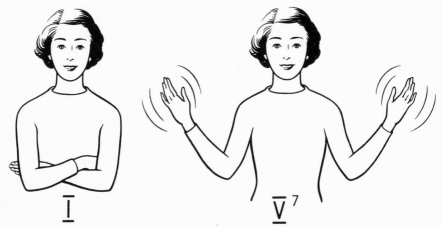

They practiced listening for chord changes and showing tension and relaxation positions while a child at the board pointed to the ocean-wave sketches. Together they worked out chord markings for three more familiar songs:

In a cav-ern, in a can-yon, ex-ca-va-ting for a mine,
  I   I   I V^7

Dwelt a min-er, for-ty-nin-er, and his daugh-ter Clem-en-tine.
V^7 I V^7 I

Oh my dar-ling, Oh my dar-ling, Oh my dar-ling Clem-en-tine.
I I I V^7

You are lost and gone for-ev-er, dread-ful sor-ry, Clem-en-tine.
V^7 I V^7 I

Here we go loo-by loo, here we go loo-by light,
I I I V^7

Here we go loo-by loo, all on a Sat-ur-day night.
I I V^7 I

Lon-don bridge is fall-ing down, fall-ing down, fall-ing down,
I I V^7 I

Lon-don bridge is fall-ing down, my fair la-dy-o.
I I V^7 I

Piano Chording with I and V^7

The following Friday after school Miss Johnson asked the music consultant to show her how to find the V^7-chords on the piano and bells in the key of C:

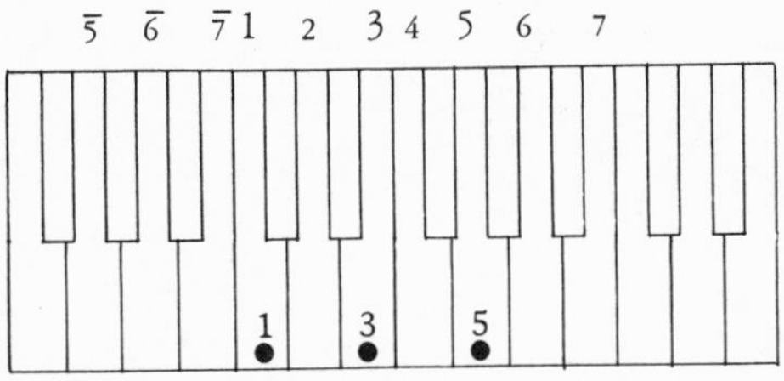

I-chord in C

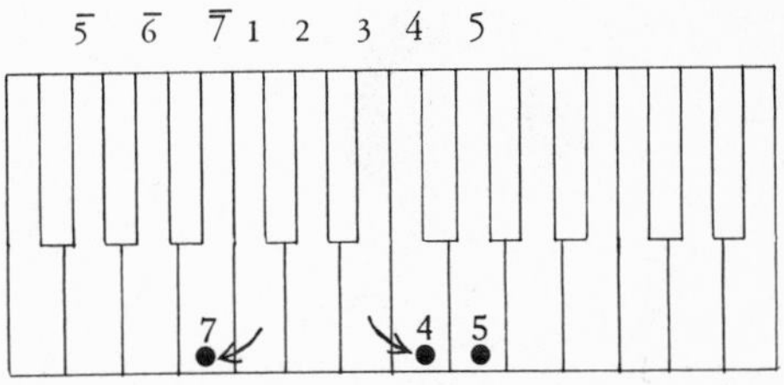

Simple V^7-chord in C

"Be sure that the children notice the two tones which move from 1 to $\overline{7}$ and from 3 to 4 because they are the tones which are a half step apart in the scale. This will help to teach the children which black keys to use in other tonalities. In the key of F, for instance,

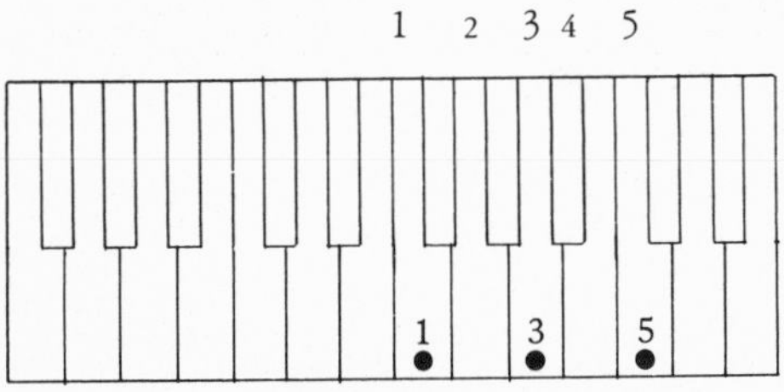

I-chord in F

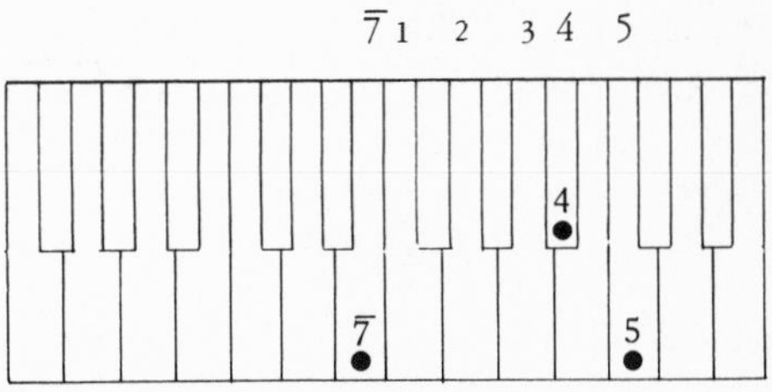

V^7-chord in G

when the tones move to the V^7-chord, the middle tone (3 to 4) will move up to a black key (B-flat) to be a half step from note 3.

"From a I-chord built on G, note 1 will move down to a black key in order to get to $\overline{7}$ a half step down":

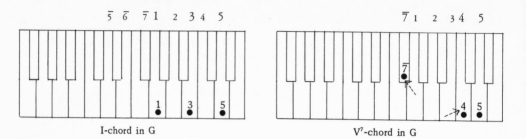

I-chord in G V^7-chord in G

When the opportunity came, Miss Johnson helped the children to find the I- and V^7-chords on the keyboard and on the bells. At first they just played on the strong beats where the autoharp was strummed, but when the bell players noticed that their bells didn't sustain notes as the autoharp and piano did, someone asked if they could play a chant rhythm as they had done on "Life is but a dream" with the I-chord. They tried various ideas before finding ways which a majority preferred.

For "Clementine" they made a chant of skip-ty walk walk, skip-ty slo-ow, which was derived from the chorus word-rhythm, "Oh my dar-ling Clem-en-tine." This rhythm was chorded on the bells, with one child playing note 1 on the I-chord and note $\overline{7}$ on the V^7-chord; another child playing note 3 on the I-chord and note 4 on the V^7-chord; and a third child playing note 5 only, because it occurs in both the I- and V^7-chords.

Clementine

Oh   my   dar - ling   Clem - en - tine.   Oh   my

They quickly discovered that "Clementine" did not sound well in the key of C because it was too low for their voices, but since their attention was on practicing chords at the moment nobody minded. When, however, they had the idea firmly in mind and could find these chords in C, Miss Johnson suggested they transpose the song to the key of F. Remembering the consultant's advice about having the children notice that 1 to $\overline{7}$ and 3 to 4 were only <u>half steps</u>, Miss Johnson soon had them finding the B-flat needed for a proper sound 4 in the V[7]-chord for the key of F.

For "Looby Loo" the class worked out a chord rhythm of <u>walk walk skip-ty walk</u> taken from the word chant "Loo, loo, loo-by loo," and they chorded it on that rhythm. Since she wanted the children to build eye-recognition of these rhythm patterns in chord clusters she wrote out the figure on the board:

This chord rhythm was still on the board after school when the music consultant dropped by to see how the class had made out with I- and V[7]-chords in various keys.

A Reminder About Compound Meter

Noticing the chant on the board; he asked, "Would you like to help the children find a better way to notate that rhythm, Miss Johnson?"

"Of course I would. Is anything wrong with it?"

"No, not really wrong. When you step out what you hear, it is <u>walk walk skip-ty walk</u>, and ♩ ♩ ♩. ♪ ♩ is the notation for that movement. But listen to this!"

When the consultant played, Miss Johnson noticed that, taking the song as a whole, the subdivision of undercurrent of the beat was not $\dfrac{\text{Run-run Run-run}}{\text{TIC} \quad \text{tok}}$; but rather $\dfrac{\text{Ta-ta-ta Ta-ta-ta}}{\text{TIC} \quad \text{tok}}$. The rhythm of the first phrase, for example, was:

Here we go loo -by loo   Here we go loo -by light
Tri- ple-it skip-ty slo-ow   Tri - ple-it skip-ty slo-ow

and the last bit was:

All on a Sat-ur -day night
Tri-ple-it tri -ple-it slo-ow

Then Miss Johnson recalled that songs with an undercurrent of <u>tri-ple-it</u>

68

either had to have permission (♩♩♩ with 3) everywhere to crowd <u>three-on-a-beat</u> where only <u>two</u> eighth-notes should be, or, most often, were written in compound meter ($\frac{6}{8}$ $\frac{2}{\text{♩.}}$) so that the beat note would be big enough to contain <u>three</u> eighth-notes instead of the customary two. They looked up a copy of the song and found it was indeed written in compound meter:

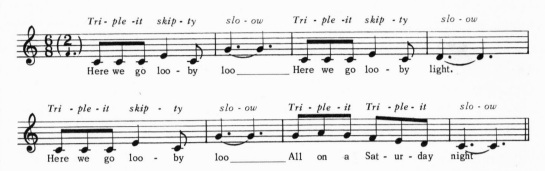

Miss Johnson asked, "In this meter shouldn't 'Loo, loo, loo-by loo' have been written this way?

$$\frac{6}{8} \quad \text{♩.} \quad \text{♩.} \quad \text{♩} \quad \text{♪♩.}$$

Walk   walk   skip - ty walk

"Yes, indeed," said the consultant. "Would you like to borrow these records of children's songs and see if you and your class can decide which are compound meters—three-on-a-beat (♩♩♩ with 3) feelings; and which are simple meters— two-on-a-beat (♩♩) feelings?"*

"I certainly would," she exclaimed, "but first I'm going to take them home and practice myself so I won't lead the children astray."

*Page 128 lists several recent song-series books for elementary grades. Each of these series provides recorded albums of a large number of songs from each grade-level book. By looking in the books available to him the teacher can locate songs in $\frac{2}{4}$ meter to contrast with other songs in $\frac{6}{8}$ meter, or songs in $\frac{3}{4}$ meter to contrast with songs in $\frac{9}{8}$ meter. By finding the corresponding phonograph recordings for these songs the teacher can provide a wealth of songs to explore for compound vs. simple meter characteristics.

POINTERS AND PRACTICE–
CHAPTER 3

PRACTICE

I. Some songs which can be sung to the I-chord alone in slow steady strumming are: "Old MacDonald"; "Row, Row, Row Your Boat"; "Are You Sleeping?"; "Little Tom Tinker"; "The Farmer in the Dell"; "Taps"; "Swing Low, Sweet Chariot"; "Shortnin' Bread"; "Goodbye, Old Paint"; "Three Blind Mice."

Try singing those which are familiar to you, and accompany yourself with the I-chord on the autoharp or the piano.

II. Learn to play the melody to "Skip to My Lou" on p. 62 in the key of C on the piano. To train ear, eye, and fingers together, sing the numbers as you play the first time, reading from p. 62.

C is 1: 3 3 1 1 3 (3 3) 5 -

2 2 7̄ 7̄ 2 (2 2) 4 -

etc.

Play it again, but sing the rhythm-movement words to be sure your song flows smoothly.

In 4s: Walk walk walk walk | run-run walk slo-ow

Walk walk walk, etc.

Play it again, keeping accurate pitch and rhythm, but sing the regular words of the song.

Find the tones of the I- and V⁷-chords in the key of C. On the diagram below mark the I-chord tones with dots (·) and the V⁷ chord tones with crosses (+).

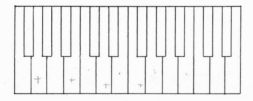

Using this keyboard diagram of the chords to guide you, find the I-chord and the V⁷-chord in the key of C at the piano. Ultimately you will want to play these chords with the left hand, leaving the right hand free to play melodies. To begin with you may find it easier to use the right hand or even to distribute the three tones between both hands, left hand taking the bottom chord tone (C) and right hand taking the middle and top chord tones (E and G).

71

Sing "Skip to My Lou" again, using the I- and V[7]-chords as indicated on p. 63

III. Use an autoharp or piano and sing to determine by ear where the I-chord will no longer fit and the V[7]-chord is needed in the following songs. Indicate the proper chord at each parentheses:

One lit-tle, two lit-tle, three lit-tle In-dians
( )   ( )   ( )   ( )

Four lit-tle, five lit-tle, six lit-tle In-dians
( )   ( )   ( )   ( )

Sev'n lit-tle, eight lit-tle, nine lit-tle In-dians
( )   ( )   ( )   ( )

Ten lit-tle In-dian boys
( )   ( ) ( ) ( )

IV. Mark the I-chord tones (·) and the V[7]-chord tones (+) for the key of F:

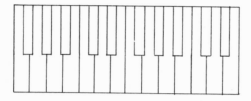

Sing "Skip to My Lou" or "The Paw-Paw Patch," accompanying yourself in the key of F.

V. Mark the I- and V[7]-chord tones for the key of E-flat and accompany your-self while you sing "Skip to My Lou" or "The Paw-Paw Patch" in that key:

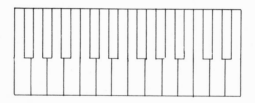

VI. Try singing and chording "Clementine," "Looby Loo," "London Bridge" (by ear, or refer to pp. 64-65) in the above, or other keys. Specifically, acquire skill in using the keys of C, F, G, and E-flat.

VII. Other familiar songs which can be accompanied with only the I- and V[7]-chords are given below. Practice those you know, striving to keep even, rhythmical strumming or piano chording throughout, with as few chord changes as possible. Indicate next to each title which is better in the key of C and which in the key of F.

_____ "Down in the Valley."   _____ "The Farmer in the Dell."

_____ "Alouette."   _____ "Leavin' Old Texas."

_____ "Long, Long Ago."   _____ "Buffalo Gals."

_____ "Billy Boy."   _____ "Yellow Rose of Texas."

_____ "Oh Where Has My Little Dog Gone?"   _____ "The More We Get Together."

_____ "Oats, Peas, Beans, and Barley."   _____ "Sweetly Sings the Donkey."

_____ "Go Tell Aunt Rhodie."   _____ "Sur le Pont d'Avignon."

_____ "Jingle Bells."   _____ "Polly Wolly Doodle."

POINTERS ON PEDAGOGY

1. Why is it desirable to use just one chord when children are first learning to use the autoharp? What problems are involved in first playing the autoharp? What additional problems would immediate use of both I- and V^7-chords introduce?

2. Consider the physical dexterity and co-ordination involved in playing the tuned water glasses, the autoharp, the violin. Which is best for a child to begin on? Why?

73

Compare the relative co-ordination difficulties involved in playing the water glasses, the melody bells, and the piano.

3. The first two paragraphs of Chapter 3 illustrate aspects of individual differences as they are often found in music participation. We sometimes tend to overlook how psychologically difficult it is for an adult with a lifetime of "I can't do music" behind him to participate freely. A classroom teacher is fortunate in being able to go back and experience music daily at the less complex level of a child—frequently near a point where the teacher's own involvement in music had ended. How did the autoharp help Miss Johnson over a psychological barrier?

Ralph had a similar problem, i.e., psychological or social, in that he joined the class after their own common experiences and their own group relationships had been established. How did Miss Johnson provide for him to make a successful start in a new activity?

Stanley's problem was perhaps less a psychological one than something else. Discuss his problem.

In what ways might Miss Johnson be justified in feeling that playing the auto-harp would be easier and better for Stanley than playing bell melodies?

Miss Johnson wanted to minimize the difficulties in order to ensure success in Stanley's first attempt with the autoharp. How did she help him the first time he tried the instrument? (This approach is particularly helpful when working with Primary grade children.)

4. For many generations the typical piano method book began by explaining how music is written, how it looks on the keyboard, and how it should be played. For example:

This is the music staff. It has five lines. It has four spaces.

This is the treble clef.

This is the bass clef.

These staves are combined to make the Grand Staff on which piano music is written.

This is Middle C.

This is a "whole note." It gets four counts.

This is how Middle C is written on the Grand Staff.

When you see it, play Middle C on the piano and count "1 2 3 4."

Educational psychology tells us something very different, namely, that a child should:

a. Listen to the musical aspect under consideration in familiar tunes, e.g., the V^7-chord.
b. Feel it in his psycho-physical being, e.g., the <u>tension</u> of the V^7-chord.
c. Express through movement and words how it makes him feel, e.g., in contrast to the more relaxed I-chord.
d. Learn how it is produced on an instrument, e.g., the V^7-chord on the autoharp, piano, or in group singing.
e. Learn its symbol—how it is written, e.g., as V^7, or G^7 in the key of C, or in music notation on the staff.

In summary these principles involve (1) how the music <u>sounds</u>; (2) how it makes the hearer feel and how he expresses that <u>feeling</u>; (3) how the instrument <u>looks</u> when specific sounds are produced, and how the music <u>looks</u> in notation.

How were these principles treated when Miss Johnson introduced walking, running, and skipping rhythms to the class in Chapter 1? When Stanley introduced chording on the autoharp to the class? When the music consultant introduced vocal chording and the I- and V^7-chords to the class?

5. In learning our native language we first heard it spoken around us, then tried to imitate the sounds we heard, then tried to use the sounds to communicate (e.g., "spoon," "ball," "broom"), learned to recognize pictures of it, and after six years or so began to read printed word symbols. What similarities do you see in learning the language of music?

6. On p. 59 it is reported that "by the end of the week all who cared to learn were able to chord ... on the autoharp." Should not each child be <u>required</u> to learn regardless of whether he "cared to learn" or not? Howard Taubman, music critic for the <u>New York Times</u>, suggests in <u>How to Bring Up Your Child to Enjoy Music</u>: "If it is humanly possible, avoid compulsion in your campaign to make music part of your children's life." Is such a philosophy compatible with the school's responsibility to pass on the fundamentals (including music) of our culture? Discuss briefly.

4

SEEING WHAT WE HEAR LEADS TO HEARING WHAT WE SEE

Reading a Familiar Song

Both Miss Johnson and her class were ready to place more emphasis on the use of notation, not only to see how their own music making looked on the printed page, but to enjoy the musical ideas written down by others. With the help of the music consultant Miss Johnson prepared a list of "mystery tunes." The first was on the board one day when the children came in:

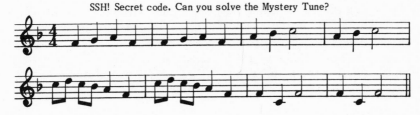

SSH! Secret code. Can you solve the Mystery Tune?

Just before lunch when there were a few spare moments, Miss Johnson said, "Let's check our mystery-tune clues now. Can anyone find a place that sounds like my clapping?" and she started to clap:

|Run-run run-run walk walk   run-run run-run walk walk

"Ah, some of you know now, don't you? Shall we clap and then say the rhythm movement for the entire song?"

They clapped and chanted:

81

```
|Walk walk walk walk        |walk walk walk walk
|Walk walk slo-ow           |walk walk slo-ow
|Run-run run-run walk walk  |run-run run-run walk walk
|Walk walk slo-ow           |walk walk slo-ow
```

"Many of us have solved the mystery. Let's see . . . who wants another clue?
. . . Stanley? Stanley, can you sing 1 2 3? . . . Good! Now can you sing 1 2 3 1?"
Stanley tried, but it came out 1 2 3 2, although he called it "1 2 3 1."

"Here, Stanley, try playing 1 2 3 1 on the pipe bells using F for sound 1. That's
fine! Now will you play and sing it twice, the way the music tells you to? Still no?
This time as you play the pattern twice, Stanley, the class will sing softly on loo
because, after all 1 2 3 1 are not really the words to the song, and that might be
throwing you off."

Miss Johnson could tell that everyone else knew the song, and by the time the
class had sung the first two measures on loo Stanley had guessed the mystery
tune also. Someone suggested that since they had the pipe bells, the bells should
sound the Ding, ding, dong at the end.

Miss Johnson suggested that since this song was a round the "1 5̄ 1 -" pattern
could be played continously. As the bell rang for lunch one row was singing:

as a continous chant and Stanley was playing it on the bells while the rest of the
class sang the melody. Gale was on the point of suggesting that the bell part could
also be used as an introduction when Miss Johnson suspended the activity in favor
of lunch.

Reading an Unfamiliar Song

The next excursion into reading notation came when the children encountered
"Sur le pont d'Avignon" in their Social Studies unit on European groups and cultures in North America. From the notation on the board they observed the two

types of rhythm patterns, ♪ ♪ ♩ and ♪ ♪ ♪ ♪, which make up the first two
phrases.
```

Sur   le pont    d'A- vi - gnon    L'on   y   dan - se,   l'on   y   dan - se,

Sur   le pont    d'A - vi- gnon,   L'on   y   dan - se   tout   en   rond.
```

Several children stepped out run-run walk, and the class picked up this pattern on the rhythm sticks. The run-run run-run pattern was given to the shakers. Then the two groups read the patterns through all eight measures, trying not to overlap each other's pattern. After that, two individuals tried it with shaker and rhythm stick, followed by other groups of two, until quite a few could do it accurately and smoothly.

When the rhythm was mastered Miss Johnson called attention to the pitches:

First phrase:
    1st measure: run-run walk on sound 1.
    2nd measure: run-run walk on sound 2.
    3rd measure: run-run run-run on sounds 3 4 5 1.
    4th measure: run-run run-run on sounds $\overline{7}$ 1 2 $\overline{5}$.
Second phrase:
    5th measure: same as 1st measure.
    6th measure: same as 2nd measure.
    7th measure: same as 3rd measure.
    8th measure: run-run walk on sounds 2 $\overline{7}$ 1.

By listening to each other play the 3rd, 4th, and 8th measures on the bells as they came to "reading" those parts, the children could soon sing the entire song using numbers for words:

In 2s: | (1 1) 1 | (2 2) 2 | (3 4)(5 1)($\overline{7}$ 1)(2 $\overline{5}$)
| (1 1) 1 | (2 2) 2 | (3 4)(5 1)(2 $\overline{7}$)1 ‖

They reviewed this once or twice in order to become familiar with it, although Miss Johnson was careful to avoid extended drill which could cause interest to lag. Then the French text was used—as closely as Miss Johnson could pronounce it, for her belief was that an attempt at French pronunciation, however faulty, was better than not trying at all. She hoped by the next day to be able to bring a tape recording—made at her request by the high school French Club—of the song properly done. The children could then check their version of both the music and the language, and correct any errors.

Miss Johnson had kept in the back of her mind the needs of Stanley and some of the other children to have more deliberate experience with hearing sounds and seeing notes and relating them to scale degrees. To provide this experience she began devoting two or three minutes each day to ear-recognition games with several variations. The important thing, she was convinced, was to limit the "vocabulary" to simple choices and then to expand it as the children gained confidence—much as the child at first learns black, white, red, yellow, blue before he becomes concerned with such refined discriminations as magenta, aquamarine, beige, and coral.

Because they were easy to find visually, she chose the three black keys of the piano. One child would play on the three piano keys or on a set of bells a short pattern such as 3 2 1 or 3 2 3 or 1 2 3 or 1 2 1 or 1 3 3 or 3 1 3 or 2 3 1. Another child would try to repeat the pattern by ear on the three keys of another instrument. Other variations of this were:

1. "Spell-down," with the teacher giving the original patterns and adapting their length and difficulty to the ability of the individual child responding.
2. Teacher or child plays a three-tone pattern. The class, the row, or the individual sings it back by numbers.

3. Teacher or capable child sings a pattern using those three tones on the syllable <u>loo</u>. Children answer with numbers.
4. Leader writes a three-tone pattern on the chalkboard or places it on a music flannelboard indicating which line or space he selects to be sound 1, e.g.:

Notice that no clef, letter name, or key signature is involved, and children may respond on the same three black keys of an instrument regardless of which line or space is arbitrarily selected to be sound 1 on the staff.
5. Leader plays a pattern. Children respond by placing flannelboard notes, or by writing notes at the board or on staff-lined paper at their seats.

Many versions of this activity were developed, but Miss Johnson was careful to limit the games to short periods fitted into other playing, singing, moving, or listening experiences, and always ending while the children were still eager for more. In a short time many children were ready to include the two black keys above or below as well as the three black keys they had been using, and from there to add the white key a half step above black note 3 and the white key a half step below black note 1, making the full octave scale. Many became skillful enough on hearing tonal patterns to be able to sing and name then, write them, or to play them on instruments. Conversely, on seeing the patterns they could name and sing them or play them on instruments.*

These same short practice experiences were adapted to rhythm and harmony as well. Miss Johnson would clap, play on the piano, or strike on the drum such rhythms as:

Children might step the patterns out on the floor, tap them at their seats while chanting (for patterns, <u>walk</u> <u>walk</u> <u>slo-ow</u>, <u>run-run</u> <u>run-run</u> <u>walk</u> <u>walk</u>, etc.), or write the symbols on paper or at the chalkboard.

To provide practice in reading rhythm symbols Miss Johnson had flash cards of individual fundamental movements. In the early stages each practice would begin with a steady walking group to establish the underlying pulse feeling:**

---

*For uses of the recorder flute to help build musical understanding see Appendix A, pp. 332-335.
**As mentioned in Chap. 1, the visual rhythm board is available commercially with an assortment of basic rhythm cards. See fn., p. 10.

In front of this strip could be superimposed other individual rhythm cards showing the rhythmic disposition of certain walking pulses:

Children could respond to these patterns by clapping, tapping, playing instruments, stepping them out, or chanting.

The IV-Chord

The three fundamental harmonies were similarly handled. The children were already quite skillful at distinguishing the restless, dominant V^7-chord from the reposeful tonic I-chord. The leader would play on the piano or autoharp a pattern such as:

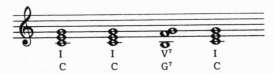

Miss Johnson showed them that the IV-chord was always found next to the V^7-chord on the autoharp. Several children experimented with using it in "Oh Susannah" and "I've Been Working on the Railroad" while the class responded with arm movements appropriate to the harmonies they heard.* As the children felt the IV-chord to be more restless than the I-chord, but not as dominant as the V^7, they decided to unfold their crossed arms, but just comfortably so instead of under tension as in the V^7-chord.

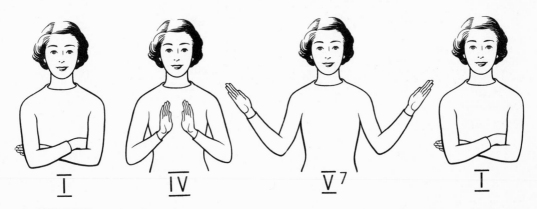

*The notation to "Oh Susannah" and "I've Been Working on the Railroad" is found on pp. 92-93 and p. 88, respectively, but it is recommended that the student discover this need of the IV by ear from the autoharp without reference to notation.

They used the new IV-chord on the autoharp, finding it in the keys of F and G as well as C. (See Pointers and Practice, p. 97.)

At a later time Miss Johnson used the IV-chord on the piano. They found the three primary chords for the key of C on the piano, and wrote them on the board.*

"Janet, will you play on the piano the C-chord just above middle C, and Linden, would you like to join Janet playing the C-chord just below middle C? If you two will both play very slowly the I-chord, the IV-chord, the I-chord, and then the I-chord again . . . and keep doing that in a rhythm of

slo-ow slo-ow slo-ow slo-ow
I   IV   I   I

I'll show you how a favorite song of ours can be sung to it. Just listen the first time, and then we'll all sing it slowly the second time.

Miss Johnson started the chording, as an introduction, and began singing the familiar Australian song:

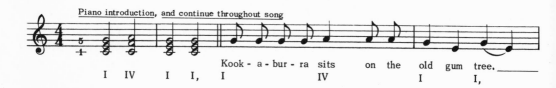

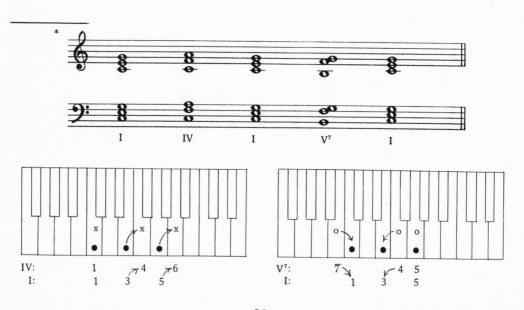

86

laugh,   kook - a - bur - ra,   Gay your life must be.
I   I,   I   IV   I I

With this understanding of the IV-chord in the key of C, Miss Johnson then encouraged piano chording and bell chording in the key of F (cautioning the children to notice the note "3 to 4" half step which requires B-flat instead of plain B-natural—B♮).* They worked out a rhythmic chant which proved to be passive in the first measure where the melody is active, and active in the second measure where the melody is passive: <u>Laugh</u>, <u>laugh</u>, fun-ny kook-a-bur-ra.

The class divided into four groups. First, two of the groups chanted on sound 1:

Laugh,   laugh   fun - ny kook - a - bur - ra

Then the other two sang the song against the chant. After that one group chanted on sound 1, another group sang the melody, and the rest of the children chanted on sound 3 (whenever a I-chord harmony was needed) or on sound 4 (whenever a IV-chord harmony was needed). Finally one group chanted on sound 1, one group chanted on sound 3 or 4, one group chanted on sound 5 or 6, and one group sang the melody:

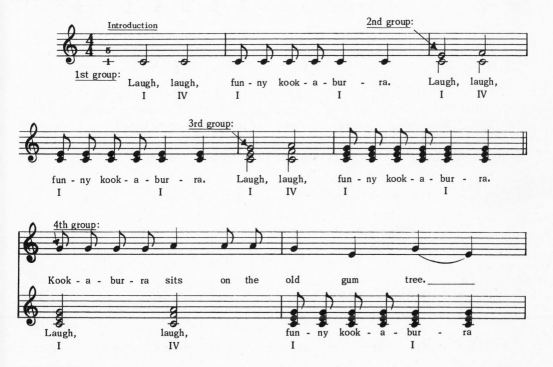

---

*See Pointers and Practice, pp. 51-52.

To complete the introductory experience with vocal chording Miss Johnson, after consultation with the music specialist, used "I've Been Working on the Railroad." This song requires all three of the primary chords.

First the children worked out the vocal chording on an <u>oo</u> sound, sustaining each chord for slo-o-o-ow duration and breathing at the end of each phrase:

I've been work-ing on the rail-road, all the live-long day.
I   I   IV   I

I've been work-ing on the rail-road just to pass the time a-way.
I   I V^7 V^7

Don't you hear the whist-le blow-ing: rise up so ear-ly in the morn?
V^7 I   IV   I

Can't you hear the cap-tain shouting: Di-nah, blow your horn!
IV   I   I V^7 I

When the rhythmic word-chant was added in this harmonic pattern the following arrangement emerged:

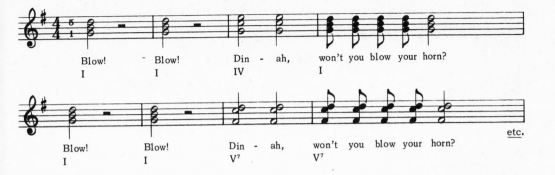

Blow!   Blow!   Din - ah,   won't you blow your horn?
I   I   IV   I

Blow!   Blow!   Din - ah,   won't you blow your horn?   etc.
I   I   V⁷   V⁷

Inverted Triads

However, something was wrong. It did not sound as well as the "Kookaburra" vocal chording had. When Miss Johnson brought the problem to the music consultant he pointed out that the top voice part was probably uncomfortably high for some of the children to stay on for the entire song.

"Why did you try to do this song in the key of G instead of doing it in C as you have done before in vocal chording?"

"We did try the melody in the key of C first," said the teacher, "and it took the children down to G below middle C and only went up to F above middle C." She diagrammed it as she spoke:

"Obviously this is too low. They told us in the workshop that children's songs should generally lie between D and D, staying within the staff," she continued, while adding another diagram:

"So we moved it up to G."

"Very good, Miss Johnson. And there's a way to get the melody to lie within the desired range, and yet not have the vocal chording so high—by using an inverted G-chord. All this means is that we take off the high note 5 (D) and put it under the other tones of the chord where it is more comfortably chanted."

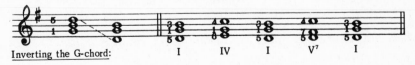

Inverting the G-chord: I   IV   I   V⁷   I

89

"Notice," he added, "that each voice still goes where it should except that low 5 ($\bar{5}$) is used instead of regular 5":

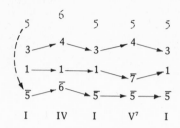

Armed with this new knowledge, Miss Johnson and the children developed their vocal chording to "I've Been Working on the Railroad" as follows:

I've Been Working on the Railroad

The Bass Staff and Chord Roots

"I have one more area in which I'd like your assistance before this year ends," said Miss Johnson to the music consultant one day toward the end of the school year. "When you use the staff and talk about letter-names of notes, I have to count everything from Middle C and it's very slow. Is there some way the children and I can develop more facility, particularly in using the bass staff?"

"We don't normally concern ourselves with the bass staff in elementary school," answered the consultant. "In Grades Five and Six we do try to acquaint the children with it to prepare the boys for the time when their voices will mature and they will be using the bass clef in choral singing. Actually, singing from the bass clef presents few problems when a child has learned to use the staff without any clef sign or letter-name, as you began your children. They learned from the start to read vocally, letting any line or space represent sound 1. In playing instruments, however, there is a decided advantage in knowing letter-names and bass-clef key signatures, so let me suggest a start that is used by some teachers.

"Your children already know the musical alphabet and its habit of repeating

91

seven letters over and over. Have you happened to notice that, beginning with F, every other letter spells the word: F-A-C-E? I tell the children if they can find F-A-C-E in three places they can easily learn the letter-names of the staff."

"On this page [diagram above] you can see the middle f-a-c-e is on lines while the lower and the upper one are in spaces. Both 'space-faces' do not begin in the first space of the staff. Children need to observe that the bass f-a-c-e begins below the staff.

"To gain facility in using the bass staff we can have the children read and play the chord roots on the piano."

Miss Johnson nodded. "They will remember your teaching them that in the key of C the root of a I-chord is sound 1 or C, and the root of a V^7-chord is sound 5 or G."

"In 'Skip to My Lou'," continued the consultant, "the chord pattern was:

$$\text{I} \quad \text{I} \quad \text{V}^7 \quad \text{V}^7$$
$$\text{I} \quad \text{I} \quad \text{V}^7 \quad \text{I}$$

"So in the key of C the chord roots are:

Lost my partner, what will I do?	Lost my part-ner, what will I do?

| I | I | V^7 | V^7 |
| (C) | (C) | (G) | (G) |

Lost my partner, what will I do?	Skip to my Lou, my darling.

| I | I | V^7 | I |
| (C) | (C) | (G) | (C) |

"Let's write out 'Oh Susannah' in the key of F with the chord roots a child could read and play."

Miss Johnson did some homework on chords and she learned that chord roots are actually the foundation blocks of the most familiar music of our culture. They also constitute the larger proportion of the bass parts found in hymns and similar choral music. The guitar, a homemade two- or three-stringed 'cello, tuned water jugs for blowing, or tunable drums are good classroom instruments for playing chord roots, producing musical effect similar to that of a bass viol (string bass) in a dance band.*

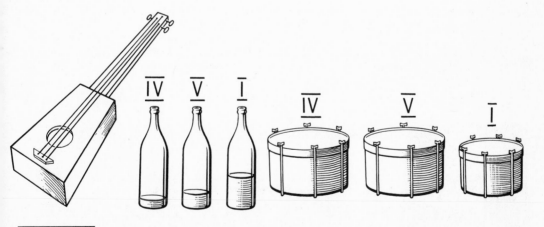

*The strings of the guitar from low to high are tuned: E A D G B E. (See also Chap. 7, p. 165.) Thus the four lowest strings—and incidentally the four strings of the orchestral bass viol—may be used for playing chord roots in the key of A (D:I, A:V, G:IV).

A Variety of Music Experiences

Two days before the close of school Miss Johnson and the music consultant met once more, quite by chance, in the main office.

"Here she is now," beamed the Principal. "Our music consultant was just telling me how much he enjoyed working with you and your class and what astonishing progress you've made. Congratulations!"

"I wish you could have heard the class sing and play their own arrangement of 'Oh Susannah' at the close of their dramatization of the Westward Movement unit," said the music consultant to the Principal. "Two children playing piano chords, one playing chord roots on the piano, another playing chord roots on the water jugs, one playing autoharp, a student violinist, vocal chording, singing, percussion rhythms, and all under a student conductor!"

"You just wait until next year," said Miss Johnson. "We'll have recorder flutes, the school has purchased two more autoharps, and we'll be composing the music for our original dramas. I've just begun to get a glimpse of how I can use music with art and dance for the enrichment of all our Social Studies units. I've arranged to take a workshop course at the university this summer where we'll learn authentic folk dances, songs, handicraft, games, lore, and instruments from all over the world. Think of the added interest for the children when we can actually re-create something live and authentic from other cultures here in our classroom. I know I'll need your help more than ever, and I do appreciate all you have done this year!"

"There goes a real teacher!" observed the Principal, as Miss Johnson walked away. "She'll continue to grow and improve with each succeeding year."

Each string may be deliberately tuned a whole step lower except the B, which is lowered to B-flat (D G C F B♭ D) making available chord roots for the convenient keys of G (G:I, D:V, C:IV) or C (C:I, G:V, F:IV), or F (F:I, C:V, B♭:IV). See also Chap. 6, p. 165.

A two- or three-string 'cello may be obtained commercially through Peripole, Inc., 51-17 Rockaway Beach Blvd., Far Rockaway 91, Long Island, N.Y., or through Canadian Music Sales, 58 Advance Rd., Toronto 18, Ont., Canada. Standard orchestral 'cellos are excellent and are often owned by school systems.

Tunable drums may be obtained commercially through Empire Music Company, 3216 44th Ave. S.W., Seattle, Wash., and 934 12th St., New Westminster, B.C., Canada.

POINTERS AND PRACTICE–
CHAPTER 4

PRACTICE

I. On the keyboard diagram, mark the I-chord tones in the key of G with dots (·), the V⁷-chord tones with crosses (+), and the IV-chord tones with small circles (o).

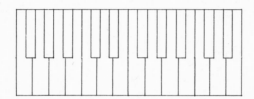

II. Practice playing these chords with one hand, particularly the left hand, until you are sure of them.

Sing and chord the "Kookaburra" song (p. 86) in the key of G.

III. Sing and chord "The Man on the Flying Trapeze." Notice it repeats the same pattern continuously: I IV V⁷ I.

He flies through the air with the greatest of ease,
  I   (I)   IV   (IV)

The daring young man on the flying trapeze.
  V⁷   (V⁷)   I   (I)

His actions are graceful, all girls he does please
  I   (I)   IV   (IV)

And my love he has stolen away.
  V⁷   (V⁷)   I   (I)

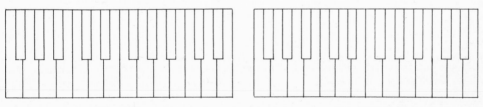

Key of D   Key of A-flat

IV. Practice using these chords until you gain facility and sufficient familiarity to make use of the further guidance in providing piano accompaniment to be given in chapters 5 and 6.

V. Write the chord roots on the bass clef to "The Camptown Races" following the "Oh Susannah" example on pp. 92-93.

The Camptown Races*

Stephen Foster

The Camp-town lad - ies   sing this song: Doo- dah! _____

I   I   V⁷

doo - dah! _____The   Camp - town   race - track   five   miles   long,

V⁷   I   I

Oh   doo - dah   day. _____   Gwine   to   run   all   night;

V⁷   I   I   I

gwine   to run   all   day.   I   bet   my   mon - ey

IV   I   I

---

*"C" is an alternate designation of $\frac{4}{4}$ meter. "¢" indicates that in performance the song should
be "compressed" to swing in two pulses per measure—$\frac{2}{2}$ instead of the usual $\frac{4}{4}$.

♩ ♪ ♪ is more commonly written ♩. ♪. Many teachers help children associate it with a known
rhythm from a familiar song: e.g., calling it a "Sleep-my-child" rhythm as in:

c ♩. ♪♩ ♩ │♩. ♪♩ ♩ │♩   ♩.   ♪ o ‖

Sleep, my child and   peace attend thee   all   through the night.

96

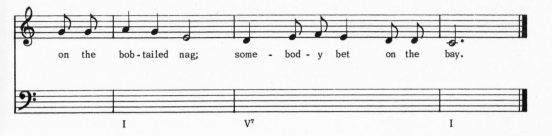

on the   bob-tailed nag;   some - bod - y bet   on the   bay.

I   V⁷   I

VI. The chord-button arrangement of the autoharp is:

The I-, IV-, and V⁷-chords are easily determined in the various keys. The key of C is shown. Complete the identification of these three basic chords for the keys of F, G, and D.

	A	B	C	D	E	F	G	A	B	C	D
Key of C:			I			IV	V⁽⁷⁾				
Key of F:								IV(♭)			
Key of G:											
Key of D:											

VII. The tendency of the beginner in music is to take his printed score immediately to the piano "to hear how it sounds," forgetting that the instrument cannot have any higher insight than the person playing it. This is particularly true with rhythm, as no instrument can generate its own rhythm. This must be supplied by the performer. Make the habit of first studying a score to awaken within yourself the same rhythmic feeling the composer had when he wrote. Likewise, to the extent of your skill at the moment, approximate the pitches which accompany the rhythm. This is one desired outcome from using Miss Johnson's mystery-tunes idea. Try it yourself with two familiar "mystery tunes" following:

1. Set up a walking pulse which swings in twos, threes or fours as the meter signature directs.
2. Talk out (or better, step out) the rhythmic movement of the melody against the steady pulse.
3. Substitute tah tah tah tah for the rhythm-movement words.
4. Substitute the pitch numbers for tah tah tah.
5. Sing the numbers on proper pitch, with the aid of piano, bells, etc., as needed.
6. Sing the word-text where given.

Mystery Tune Number One:*

---

*This is the first use of the meter designation "C"; its meaning can be determined by studying the music. The pulse of this song moves in groups of _____ . The walking pulse is represented by
(2, 3, 4)
the _____ (?) note. By putting the first answer over the second we determine that
(eighth, quarter, half)
"C" means a key signature of $\frac{4}{4}$.

Complete the
following:

Pulse accent
pattern.

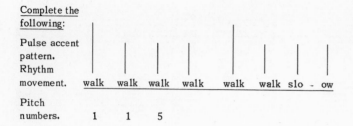

Rhythm
movement. walk   walk   walk   walk   walk   walk slo - ow

Pitch
numbers.   1   1   5

Sing and play at the piano or bells, using number notation. (The key of C is recommended for playing as all of its pitch numbers are found on white keys.)

The title of this familiar song is:_____.

Mystery Tune Number Two:

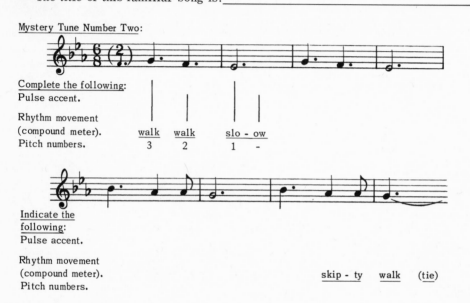

Complete the following:
Pulse accent.

Rhythm movement
(compound meter).   walk   walk   slo - ow
Pitch numbers.   3   2   1   -

Indicate the
following:
Pulse accent.

Rhythm movement
(compound meter).   skip - ty   walk   (tie)
Pitch numbers.

Sing and play by number notation. Once again, the playing by numbers in the key of C is recommended as being easier for a nonpianist. Songs in any key can be put into number notation and played by numbers in the key of C (or for that matter any other key) to discover the sound.

The name of this familiar song (a round) is:_____.

Mystery Tune Number Three:

Complete the following:
Pulse accent.

Rhythm
movement.   walk   skip - ty   walk   walk
Pitch numbers. 5   6   5   3   3

Indicate the
following:
Pulse accent.

Rhythm
movement.
Pitch numbers.

Sing and play by number notation:

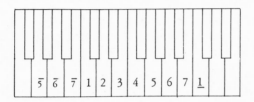

The name of this familiar song from Bizet's opera, <u>Carmen</u>, is:_____.

VIII. Sing and chord "I've Been Working on the Railroad," (p. 88) in the key of G.

Here are more familiar songs which can be chorded with I-, IV-, and V⁷-chords. Be sure your chords emphasize the strong accent of the song's pulsing. Try them in the keys of G and C before going on to other keys.

1. "The Camptown Races"
2. "Home on the Range"
3. "Jingle Bells"
4. "Auld Lang Syne"
5. "Old Black Joe"
6. "Silent Night"
7. "The Muffin Man"
8. "You Are My Sunshine"
9. "Battle Hymn of the Republic"
10. "Twinkle, Twinkle Little Star"

11. "Brahms' Lullaby"
12. "Comin' Round the Mountain"
13. "Red River Valley"
14. "Aloha Oe"
15. "Goodnight Ladies"
16. "Nelly Bly"
17. "Oh Dear, What Can the Matter Be?"
18. "Blue-Tail Fly"
19. "Little Brown Jug" (uses same chord pattern as "Man on the Flying Trapeze": I IV V⁷ I)

As in practice exercise I above, mark the tones used to build the I-, IV-, and V⁷-chords in the keys suggested. Remember that while all other scale tones are one step apart, 3 to 4 and 7 to 1 are only half steps apart.

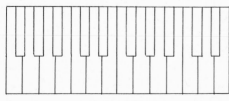

Key of F

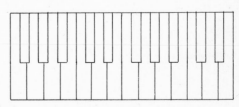

Key of E-flat

A resourceful teacher, we might assume, is a teacher full of resources. To what resource did Miss Johnson turn for French-language pronunciation?

Does this example suggest sources for bringing "live" music performance and standard band and orchestral instruments into the elementary classroom from time to time?

Would such a request be merely annoying to the group asked or might there be mutual benefits?

Have you known people who have lived abroad and acquired an enviable skill in a new language? Have you known of other persons who have similarly experienced foreign cultures, but have returned still unskilled in the foreign language? Is it possible to live in a musical environment and yet remain ignorant of that language?

What does this suggest for the elementary classroom beyond the mere listening to, and singing of, songs?

Review pp. 85 and 86. Would not Miss Johnson have saved a great deal of time by just <u>telling</u> the children which tones are used in the IV-chord? Comment.

In all phases of education inexperienced teachers often fail to realize the thought-provoking potential of a question, and call on the first child who raises his hand—thus releasing the rest of the children from the challenge of thinking the problem through. How did Miss Johnson handle this matter in regard to the "mystery tune"?

The skilled elementary teacher tries to help a child through to the correct response when he comes forward to do something, rather than saying: "No, that's wrong. Who knows how to do it correctly?" How did Miss Johnson attempt to ensure that Stanley would succeed?

When this failed, how did she assist him?

How would singing a melody on a neutral syllable such as loo help an uncertain child to recognize a melodic pattern?

Sometimes rounds, descants, chant repetitions, and other part-singing deteriorate into chaos under a new teacher. The fault is apt to be in feeling the pulse (meter) of the song. Have the children prepare this pulse feeling before they begin to sing (see p. 12) and continue it in bodily movement while singing. It is not apt to be a problem if the children have had ample experiences in responding to music through physical movement.

Music study has long been associated with exercises and drills. Creative teachers learn to provide these special-attention experiences directly from the songs themselves. For example, a class can drill on the tonal pattern 1 $\overline{5}$ 1 as an isolated problem or the child can play and sing a repetitive pattern like

Ding,   ding,   dong

in "Are You Sleeping?" while the class is singing and playing the song. Which is more desirable and why?

There are many advantages to introducing children to the keyboard via the black keys, using the "three blacks" as sounds 1 2 3, and the "two blacks" as 5 and 6 or low $\overline{5}$ and $\overline{6}$. These tones give the penta-tonic or five-toned scale from which much folk music is derived:

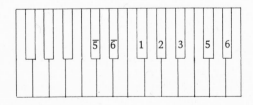

Swing Low, Sweet Chariot

In 4s: 3 |1 - - 3 | 1 (1̸ 1) (6̄ 5̄) 5̸ | (1 1) (1 1) (3 3) 5 | 5 - -

(6̄ 5̄) 3 - - 5 | 1 (1̸ 1) (6̄ 5̄) 5̸ | (1 1) (1 1) (3 3) 2 | 1 - - ‖

Shortnin' Bread

In 4s: (1 . 1) (6̄ . 6̄) (5̄ . 5̄) 6 | 1 6 5 6 (1 . 1) (6̄ . 6̄) (5̄ . 5̄) 6 | 3 2 1 - ‖

Auld Lang Syne

In 4s: 5̄ | 1 (1̸ 1)* 1 3 | 2 (2 1̸) 2 3 | 1 (1̸ 1) 3 5 | 6 - - ‖

6 | 5̄ (. 3̄)* 3 1 | 2 (. 1̄) 2 (3̄ 2) | 1 (. 6̄) 6̄ 5̄ | 1 - - ‖

Bury Me Not on the Lone Prairie

In 4s: 5̄ (1 1) 3 | 5 - - - | - (6̄ 5̄) 3 1 | 3 - - - | -

5̄ 1   3 | 2 - - - | - (3̄ 2) 1 6̄ | 1 - - - | - ‖

When well-learned on the black keys these patterns can be easily transposed to various white keys**

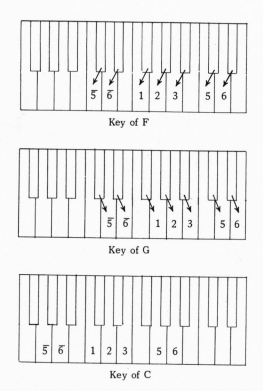

Key of F

Key of G

Key of C

---

* Note two ways of writing the same rhythm.

** In the matter of a functional approach to the piano keyboard the authors highly recommend Robert Pace, Piano for Classroom Music (Englewood Cliffs, N.J.: Prentice-Hall, 1956). The interested student can readily learn to use the piano through the instruction in this book.

In the history of mankind the preponderant use of major scales is a recent innovation. Many lovely songs in minor modes have come down to us from older times and cultures. Notice the familiar "We Three Kings of Orient Are":

The song ends on D, and D gives the feeling of "home base," or sound I. Yet the key signature tells us the key of F. We can generalize by saying that, in relation to the key signature, a minor song tends to run from note $\bar{6}$ to note 6 of the major key and scale, and tends to end on note $\bar{6}$ of the major key's signature.

Some music educators number the pitches from the key signature, in which case the above tune would be:

$$\boxed{3 - 2}\,\boxed{1 - \bar{6}}\,\boxed{\bar{7}\ 1\ \bar{7}}\ \bar{6}$$

Others recognize this as a minor tonality and call the tone we hear and see as the tonal center, sound 1. In this case the above tune is:

$$\text{Minor mode: }\boxed{5 - 4}\,\boxed{3 - 1}\,\boxed{2\ 3\ 2}\ 1$$

This latter has the advantage when it comes to chording, for the three primary chords are then still built of the same scale degrees:

$$
\begin{array}{ccccc}
5 & {}^{6} & 5 & 5 & 5 \\
3 & {}^{4} & 3 & {}^{4} & 3 \\
1 & 1 & 1 & {}_{7} & 1 \\
\text{I} & \text{IV} & \text{I} & \text{V}^7 & \text{I}
\end{array}
$$

with label "Minor mode:" to the left of the chord numbers.

In order to give the V^7 chord the true restless, dominant feeling it characteristically has, the sound 7 is raised:

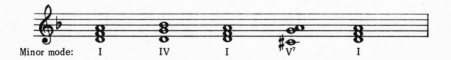

Minor mode: I   IV   I V^7 I

This raising of the seventh degree is so common that many minor songs can frequently be detected at a glance by the sharp (♯) or natural sign (♮) consistently found in front of the same note every time it occurs:

105

Let My People Go

The signature indicates that B-flat will be sound 1, yet the melody itself comes to rest on G, note 6 of the B-flat scale. This confirms the minor mode, which we surmised from the consistent occurrence of the "accidental" sign in front of each note F—sound 7 in the G scale.

Children can be encouraged to explore the qualitites of the minor mode if the teacher will give them the notation to familiar minor tunes transposed to the major:

Example 1

1 3 5 1 6 - (5 4)(3 2) 1

Example 2

1 2 3 2 1 1 2 3 5 2 3 1

Example 3

5 - 4 3 - 1 2 3 2 1 - -

5 - 4 3 - 1 2 3 2 1 - -

After a child has played a tune, the teacher should invite him to play it again, but instead of using C as the final tone, call A sound 1 and have the child play on the white keys by number:

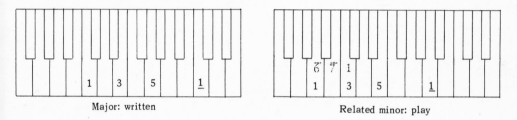

Major: written   Related minor: play

Another experiment with this new "flavor" is to take familiar major-scale tunes and transpose them to minor in much the same fashion as above.

Hot Cross Buns

| 3 2 1 - | 3 2 1 - |(1 1) (1 1) (2 2) (2 2)| 3 2 1 - ||

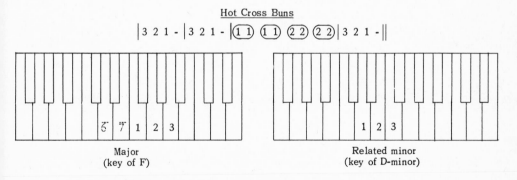

Major
(key of F)

Related minor
(key of D-minor)

Merrily We Roll Along

| 3 (3 2) 1 2 | 3 3 3 - | 2 2 2 - | 3 5 5 -

| 3 (. 2) 1 2 | 3 3 3 - | 2 2 3 2 | 1 - - - ||

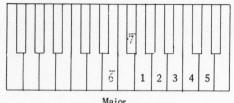

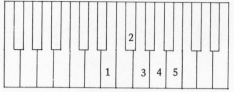

Major	Related minor
(key of G)	(key of E-minor)

As the minor mode is not heard often in the casual music of our culture today the children should be given particular opportunity to hear recorded music in minor mode such as the following—and this in addition to learning minor songs from the various elementary song sources:

1. <u>Prelude in C♯ Minor</u> (Rachmaninoff), Bells of Moscow.
2. <u>March Slav</u> (Tchaikovsky). A still different form of minor.
3. <u>I Wonder as I Wander</u> (Appalachian folk song).
4. <u>Dark Eyes</u> (Gypsy air).
5. <u>What Shall We Do with the Drunken Sailor?</u> (American sea chantey).
6. <u>Peer Gynt Suite</u> (Edvard Grieg).
   "Ase's Death"
   "In the Hall of the Mountain King"
   "Anitra's Dance"
   "Solveig's Song"
7. <u>Hungarian Dances</u> (Brahms).
8. <u>Carnival of the Animals</u> (Saint-Säens).
   "Introduction and Royal March"

The children will enjoy playing the main theme of the lion on their instruments (minor scale):

In 4s: 1 5 5 5 | 6 (·5) 4 5 | (3 4) (5 4) 3 2 | 3 (·2) 1 - |

9. <u>Swan Lake Ballet</u> (Tchaikovsky).

Children will especially enjoy playing this graceful, haunting theme on bells and recorder flutes. Once they've captured the mood and the story, they might want to write their own words to it about the white, silent, graceful creature (really a princess bewitched) who so entranced the young hunter prince:

108

5
WHAT GRADE LEVEL

"Child Music" vs. "Adult Music"

The answer to the question "What grade level?" is that "grade level" exists for a piece of music primarily in terms of what the child or teacher is going to do with it. The most experimental contemporary "adult" music often evokes more favorable response from children than from adult audiences, while the simple three-note "Hot Cross Buns" can challenge even a sophisticated adult just learning to improvise chordal accompaniments or to play the recorder flute. Nursery tunes have provided impetus to creative expression for such contemporary composers as Ernst von Dohnanyi* and Edward Ballantyne,** to say nothing of Mozart's piano variations on the tune for "Twinkle, Twinkle, Little Star."† True, words may occasionally force a song into an adult or a child category, but it would be difficult to make a comparable case for the music. The real criteria, then, are in terms of the experience level, understanding and skill of the student.

The first four chapters describing Miss Johnson's activities outline a developmental pattern of human growth in becoming more perceptive to the various elementary aspects of rhythm, pitch, and harmony, and are independent of grade level. These are phases of experience through which students of all elementary grades might well progress, be they primary or upper elementary grades still needing the introductory awarenesses. In every instance the student encounters musical sound—usually arising out of an appealing song. He is encouraged to do something about some aspect of what he hears, and in the process he clarifies his perception and understanding. Having heard and come to know through expressive physical movement, he is ready to understand, and to communicate through, more or less abstract symbols leading to standard music notation. Indeed, the visual and kinesthetic senses assist the student to interpret what he is hearing.

What sorts of activities are appropriate within the framework of musical participation (listening, moving, and making music through singing and playing instruments) for the various elementary grade levels? The following suggestions are modified from material developed by the author in collaboration with Professor Florence Hutchinson, Oregon College of Education.‡

---

*"Variations on a Nursery Tune."
**"Variations for Piano on 'Mary Had a Little Lamb' in the Styles of Ten Composers."
† "Ah, vous dirai-je, maman."
‡ This grade-level organization of music activities is available in its original form as: Music Education in Oregon Public Schools. It may be obtained for 25¢ from the state Department of Public Instruction, Salem, Ore.

EDUCATIVE OUTLINE OF THE SCHOOL MUSIC PROGRAM

Music Experiences of these general types . . .	SHOULD be carried on in such a way as to . . .	Achieve These Educational Goals:
Listening to Music.		Give Pleasure.
Moving to Music		Develop Music Skills.
Making Music by Singing. by Playing.		Develop Creative Capacities.
		Develop Familiarity with a Wide Variety of Music Literature.
		Develop Understanding of the Symbols and Vocabulary of Music.
		Develop Understanding of the Structure of Music.
		Develop Understanding of Human Feelings and Their Expression.

KINDERGARTEN AND PRIMARY GRADES

LISTENING TO MUSIC SHOULD:

GIVE PLEASURE. For example:
Listening to music as preparation for pupil response.
Listening to music for quiet enjoyment and relaxation, such as:
Teacher making music for children;
Individual children making music for the other children;
Guests making music for the children;
Radio, television, recordings, and other reproductions of music.

DEVELOP MUSIC SKILLS. For example:
Learning to recognize tunes.
Learning to recognize pitch changes.
Learning to match pitch.
Learning to sing rote songs.
Learning to improve tone quality.
Learning to respond to music by movement.
Learning to recognize sounds of instruments.
Learning concert-audience manners.

DEVELOP CREATIVE MUSIC CAPACITIES. For example:
Individual planning of responses to music through art and bodily movement.
Making up stories and planning dramatizations to music.

DEVELOP KNOWLEDGE OF MUSIC LITERATURE. For example:
    Listening to recordings of familiar songs.
    Listening to selected instrumental recordings.
    Listening to recordings which children bring from home.
    Listening to school concerts.
    Listening to radio and television music.

DEVELOP UNDERSTANDING OF MUSIC SYMBOLS AND VOCABULARY. For example:
    Hearing the "up and downness" of notes.
    Hearing long and short notes.
    Hearing scale (step patterns) and chord patterns (skip patterns).
    Hearing characteristics such as holds, slurs, repeats, and accents.

DEVELOP UNDERSTANDING OF MUSIC STRUCTURE. For example:
    Becoming aware of phrases.
    Becoming aware of introductions, interludes, and codas.

DEVELOP UNDERSTANDING OF HUMAN FEELINGS AND THEIR EXPRESSION. For example:
    Hearing and recognizing the musical expression of basic childhood emotions.
    Becoming aware of group and individual interpretations of moods.
    Reaching out toward other peoples so far as readiness and maturity of children permit.

MOVING TO MUSIC SHOULD:

GIVE PLEASURE. For example:
    Free rhythmic interpretations of songs, instrumental and recorded music.

DEVELOP MUSIC SKILLS. For example:
    Keeping time (accent and beat) with large muscles while walking, running, skipping, swinging, galloping, clapping, etc.
    Responding to fast and slow tempo.

DEVELOP CREATIVE MUSIC CAPACITIES. For example:
    Free rhythmic responses through art, bodily movement, and dramatizations.

DEVELOP KNOWLEDGE OF MUSIC LITERATURE. For example:
    Taking part in rhythmic songs and folk dances.
    Creating dramatizations of instrumental music.

DEVELOP UNDERSTANDING OF MUSIC SYMBOLS AND VOCABULARY. For example:
    Responding to long and short notes as they appear in songs.
    Responding to accent and observing accent in songs.
    Responding to the swing of music and discovering the meaning of the top number of the meter sign.
    Observing notations of common rhythmic patterns.

DEVELOP UNDERSTANDING OF MUSIC STRUCTURE. For example:
    Showing phrase lines by movement.

111

DEVELOP UNDERSTANDING OF HUMAN FEELINGS AND THEIR EXPRES-SION. For example:

Expressing basic childhood emotions in movement.

Appreciating the feelings of self and others through the playing of singing games, and simple folk dances.

MAKING MUSIC BY SINGING SHOULD:

GIVE PLEASURE. For example:
Singing for the joy of singing, alone and with others.

DEVELOP MUSIC SKILLS. For example:
Learning to sing with others.
Learning to sing with a tone expressive of the song.
Learning to sing smoothly.
Learning to sing words clearly.

DEVELOP CREATIVE MUSIC CAPACITIES. For example:
Taking part in singing conversations.
Making up songs and chants.

DEVELOP KNOWLEDGE OF MUSIC LITERATURE. For example:
Learning many songs of child interest, of permanent interest, and of cultural value.

DEVELOP READINESS FOR UNDERSTANDING OF MUSIC SYMBOLS AND VOCABULARY. For example:
Following a song in a songbook while singing.
Recognizing tonal patterns aurally and visually by intervals, numbers, or syllables.
Encouraging self-reliance in reading familiar patterns in new songs.
Helping to write down a song composed by the class.

DEVELOP UNDERSTANDING OF MUSIC STRUCTURE. For example:
Becoming aware of phrases in songs.

DEVELOP UNDERSTANDING OF HUMAN FEELINGS AND THEIR EXPRES-SION. For example:
Recognizing and expressing basic childhood emotions through songs.
Expressing and recognizing the expression of these basic emotions by others, through songs.

MAKING MUSIC BY PLAYING SHOULD:

GIVE PLEASURE. For example:
Free exploration in playing upon rhythm and melody instruments.
Discovering effects which are musically pleasing.

DEVELOP MUSIC SKILLS. For example:
Learning ways of using rhythm and melody instruments to keep time and en-rich the melody.

DEVELOP CREATIVE MUSIC CAPACITIES. For example:
Discovering effects which are musically pleasing.
Making up tunes with instruments.

DEVELOP KNOWLEDGE OF MUSIC LITERATURE. For example:
Playing many songs with rhythm and melody instruments.
Playing these instruments with piano and recorded music.

DEVELOP UNDERSTANDING OF MUSIC SYMBOLS AND VOCABULARY. For example:
Associating aurally and visually the "up and downness" of pitch with instruments.
Learning that the lines and spaces of the staff represent these pitches.
Following symbols while playing rhythm instruments.
Learning piano keyboard.

DEVELOP UNDERSTANDING OF MUSIC STRUCTURE. For example:
Recognizing phrases while playing.
Playing introductions, interludes, and codas for songs.

DEVELOP UNDERSTANDING OF HUMAN FEELINGS AND THEIR EXPRESSION. For example:
Recognizing and expressing basic childhood emotions with instruments.
Recognizing and portraying instrumentally the basic emotions of self and others.

To interpret these music activities and educational outgrowths at various grade levels—or more properly, experience levels—sample lessons are recounted in the following pages illustrating the use of the same music material at Grade Two and at Grade Six levels.

It cannot be stressed too emphatically that grade levels, as such, are meaningless unless the children have had preparatory experiences in preceding grades. Often it is necessary to involve children of upper grades in awareness activities which ideally should have been initiated in the Primary grades. Fortunately, music lends itself well to such flexibility.

Miss Harbrecht, a second-grade teacher, and Mr. Penn, a sixth-grade teacher, each heard the Roger Wagner Chorale recording of "On Top of Old Smoky,"* and added it to their personal record libraries. Each teacher wanted to share it with the children, and each developed an individual approach suitable to the particular group of children.

Sample Lesson for Primary Grades: Miss Harbrecht

"How does this feather make you feel as it floats to the floor? . . . Show me with your hands . . . How light would you have to be to float on a feather? What

---

*Folk Songs of the New World, sung by the Roger Wagner Chorale; Capitol Recording P-8324.

if you really were all light and feathery and could just float off into space? Look at the clouds outside our window. If you were a feather where would you like to go? ... To that patch of blue out there? ... Up and up to the top of that high, towering cloud, or would you prefer to drift down into that white, fluffy part? Continue on your journey while this music helps you to soar."

Miss Harbrecht started the phonograph, and through light, floating bodily movement several children portrayed the sensation they felt on hearing the music. She had them hum the tune with her and show the pitch levels.

"Does the melody seem to go up by little bits? Or by bigger skips?

```
                                                    ___
                                  _              _
                        _ _ _ ‾        _ _
```

Does the second phrase pattern start exactly the same as the first phrase did?"

```
                        ___
                 _                        _ _
          _ _           _          _ _
```

"Do you think the song will be played on these bells by playing (pointing with her finger on the bells) 1 1 2 3 5 or by playing 1 1 3 5 1?"

The children tried it, and discovered the latter pattern was right. By experimenting they found that the second phrase was 1 1 3 5 5. As they sang, a child played these two five-note patterns, choosing the appropriate one each time.

"Let's listen to the introduction again. Does it make you feel all alone or as though you were in a crowd? Are you down in a valley under the trees or out in the open sky? Yes, I feel that the one instrument playing the melody is lonesome—out in the wide open country. By the way, do you think that instrument is one you play by striking it like our bells, or by blowing it? Blowing! Good for you! Yes! John knows what it is ... a harmonica.

"Do you suppose this song was made by mountain people who loved their mountains very much? Yes, I think so, too. And the harmonica is an instrument they favored. They weren't wealthy and this was not too expensive to own—and one could carry it in his pocket handy for playing as he walked or rode along.

"Would you rather listen once again to the chorus sing it on the record or to sing it yourself while I play the chords on the autoharp? You'd rather sing it yourself? Do you suppose our voices can create that same lonesome feeling which the harmonica gave us in the introduction?"

Notice that in this simple lesson Miss Harbrecht has involved the children in listening, in singing, in playing instruments, and in expressive bodily movement. They have found pleasure in listening for quiet enjoyment as well as in moving, playing, and singing. They have had experience in recognizing pitch changes and learning to match pitch, in singing rote songs with encouragement to seek for an appropriate expressive tone quality, in recognizing the sounds of an instrument. They gained in understanding of the "up and downness" of notes, similar phrases, and introductions. They were helped to understand human feelings and their expression.

INTERMEDIATE GRADES

(Note: Review Primary-type experiences as necessary.)

LISTENING TO MUSIC SHOULD:

GIVE PLEASURE. For example:
Listening to music as preparation for pupil response as well as listening for quiet enjoyment and relaxation.
Listening to favorite records, radio and television programs.
Listening to schoolmates perform.
Listening to skilled performers in person.

DEVELOP MUSIC SKILLS. For example:
Listening to longer compositions.
Listening to more unusual orchestral instruments.
Listening to identify major and minor modes.
Listening to the teacher singing a second part to a song.
Listening to recognize common intervals as needed.
Listening to distinguish voices singing rounds or part-songs.
Listening for growth in awareness of mood, rhythms, pitch, harmony, and tone quality.

DEVELOP CREATIVE MUSIC CAPACITIES. For example:
Listening to respond to music by movement.
Listening to respond to music with an accompaniment.
Listening to harmonize with another part.

DEVELOP KNOWLEDGE OF MUSIC LITERATURE. For example:
Listening to program music (music with a story).
Listening to music without a story.
Listening to become acquainted with composers through their music.
Listening to music for recognition of folk and national characteristics.

DEVELOP UNDERSTANDING OF MUSIC SYMBOLS AND VOCABULARY. For example:
Identifying notations of themes which appear in music.
Following notations of a harmony part as the teacher sings.

DEVELOP UNDERSTANDING OF MUSIC STRUCTURE. For example:
Becoming aware of two- and three-part song forms.
Becoming aware of fugues, air with variations.

DEVELOP UNDERSTANDING OF HUMAN FEELINGS AND THEIR EXPRESSION. For example:
Developing a sense of belonging by sharing records.
Developing sympathetic understanding of others through their music.
Developing an independent recognition of beauty.

115

MOVING TO MUSIC SHOULD:

GIVE PLEASURE. For example:
Free rhythmic interpretations of songs, instrumental and recorded music.
Enjoyment in moving rhythmically with others.

DEVELOP MUSIC SKILLS. For example:
Responding to the beat through movement.
Responding to the note pattern through movement.
Responding to the rhythm of a dotted quarter followed by an eighth through movement.
Gaining ability in conducting songs.

DEVELOP CREATIVE MUSIC CAPACITIES. For example:
Taking part in original rhythmic interpretations of songs and instrumental compositions.
Stepping rounds and canons.
Creating original dance patterns.

DEVELOP KNOWLEDGE OF MUSIC LITERATURE. For example:
Moving to many types of songs, instrumental and recorded music.
Learning folk dances native to our country.
Learning folk dances brought from other countries.
Responding to and identifying rhythmic patterns characteristic of different countries.

DEVELOP UNDERSTANDING OF MUSIC SYMBOLS AND VOCABULARY. For example:
Transferring rhythmic patterns from movement into notation.
Interpreting the meter sign.
Learning terms such as tempo, ritardando, ties, etc.

DEVELOP UNDERSTANDING OF MUSIC STRUCTURE. For example:
Recognizing dance forms—waltz, polka, minuet, mazurka, tango, etc.

DEVELOP UNDERSTANDING OF HUMAN FEELINGS AND THEIR EXPRESSION. For example:
Gaining poise through self-expression in movement.
Developing a sympathetic understanding of other peoples through their rhythms.
Developing a sympathetic attitude toward the efforts of others in rhythmic expression.

MAKING MUSIC BY SINGING SHOULD:

GIVE PLEASURE. For example:
Singing for the joy of self-expression alone and with others.
Feeling the blend of harmonizing with others.

DEVELOP MUSIC SKILLS. For example:
Singing with a tone expressive of the song.
Using clear-cut attacks and releases.

Achieving good posture habits.
Singing in harmony.
Blending with other voices.

DEVELOP CREATIVE MUSIC CAPACITIES. For example:
Adding harmonic endings.
Adding new verses to songs.
Creating descants.
Creating harmony in thirds.
Creating songs.
Creating musical plays.

DEVELOP KNOWLEDGE OF MUSIC LITERATURE. For example:
Singing songs of permanent interest and cultural value.
Singing many unison, two-part songs, songs with descants, rounds, canons,
and some three-part songs.
Singing songs in major and minor keys.

DEVELOP UNDERSTANDING OF MUSIC SYMBOLS AND VOCABULARY. For
example:
Seeing how the music looks after learning how it sounds.
Scanning a new song before singing it.
Singing parts of new songs (cadences and familiar patterns) with little help
from the teacher.
Attempting new songs without the teacher's help after establishing the rhythm
and observing like phrases.
Building chords vocally and using them in accompanying songs—in cadences,
as "amens" to hymns.
Telling the key.
Recognizing common intervals.
Using sharps and flats.
Using dynamics.

DEVELOP UNDERSTANDING OF MUSIC STRUCTURE. For example:
Recognizing similar and contrasting sections.
Learning the use of climax.

DEVELOP UNDERSTANDING OF HUMAN FEELINGS AND THEIR EXPRES-
SION. For example:
Developing sympathetic understanding of other peoples through their songs.
Expressing the mood of a song.
Understanding the appeal of favorite songs of classmates.

MAKING MUSIC BY PLAYING SHOULD:

GIVE PLEASURE. For example:
Free exploration in playing upon rhythm, melody, and chording instruments.
Discovering effects which are musically pleasing.

DEVELOP MUSIC SKILLS. For example:
Using accompanying instruments such as the autoharp, guitar, ukulele, piano.

Playing roots of chords on instruments to accompany songs.
Using instruments to play a descant, to assist a singing part, and for giving pitch.

DEVELOP CREATIVE MUSIC CAPACITIES. For example:
Creating and improvising tunes on instruments.
Playing instruments "by ear."
Selecting appropriate instrumentations.

DEVELOP KNOWLEDGE OF MUSIC LITERATURE. For example:
Playing many songs with rhythm and melody instruments.
Accompanying many songs with chordal instruments.

DEVELOP UNDERSTANDING OF MUSIC SYMBOLS AND VOCABULARY. For example:
Following the notation of a song in order to play a chordal accompaniment.
Notating original songs and instrumental compositions.
Following the notation to play a song on an instrument.
Learning the pitch names of the lines and spaces.
Learning the keys of the piano.

DEVELOP UNDERSTANDING OF MUSIC STRUCTURE. For example:
Learning the meaning of accompaniment, obbligato, ensemble, trio, tonic, subdominant, dominant.

DEVELOP UNDERSTANDING OF HUMAN FEELINGS AND THEIR EXPRESSION. For example:
Exploring one's own potentialities on instruments.
Realizing the responsibility and satisfactions in contributing to the group.
Achieving a helpful attitude toward the efforts of others in playing instruments.
Identifying and exploring instruments characteristic of peoples and cultures.

Sample Lesson for Intermediate Grades: Mr. Penn

"Last weekend I heard a chorus arrangement of a song we sing in our class, and I liked it so much that I bought the record for my own library. I think you'll hear a combination of instruments in the introduction which you've never heard together before and yet which would be a perfectly natural combination for the people who made this song. See if you can tell what instruments they are. And notice how the introduction and first verse make you feel. And, by the way, there's a chord near the end of the piece which we can't find on our autoharp. Raise your hand if you think you hear it."

Mr. Penn played the record. They discussed it, commenting on the odd but appropriate combination of harmonica, and harp, and men's voices on the first verse.

"I was able to borrow an instrument from the high school band for a couple of weeks. It's hidden behind the piano. I'm going to go play a few notes on it, and see if you can tell me what instrument you are hearing. . . . That's right, a bass

118

viol or string bass. I was wondering if you would like to use the bass viol—by the way who can spell that on the board for us?—and other instruments to make our own special arrangement of "On Top of Old Smoky." What other instruments would be appropriate—bass drum and cymbals?"

"The autoharp," added one of the children.

They recalled chord patterns they had used before, and Mr. Penn wrote them on the board:

	1	1　3　5	1- -	6- -	- - 6	4　　5　　6
Introduction: On	top of Old	Smo -	ky	all	cov-ered with
I　　I　　I	I		IV	IV	IV	IV

5 - -	- - -	- - 1	1　3　5	5 - -	2 - -	- - 3
snow	- - -	I	lost my true	lov-	er	come
I	I	I	I	V⁷	V⁷	V⁷

4　　3　　2	1- -	- - -	- -
court-ing too	slow		
V⁷	I	I	I

"That sounds so loud," remarked one of the students after they had played a few chords. "Couldn't we use the soft felt pick instead of the hard plastic one for strumming?"

"Why not just use our thumb for strumming the way we did on 'Silent Night'?" asked another child.

"Since it has a soft, lonely feeling, couldn't we have a soft kind of rhythm under it—like the sandpaper blocks or shakers?" someone else queried.

"Of course we could," replied Mr. Penn. "You experiment until you find a rhythm pattern you like."

Then the string bass was brought into the song and the children learned about playing chord roots. Mr. Penn retuned the strings from their usual E-A-D-G tuning to G-C-F-G so that in the key of C they could play the roots of I (C), IV (F) and V⁷ (G). The children decided that for this song they preferred the legato quality made with the bow to the more abrupt sound of the plucked string.

To achieve the quality of the Roger Wagner Chorale on the phonograph record, Mr. Penn had the children interpret the long phrases of the song in bodily movement, by starting the phrase standing, with arms extended down, palms of hands together; then, as the phrase progressed, moving hands and arms out to the side and upward in right-and-left-arm arcs until palms met again extended overhead at the close of the phrase. This helped the children experience and appreciate the extended phrases. They were quick to observe that this was the first song they had noticed with only two phrases.

When the shaker instruments settled into an appropriate pattern, the entire class tapped or stepped it out to discover that it went:

| Walk run-run run-run | walk run-run run-run | walk walk walk | walk walk 𝄾 |

Then the autoharp players experimented with an ornamental strumming. By pinching thumb and index fingers and brushing the strings with the fingernails of the thumb and index finger in a side-to-side motion they produced an attractive pattern. A couple of days later the pipe bells (such as Henry had made for Miss Johnson's class, see pp. 36-38) were decorating the long melodic holds by going up and down the appropriate I-, IV-, or V⁷-chord pattern, with three children each responsible for one of the bell chord patterns:

$$I \begin{smallmatrix} 1 \\ 5 \\ 3 \\ 1 \end{smallmatrix} \begin{smallmatrix} 1 \\ 5 \\ 3 \end{smallmatrix} \quad IV \begin{smallmatrix} 1 \\ 6 \\ 4 \\ 1 \end{smallmatrix} \begin{smallmatrix} 1 \\ 6 \\ 4 \end{smallmatrix} \quad V^7 \begin{smallmatrix} 7 \\ 5 \\ 4 \\ 2 \end{smallmatrix} \begin{smallmatrix} 7 \\ 5 \\ 4 \end{smallmatrix}$$

The children wanted to perfect their arrangement of the song and then play it at the school assembly. The arrangement which they worked out was:

On Top of Old Smoky*

---

*See also Chap. 10, p. 265, for different arrangement.

snow _____ I lost my true lov -

er _____ come court - ing too slow. _____

It was possible to sing any number of verses, and the instrumental introduction could be used again as an ending or a coda. When later they presented the song at the school assembly they highlighted the introduction by having the harmonica player stroll across the stage as he played and then return across the stage after the singing, playing an instrumental coda at the end.

In this group, as in the Primary class, the teacher involved his students in listening, singing, the playing of instruments, and expressive bodily movement— but at a deeper level. There was a functional use of notation and the opportunity to discover and to create. Mr. Penn "lived" an important lesson in indicating his habitual regard for music as a wholesome pleasure to be brought into one's daily life and shared with others. In borrowing the string bass from the high school he used a type of resource often ignored by classroom teachers. The activity was planned and developed jointly by teacher and pupils.

121

That the class derived pleasure from their creation is indicated in the desire to perform for their schoolmates. Playing the chordal notes on the bells was a most natural and effective way to learn how the I-, IV-, and V^7-chords are formed. Creative capacities were encouraged by experimenting with different ideas such as the tone qualities obtained from the plastic strumming pick, the felt pick, and fingernails brushed sideways across the autoharp strings. By rebuilding their own arrangement of this Appalachian folk song the children learned more of the structure of music, and deepened their understanding of the musical feelings within themselves and others.

Upper Elementary Grades and Junior High School

Some suggestions of the scope and sequence of the music program are projected into grades Seven, Eight, and Nine and are given now in conclusion:

UPPER ELEMENTARY GRADES AND JUNIOR HIGH SCHOOL

(Note: Review Primary and Intermediate-type experiences as necessary.)

LISTENING TO MUSIC SHOULD:

GIVE PLEASURE. For example:
Listening to music as preparation for pupil response as well as listening for quiet enjoyment and relaxation.
Listening to favorite records, radio programs, sound films, and television programs.
Listening to schoolmates, teacher, or guests perform.

DEVELOP MUSIC SKILLS. For example:
Listening to distinguish the different parts in part-songs.
Developing the habit of listening to one's own voice as well as to the voices of others.
Listening to tape recordings of class singing.
Identifying I-, IV-, and V-chords by sound.
Listening for growth in awareness of mood, rhythm, pitch, tone quality, and harmony.
Identifying instruments of the orchestra by sound and sight.
Listening to music using pentatonic and whole tone scales, major and minor scales.
Learning concert audience behavior.

DEVELOP CREATIVE MUSIC CAPACITIES. For example:
Listening to respond to music by movement.
Listening to respond to music with an accompaniment.
Listening to harmonize with another part.
Listening to discover nationalistic tendencies in composers.
Listening to learn uses of dissonance in music.

DEVELOP KNOWLEDGE OF MUSIC LITERATURE. For example:
  Listening to music for recognition of folk and national characteristics.
  Listening to music of great composers from countries associated with units
    of classroom study.
  Listening to music of composers who were influenced by nationalism.
  Listening to music representative of great religions.
  Becoming acquainted with the music of North American composers.
  Learning the evolution of jazz in America.
  Learning the influence of industry on music.

DEVELOP UNDERSTANDING OF MUSIC SYMBOLS AND VOCABULARY. For
example:
  Identifying notations of themes which appear in music.
  Following notations of a harmony part as a song is played or sung.

DEVELOP UNDERSTANDING OF MUSIC STRUCTURE. For example:
  Becoming aware of how composers have used folk music.
  Comparing the form of a composition with a poem, a building, a painting.
  Becoming acquainted with oratorios, operas, symphonies, and string quartets.
  Discovering the form of spirituals, Stephen Foster's songs, Edward Mac-
    Dowell's music, some popular music.
  Becoming aware of the ways in which the music of great composers has been
    used by popular composers.

DEVELOP UNDERSTANDING OF HUMAN FEELINGS AND THEIR EXPRES-
SION. For example:
  Recognizing universal emotions expressed in the music of other peoples.
  Recognizing that music reflects the same thoughts and feelings that are found
    in literature and art.
  Acquiring a habit of being fair-minded when forming an opinion about music.
  Recognizing the contributions of foreign-born Americans to music.
  Becoming aware of how music expresses human feelings in American history
    as evidenced in spirituals, work songs, cowboy songs, hymns and patriotic
    songs.
  Becoming aware of how mankind uses music in contemporary life.

MOVING TO MUSIC SHOULD:

GIVE PLEASURE. For example:
  Participating in free rhythmic interpretations of song, of instrumental and
    recorded music.
  Moving rhythmically with others.
  Relieving muscular and emotional tension through physical release.

DEVELOP MUSIC SKILLS. For example:
  Learning dance steps suggested in songbooks or by demonstration, and using
    these dance steps in other songs.
  Conducting songs.
  Using walking, running and skipping movements as suggested by the musical
    phrases of some songs.
  Learning square dancing and the Virginia Reel, clapping off-beats, synco-
    pated rhythms.

123

DEVELOP CREATIVE MUSIC CAPACITIES. For example:
Creating dances to accompany songs.
Dramatizing ballads.
Creating responses to special rhythms, such as jazz, calypso, conga.

DEVELOP KNOWLEDGE OF MUSIC LITERATURE. For example:
Learning the dances which became composition forms, such as the minuet, gavotte, mazurka, polonaise, waltz, tango.
Responding to and identifying rhythmic patterns characteristic of different countries.
Recognizing dance forms such as those of the American Indian, quadrilles, and reels.

DEVELOP UNDERSTANDING OF MUSIC STRUCTURE. For example:
Observing repeated rhythms.
Recognizing dance forms such as the waltz, polka, minuet, tango.
Applying the form of songs to dancing.

DEVELOP UNDERSTANDING OF HUMAN FEELINGS AND THEIR EXPRESSION. For example:
Gaining poise through self-expression in movement.
Developing an understanding of other peoples through their characteristic rhythms.
Respecting each classmate for his particular offering in rhythmic expression.

MAKING MUSIC BY SINGING SHOULD:

GIVE PLEASURE. For example:
Singing for the joy of self-expression, alone and with others.
Building a repertoire of songs the class can sing with musical enjoyment.
Singing for the joy of harmonization.

DEVELOP MUSIC SKILLS. For example:
Give emphasis to proper breathing, good posture, care of the adolescent voice, good diction, tone quality, and appropriate interpretation.
Performing in both melody and harmony parts.
Developing the habit of looking at and comprehending groups of notes when reading.
Learning I-, IV-, and V-chords and using them in vocal chording.

DEVELOP CREATIVE MUSIC CAPACITIES. For example:
Writing original songs.
Writing descants or harmony parts to songs.
Arranging programs, pageants, and plays.

DEVELOP KNOWLEDGE OF MUSIC LITERATURE. For example:
Studying simple folk songs, hymns of various faiths, work songs, chanteys, and art songs.
Building a repertoire of songs that are of lasting musical significance.
Singing early American hymns, spirituals, patriotic songs, and work songs.

DEVELOP UNDERSTANDING OF MUSIC SYMBOLS AND VOCABULARY. For example:

Hearing and recording melodies in staff notation.

Learning the minor scale from a familiar song.

Learning the pentatonic scale from a familiar song using that scale.

Learning to locate the key of a song from its signature and finding the music scale tones 1 3 5.

Identifying familiar tunes from the chalkboard ("hearing with the eyes").

Learning the use of the bass clef in singing.

Learning the meaning of *a cappella, soprano, alto, alto-tenor, bass.*

DEVELOP UNDERSTANDING OF MUSIC STRUCTURE. For example:

Noticing the use of repeated phrases, melodic patterns, and rhythmic patterns.

Analyzing the structure of American folk songs.

Becoming aware of two-part and three-part song forms.

DEVELOP UNDERSTANDING OF HUMAN FEELINGS AND THEIR EXPRESSION. For example:

Discovering basic similarities in home songs of the world, love songs of the world, great hymns of faith.

Growing in respect and friendship for people who love music.

Gaining an appreciation of the contributions which each race and nationality has brought to our cultural heritage.

MAKING MUSIC BY PLAYING SHOULD:

GIVE PLEASURE. For example:

Using percussive instruments as an accompaniment to songs.

Adding instruments from the instrumental classes to an ensemble.

Experiencing free exploration in playing upon rhythm, melody, and chording instruments.

DEVELOP MUSIC SKILLS. For example:

Learning I-, IV-, and V^7-chords and using them in playing piano, guitar, ukulele, and autoharp.

Writing out scores for rhythmic accompaniments to songs.

Using the black piano keys to play pentatonic scales.

Finding beginning pitches of singing parts at the piano.

DEVELOP CREATIVE MUSIC CAPACITIES. For example:

Making rhythm and melody instruments to accompany songs and dances.

Learning to make a bass part on a string bass.

Making up pentatonic tunes on piano and other melody instruments.

DEVELOP KNOWLEDGE OF MUSIC LITERATURE. For example:

Playing accompaniments and playing as part of an ensemble for the song repertoire.

DEVELOP UNDERSTANDING OF MUSIC SYMBOLS AND VOCABULARY. For example:

Studying the evolution of notations, the history of syllables, the major and minor scales, the pentatonic and whole-tone scales.

DEVELOP UNDERSTANDING OF MUSIC STRUCTURE. For example:
  Learning the meaning of contrasting sections, two- and three-part forms
    contrapuntal devices.

DEVELOP UNDERSTANDING OF HUMAN FEELINGS AND THEIR EXPRES
SION. For example:
  Exploring one's own responsibility and satisfactions in contributing to th
    group.
  Exploring one's own potentialities on instruments.
  Achieving a helpful attitude toward the efforts of others in playing instru
    ments.
  Identifying and exploring instruments characteristic of peoples and cultures

PART II
A Way of Looking at Music—
The Printed Score

INTRODUCTION

There is a marked change in the contents of present-day elementary songbooks compared with those of a few years ago. Music texts, even as recent as ten to fifteen years ago, generally contained only the melodies and words of songs. Very rarely was a piano accompaniment included. Today, with some songs, additional parts for autoharp, melody bells, recorder-flutes, rhythm instruments, and even 'cellos and basses are not uncommon, particularly in texts for the upper elementary grades. Other songs have suggestions and hints relating to keyboard understanding, recorded literature, historical and biographical data.

This is all to the good, particularly when teachers' manuals accompanying the texts have detailed explanations. Nevertheless, to the new and inexperienced classroom teacher, faced with a myriad of seemingly unrelated musical arrangements and suggestions, the outlook can be disheartening. Too often, the eye sees the printed page merely as a hodge-podge of notes and unintelligible applications. The significance of the treatment given to a particular melody, perhaps a descant, a drum part, or some historical-geographic data, is not always apparent. What is needed is an insight into the composer's or arranger's world, at least into his more tangible and pertinent reasonings and feelings.

Any attempt which might help the teacher to understand the principles involved, to develop confidence, competence, and discrimination in applying these principles is therefore eminently worthwhile. The remainder of this text is devoted to this task.

One of the immediate, practical problems facing the new teacher in the school is that of organizing the musical activities for the year ahead. Apart from the concern with individual differences and learning processes (Chapters 1-4), there is the matter of average age and interest level of the pupils, the amount and kind of previous instruction, and the considerable task of planning a balance of musical experiences—a balance not only of the different media to be stressed (voice, ear, theory, instrument), but also the types of music materials to be included.

Fortunately, there are now excellent guides to help the teacher in the planning. Among the more complete are the series texts now widely in use in most schools. Considerable reference will be made in the following chapters to:

1. Birchard Music Series, Summy-Birchard Co., Evanston, Ill.
2. Growing with Music Series, Prentice-Hall, Inc., Englewood Cliffs, N.J.
3. Basic Goals in Music Series, McGraw-Hill (Can.) Ltd., Toronto, Ont.
4. Music for Living Series, Silver Burdett Co., Morristown, N.J. W. J. Gage Co., Toronto.
5. Music for Young Americans Series, American Book Co., New York; W. J. Gage Co., Toronto, Ont.
6. Our Singing World Series, Ginn and Co., New York and Toronto, Ont.
7. This is Music Series, Allyn and Bacon, Inc., Boston; Macmillan Co. of Canada.
8. Together We Sing Series, Follett Publishing Co., Chicago; Ryerson Press, Toronto, Ont.

General characteristics of series texts:

1. There are books for each grade.
2. There are teachers' manuals for all grades.
3. Many of the songs in each book are recorded and contained in albums accompanying each grade book.
4. They are recent editions or publications.
5. The selections included for each grade are generally of a kind and variety to appeal to a particular age group.
6. The organization of the material in each book is planned to parallel the physical and social changes of the school year. Thus, we can expect to find fall and winter songs before spring songs in the text, and Thanksgiving selections before Easter songs, and so on. This is probably more apparent in texts for the primary grades than for upper elementary ones.
7. There is an increasing emphasis on the inclusion of music of genuine intrinsic appeal rather than on extra-musical interests whose effects are generally secondary and transitional. For example, notable art songs and significant folk songs are preferred over contrived reading songs, Valentine ditties, and the like. Discrimination in the choice of music literature to be used in the classroom is obviously desirable and important.
8. The music included in most music texts, as in the texts for other subjects, is also arranged in order of complexity. In music, this is not readily accomplished because complexities are of different kinds and forms. There are differences in skill and manipulation, in theoretical concepts, or in mood and feeling. Stated in another way, there are differences in degree of complexity in ear apprehension, in singing or playing skills, eye co-ordination in music reading, harmonic or rhythmic sense, or in the degree of abstraction demanded by the text. It is not nearly so easy to devise a page-by-page treatise for music as it is for a subject in which the content lends itself to logical development. Add to this the challenge posed by the varying skills, tastes, and abilities found in any classroom of twenty to thirty or more children, and the problem becomes even more intricate. The teaching of music involves picking and choosing, trial and error, experimentation and guesswork. Some songs or instrumental selections, chosen for their theoretical challenge, may otherwise be boring; others again, though stirring in mood and feeling, may make technical demands beyond the pupils' capacity to execute successfully. Certain technical skills may be necessary to the

successful rendition of one selection, whereas an extended and artistic phrase line may be the crucial feature in another. Thus the teacher must be able to exploit the teaching opportunity that a particular selection offers.

Ideally then and in order to meet demands associated with any particular musical selection chosen, it is imperative that the teacher be:

1. Literate in the notational aspects of the selection.
2. Skillful enough (vocally, instrumentally) to execute the selection.
3. Aware of the significance—literary thought, beauty, mood or feeling pertinent to the selection.

These three requirements are the concern of the remainder of this book. Although the selections used in this text are primarily from series texts, others also are included. Original sources—collections of songs by famous composers, anthologies, etc.—should also be investigated. There is a wealth of fine music that has not yet found its way into school texts, but which is awaiting the enterprising teacher. It is hoped that a close study of these selections will increase the teacher's competence, and hence his confidence in the teaching of music.

6

THE MUSICAL SCORE

What the Musical Score Tells Us by Analysis

What Theoretical or Notational Concepts Are Common and Applicable to Most Songs or Selections Used in the Elementary Grades?

Answer:

1. Key or tonality.
2. Scale.
3. Chords or harmony.
4. Rhythmic patterns.
5. Melodic patterns.
6. Harmonic patterns.
7. Form or design.

1. KEY OR TONALITY

What Is Meant by Key?
Any pitch may be the tonal center of a key. Sharps or flats are used to ensure proper positioning of steps and half steps for the sounds appropriate to that particular key. (See also pp. 39-42 and 50-54.)

What Kinds of Scales Are Indicated by a Given Key Signature?
Two types are common: major and minor scales.

How Do They Differ?
In general, a song or melody in a major key ends on note 1 (do), whereas a song or melody in a minor key ends on note 6 (la).

What Are the Common Major Keys?
a. Sharp keys are:

b. Flat keys are:

Key: F   B♭   E♭   A♭   D♭

c. The key of C has no sharps or flats:

Key: C

How Do You Find the Key?

a. Major keys:

In order to find the key, two rules may be observed:

Rule 1: <u>For sharp keys</u>, the last sharp (the sharp farthest to the right) always represents sound 7 (ti), hence to find 1 (do), count <u>one above</u> the last sharp:

One above last sharp (♯), hence key of D

Rule 2: <u>For flat keys</u>, the last flat (the flat farthest to the right) always represents sound 4 (fa), hence to find 1 (do), count <u>three below</u> the last flat:

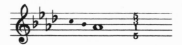

Three below last flat, hence key of A♭

b. Minor Keys:

In order to find the minor key, find the keynote, then count <u>two below</u> the keynote. Thus:

Two below 1 or A, hence key of F♯m*

and

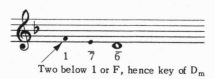

Two below 1 or F, hence key of Dm

*Note the subscript "m" added to minor key to distinguish from major keys. Often, uncapitalized letters are used: e.g., f♯m and dm, etc.

Why Are Keys Important?

The key determines the position or placing of a melody. For example, the fol
lowing excerpt may be in a key appropriate to a violinist or flautist, but not t
children's voices:

For singing, a lower key would be preferred:

The melody has been <u>transposed</u> (transferred) to a lower position. Note that th
scale arrangement of sounds, as given by the number notation shown, is identical

How Might One Explain the Meaning of Key?

Tunes "live" in certain keys in the same way that people live in certain home
and towns. Melodies finally return to the "home note" (key note) in the sam
way that people return to their homes at the end of the day. The last note of
melody in the key of G, for example, is almost invariably G; similarly, the las
note of a melody in the key of A is A, and so on.

In minor keys, where the scale runs from note 6 to note 6 of the major scale
the answer, of course, would be E and F♯ respectively.

2. THE SCALE

What Is Meant by a Scale?
A scale is a pattern of sounds from which melodies are constructed.

What Different Types of Scales Are There?
Among the more common are: the major scale; the minor scale; the penta
tonic scale*; the chromatic scale.

Of these, only the major scale will be considered here.

The Major Scale
Each key implies a different scale. Thus, the scale for the key of G:

is the pattern of sounds given by:

---
*See Chap. 11 for discussion of this scale.

```
G A B C D E F♯ G
1 2 3 4 5 6 7  8
     half      half
     step       step
```

The scale for key of A:

is the pattern of sounds represented by

```
A B C♯ D E F♯ G♯ A
1 2 3  4 5 6  7  8
    half      half
    step       step
```

The sharps (or flats in flat keys) are inserted as shown from the key signature.

How May Scale Be Explained?

The scale may be considered to contain the raw materials from which melodies in that key are made, in the same way that concrete, wood, nails, etc., are raw materials for homes; or letters of the alphabet are raw materials for words. An analysis of the following melody reveals, for example, that only notes of the G-scale are used in constructing the finished product—the melody:

Notice that within the first three measures of this melody, "Home on the Range," all the scale sounds have been used. The remainder of the tune merely contains more of the same seven sounds. Occasionally, there are melodies which also use sounds from other keys, usually keys closely related to the original; or melodies which do not appear to have any key center (see Chapter 11), such as some of the more modern types of melodies. Generally, however, melodies encountered in elementary school music books and in folk literature contain only the sounds which are common to that key.

It may be stated again that the sharps or flats in a particular key are there merely to make the tune written in that key sound "right." Thus, a tune written in the key of G, hence using the raw materials of that key, i.e., G A B C D E F♯ G, would not sound correct if the F-natural were substituted for the F♯ called for in the signature. A simple example will suffice:

The ear immediately resents hearing sound 7 (ti) a whole step from sound 1 instead of the accustomed half step.

3. CHORDS OR HARMONY (PRIMARY CHORDS)

What Is Meant by Chord?

A chord is a combination of three or more notes sounded simultaneously. On p. 60 we learned that a I-chord is formed by taking every other tone beginning on sound 1 (do), which becomes the <u>root</u> of that chord. This may be done beginning on any degree of the scale and using it as the root of a chord:

$$
\begin{array}{cccccccc}
 & & & & & \underline{4} & & \\
 & 5 & 6 & 7 & \underline{1} & \underline{2} & \underline{3} & \underline{4} \\
\text{Chord:} & 3 & 4 & 5 & 6 & 7 & \underline{1} & \underline{2} \\
\text{Scale:} & 1 & 2 & 3 & 4 & 5 & 6 & 7 \quad \underline{1}\,\underline{2}\,\underline{3} \text{ etc.}
\end{array}
$$

Name of
chord: I II$_m$ III$_m$ IV V^7 VI$_m$ VII$_d$*I etc.

To any chord a fourth tone (or more) may be added. Such added tones are designated according to their distance from the chord root. It is common for the V-chord to have an added tone, hence the designation V^7. A tone has been added to the V-chord which is a seventh away from the root tone 5, for example:

5 6 7 <u>1</u> <u>2</u> <u>3</u> <u>4</u>

a seventh

The theoretical derivation of the simple IV and V^7-chords which Miss Johnson taught her class (Chapter 3) is easily seen.

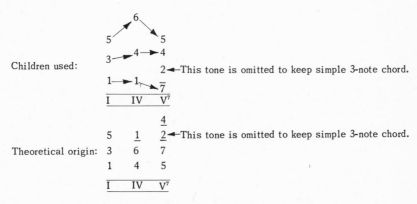

These I, IV, and V^7-chords are called <u>primary</u> chords. The primary chords for the keys of C, F, and G. are:

---

*The chord on the seventh degree of the major scale is called a <u>diminished</u> (d) chord. It is not commonly used as such.

Key of C:

```
                                    F
                       ⎧G      C  D
               Chord:  ⎨E      A  B
               Scale:  ⎩C  D  E  F  G  A  B  C

               Name    I      IV V⁷
               of      or
               chord:  C      F  G⁷
```

Key of F:

```
                                    B♭
                       ⎧C      F  G
               Chord:  ⎨A      D  E
               Scale:  ⎩F  G  A  B♭ C  D  E  F

               Name    I      IV V⁷
               of      or
               chord:  F      B♭ C⁷
```

Key of G:

```
                                    C
                       ⎧D      G  A
               Chord:  ⎨B      E  F♯
               Scale:  ⎩G  A  B  C  D  E  F♯ G

               Name    I      IV V⁷
               of      or
               chord:  G      C  D⁷
```

Why Are Primary Chords Important?

When these chords are sensitively played on autoharp, piano, or other chordal instrument along with the melody, they provide support or color for the melody with which they are allied. The added sounds blend with the melody being sung or played, thus enriching and giving depth to the total effect. Chord notations are therefore provided with many of the songs given in the series texts. They are shown in the form of either Roman numerals or capital letters and placed just above or below the melody line. Leaf through almost any song text and note this fact.

Chord I, also called the tonic or keynote chord, is of particular importance. The last note of most songs in the major key is usually the first note (root) of the tonic chord, and the first note of a song is usually either the root (sound 1), third (sound 3), or fifth (sound 5) of that chord. For this reason, immediately before singing a certain song, the tonic chord should be sounded and placed on the staff for children to see. It will contain the first note to be sung or played.

Other Chords—IIₘ and VIₘ

In addition to the primary chords I, IV, and V⁷, others also are used, particularly IIₘ and VIₘ, or those found upon the second and sixth degrees of the scale. In the key of G, for example, IIₘ and VIₘ will be shown as follows:

```
                                    C
                      ⎧D  E      G  A  B
              Chord:  ⎨B  C      E  F♯ G
              Scale:  ⎩G  A  B  C  D  E  F♯ G

              Name    I  IIₘ     IV V⁷ VIₘ
              of      or
              chord:  G  Aₘ      C  D⁷ Eₘ
```

136

The well-known melody "Au Clair de la Lune," or "By the Light of the Moon" as it is called in one text, features chord II_m in addition to the I- and V^7-chords:

By the Light of the Moon*
(Au Clair de la Lune)

French Folk Song

| G | | G | D⁷ | G | D⁷ | G |

Now the moon is shin - ing, My good friend Pier - rot,
Wak - en from your slum - ber, hear me knock - ing low.
Au clair de la lu - ne, Mon a - mi Pier - rôt,
Prêt - ez moi ta plu - me, pour é - crit un mot;

| Am | | Am | | Am | D⁷ | G |

I must write a let - ter, lend your pen to me,
Ma chan - delle est mor - te Je n'ai plus de feu.

| G | | G | D⁷ | G | D⁷ | G |

Won't you strike a match, please, I can hard - ly see.
Ouv - re moi ta por - te, Pour l'a - mour de Dieu.

Another folk song, this time in the key of C, features two minor chords, VI_m and III_m, in addition to the three primary chords:

Come Rowing with Me**
(Record #3503A)

Italian Folk Song

| I | V⁷ | I | IV |

Come, row - ing with me,_____ Come,

| I | VI_m | III_m |

jour - ney with me,_____ Float - ing so peace - ful - ly

| IV | I | I | V⁷ | I |

down to the sea, Come, row - ing with me._____

*Richard C. Berg, Daniel S. Hooley, Josephine Wolverton, and Claudeane Burns, <u>Music for Young Americans</u>, Book Four (New York: American Book Company, 1960), p. 20. Used by permission of the publisher.

**Irving Wolfe, Beatrice Perham Krone, Margaret Fullerton, <u>Music Round the Town</u> (Chicago: Follett Publishing Company, 1959), p. 41. Used by permission of the publisher.

Minor chords are unlike either of the other three chords, thus providing a contrast. Because of their quality, they are called <u>minor</u> chords to distinguish them from the I, IV, and V^7-chords, which are called <u>major</u> chords.

Chords for Melodies in Minor Keys

Primary chords are not confined merely to melodies in major keys. They are used equally with melodies in minor keys. Thus, for example, in the key of D minor (D_m)

the scale would be D E F G A B♭ C D, and the primary chords, as with major scales, would be shown as follows:

Chord:	{ A F D		D B♭ E F G	G E C♯ A B♭ C D		
Scale:						

Name of chord:	I_m *or* D_m		IV_m V^7 G_m A^7

Note that in the case of the V^7-chord, one note has been altered—C to C♯. The V- or V^7-chord will not sound convincing without this change. A similar change must be made for V- or V^7-chords in all minor keys.

4. RHYTHMIC PATTERNS

Another observable characteristic of most musical selections is the use of rhythmic <u>motives</u> or <u>figures</u> (short rhythmic grouping of notes). Thus, for example, if a certain rhythmic configuration (motive) such as ♩. ♪♩ is used, it is often repeated once or several times, as well as placed within a larger rhythmic structure which binds it to other rhythms. These larger units, or rhythmic phrases, are usually of two or four measures duration, and these too may be similar or identical. Note, for example, the rhythmic structure of this patriotic hymn:

The motive (♩. ♪♩) occurs five times. This motive is grouped with other rhythms to reveal seven rhythmic phrases. The over-all effect is one of unity.

There is an ongoing effect, marked off by places of relaxation, and several of these (seven in this case) constitute a complete song.

It is important, when learning a new song, to identify and sound out the phrase-like rhythmic patterns and to note similarities and contrasts before proceeding to play or sing the selection.

5. MELODIC PATTERNS

Like rhythmic patterns, the melodic contours of a particular selection often reveal similarities and contrasts. Note, for example, the melodic patterns of the well-known folk song "All through the Night":

Phrases 1, 2, and 4, are identical, but phrase 3 provides variety and contrast.

The rhythmic motive (♩. ♪♩) or (♩. ♪𝅝) occurs eleven times, and is grouped with other note values to form four distinct phrases. The over-all effect is one of unity. This is achieved partly by a restatement of the initial melody at the end. Within each phrase there is a feeling of rhythmic motion marked off by places of relaxation (ends of phrases), and four of these constitute the whole song.

6. HARMONIC PATTERNS

When students or teachers first attempt to play an autoharp or a chordal piano accompaniment to a song, they often have difficulty playing the chords at the proper time. The problem of watching for chord changes in the notation and playing the instrument at the same time is often a frustrating experience.

The memorization of the chord patterns given for a particular song, on the other hand, makes it possible for the player to devote all his attention to the actual playing of the instrument, thus effecting a more accurate and sensitive accompaniment. Note, for example, the chords given for "By the Light of the Moon" (p. 137). The chords, shown two to a measure, are:

1st line	I	I	I	V⁷	I	V⁷	I	-
2nd line	I	I	I	V⁷	I	V⁷	I	-
3rd line	II	II	II	II	II	V⁷	I	-
4th line	I	I	I	V⁷	I	V⁷	I	-

Notice that the harmonic pattern for the first, second (repeated), and fourth lines are identical, and easily memorized. Even a brief glance to reveal such patterns, and then to chart them as shown above, helps the beginner to provide a more satisfactory accompaniment.

Note also the harmonic pattern for "Tell Me, Little Maiden" (pp. 153-154). Although the melody is different for each line of the song, the harmonic pattern is identical for each.

The identification of all types of patterns—rhythmic, melodic, and harmonic—can speed up the apprehension and performance of most songs. A glance through any new song for the purpose of identifying, isolating, and comprehending such units should become commonplace and, in addition, provide a means for identifying the kind of tonal architecture (form) used.

7. FORM OR DESIGN

Form refers to the architectural plan of a composition. In the same way that architects use lines to create squares and triangles, in designing rooms and finally buildings, composers work with motives—rhythmic, melodic, and harmonic—when creating phrases and, finally, complete musical compositions.

Two-part Song Form (Binary Form)

In order to provide a satisfying musical experience, an art form must reveal a balance between <u>unity</u> and <u>variety</u>. Unity, or the binding force within a musical line, may be achieved by judicious repetitions of a simple motive, but variety implies the introduction of new details or alternations of contrasting ideas.

Two-part song form, or binary form, reveals how the element of contrast plays its part in a musical composition. Note, for example, the structure of the familiar "Lullaby" by Johannes Brahms:

Part A

Phrase 1

Part B

Phrase 2 Phrase 3

140

Phrase 4

Using the letters A and B to identify the different sections, the form of this melody may be shown to be AB, or A A₁ B B₁, a variant of AB. Note that in the two-part song form each part ends in the tonic key, here the key of C. In other words, the melody comes to a full stop in both sections.

Three-part Song Form (Ternary Form)

The next largest of song forms is the three-part, or ternary, form, which may be designated by the letters ABA. The four-line song, "All Through the Night," shown on p. 139, is of the AABA type, a variant of ABA. Note that the B-part, or third phrase, ends on the dominant chord, hence the need for the repetition of the A-part following.

Note: A form which combines either binary or ternary or both into a larger form of ternary form is the Minuet and Trio form. The minuet, a favored dance in the courts of seventeenth century Europe, was later incorporated into symphonic form where it served as the third movement. The minuet and trio consist of two dances or songs, the second of which is repeated according to the outline below:

A	B	A	Coda
First dance, the form of which is either AB or ABA	Second or subordinate dance (trio), the form of which is either AB or ABA	First dance (Da Capo), of which the form is AB or ABA	Optional

Some examples featuring the Minuet and Trio form (ternary form) in orchestral literature are:

Haydn: *Surprise Symphony*, third movement.
Mozart: *Eine Kleine Nachtmusik* (A Little Night Music), third movement.
Beethoven: *Symphony No. 5*, scherzo.
Chopin: *Polonaise Militaire in A major*
Prokofiev: *Sonata No. 6, Op. 82*, third movement.

Other extended forms, as applied particularly to instrumental music are:

1. Rondo form—ABACADA, etc.
Examples: Beethoven: *Sonata No. 2 Op. #2*, last movement.
Wieniawski: *Polonaise in A major*, for violin and piano.
Ravel: *Sonatine*, for piano, second movement.

2. Variation form—AA₁A₂A₃, etc. (see also p. 000).
Examples: Brahms: *Variations on a Theme by Handel, Op. 24.*
Calliet: *Variations on "Pop Goes the Weasel."*
Copland: *Variations for Piano.*
Dohnanyi: *Variations on a Nursery Theme* (Baa, Baa, Black Sheep).
Elgar: *Enigma Variations for Orchestra*
Haydn: *Surprise Symphony*, fourth movement.

Haydn:	*Emperor Quartet.*
Schubert:	*"Trout" Quintet.*

3. Sonata form—Sonata form is the most highly organized of all musical forms. It is usually found as the first movement in symphonies, and for this reason is sometimes referred to as first-movement form.

Examples: Haydn: *Symphony No. 101* (Clock), first movement.
          Beethoven: *Sonata Op. 2, No. 1*, first movement.
          Mozart: *Eine Kleine Nachtmusik*, first movement.

4. Suite—The traditional classic suite consists of a group of contrasting dances.

Examples: Bach: *Suite No. 3 in D major.*
          Corelli: *Suite for Strings.*

The ballet suite consists of ballet music arranged for concert performance.

Examples: Tschaikowsky: *The Nutcracker Suite.*
          Delibes: *Coppelia Suite.*

Orchestral suites:

Examples: Ravel: *Mother Goose Suite.*
          Grieg: *Peer Gynt Suite.*
          Copland: *Billy the Kid.*

5. Overture:

Examples: Smetana: Overture from *The Bartered Bride.*
          Rossini: *William Tell* Overture.

REFERENCES

Robert E. Nye, and Bjornar Bergethon, Basic Music for Classroom Teachers (Englewood Cliffs, N. J.: Prentice-Hall, 1962).

Robert Pace, Music Essentials for Classroom Teachers (Wadsworth Publishing Co., 1961).

Gene C. Wisler, Music Fundamentals for the Classroom Teacher (Boston: Allyn and Bacon, Boston, 1961).

See sections entitled "Form in Music," in Harry R. Wilson, Walter Ehret, Alice M. Snyder, Edward J. Hermann, Growing with Music, Books 4 and 5 (Englewood Cliffs, N. J.: Prentice-Hall, 1963).

What the Musical Score Tells Us by Listening

An understanding of theory is essential when considering the significance of arrangements of notes on the printed page. But the situation is quite different with heard music. Here the response is primarily an emotional one. Intellectual appreciation, though applicable, is secondary. A song, sung or heard by the class, is first liked as sound before it is appreciated as arrangements of notes. It is more a situation of liking or disliking what is heard, of approving or disapproving, than one of knowing or not knowing in a strictly intellectual sense. Listening to

142

music is an activity deserving the fullest attention and support of both teacher and class. One authority states that "of all types of musical activity, whether in or out of school, listening is the most basic."*

Upon reflection, one cannot easily disagree. Consider, for example, the post-school years of the majority of pupils. It is not likely that many graduates will become professional musicians, or join various community choruses, bands, or orchestras. For most, any contact with music will be with music that is heard through radio, television, recordings, and occasional concert performances. The importance of listening opportunities in school music activities, therefore, cannot be overestimated.

WHEN SHOULD MUSIC LISTENING OCCUR?

From the outset, an atmosphere of listening intentness should pervade and be a part of all music learning—as we observed in the listening activities of Miss Harbrecht (p. 113) and Mr. Penn (p. 118)—and not merely appear as a formal, structured "appreciation" period. Even apart from the use of recordings, for example, there are numerous occasions when rewarding listening attitudes and experiences may occur. For example,

1. When part of a class sings and the rest are attending to their efforts (pp. 9-10).
2. When a class is conscious of improving their tone quality, i.e. when they try to realize a prior ideal of vocal sound (p. 114).
3. When they are attempting to sight-read a song.
4. When part of a class is learning to sing a chant or obligato to a melody sung by others—allowing the ear to help in placing the sound (p. 28).
5. When humming, singing, or playing (recorders or plastic flutes) chord patterns along with a melody (p. 90).
6. When playing simple instruments, noting errors in fingering, improving intonation, etc. (p. 62).
7. When playing an autoharp accompaniment, feeling its vibrations and anticipating chord changes (pp. 62-63).
8. When playing even a simple rhythm instrument to highlight the mood of a particular phrase or section (p. 29).
9. When singing a root-bass or harmony part by ear or by sight (pp. 92-93).
10. When dramatizing or moving about to the rhythm of a melody (p. 10).
11. When learning a song by rote (p. 114).
12. When writing original melodies or parts (Chapter 11).
13. When extracting chord accompaniments for given melodies, thence sounding them (Chapter 9), and so on.

Listening possibilities are enriched and extended even further through the use of recordings. First, there is added a vast and varied quantity of music both past and present which goes far beyond the performing capabilities of even the most versatile of school performing groups. Second, there is added an excellence of tone quality and of interpretive power unmatched by the best of choruses, bands, or orchestras found in schools. The appreciation of these new dimensions is for

---

*William C. Hartshorn, "Listening a Basic Part of Music Education," from Music Education for Elementary School Children (Washington, D.C.: Music Educators National Conference, 1960), p. 31.

many pupils a considerable but valuable accomplishment. Some suggestions which may help the teacher to guide pupils toward a growing realization of this goal are therefore in order.

WHAT ARE SOME GUIDING PRINCIPLES IN CHOOSING RECORDINGS FOR CLASSROOM NEEDS?

What should guide the teacher's choice of recordings for classroom use? Basically, the answer is simple: melody, rhythm, harmony, and form. These four elements, together with dynamics, tempo, and tone color, factors that are apparent in performance, constitute the essence, the substance of music. It is to these that man everywhere (the child not excepted) in greater or less degree is sensitive. The degree of acceptability of music is a variable factor depending upon age, environment, training, experience, and native endowment. Whatever the level of acceptability may be for any individual at any given time, it is generally known that this is not a static state and is therefore subject to change. Whether the level goes down or goes up, depends to a great extent upon the quality of the music teaching and music listening taking place.

In order to ensure a favorable environment for effective listening, the following principles may be observed:

1. The music selected should be appropriate to the maturity level of children. Although there is wide variation of appeal and meaning in any age group of children, in general one would avoid what in mathematics would be "differential equations before fractions," in English literature "Hamlet" before "Kon-Tiki," yes, and in music a Bach fugue before "Carnival of the Animals."

2. The music chosen should be of intrinsic merit. Although this is difficult to define, certainly one criterion of "good" music is its lasting quality. Popularity of a selection at a given time is no indication it is "good"! Generally speaking, the preselected educational albums prescribed by educational and musical authorities are to be recommended. (See p. 160 for a partial listing.)

3. Use good quality recordings and record players. The basic and unique appeal in music is tone, hence this should be of the best.

4. A sensitivity to the attention span of children is essential. The good intentions and planning of the teacher may be undone if selections are too long for children to listen to comfortably.

5. In general, children appreciate music which has nonmusical or extramusical connotations (program music) before they appreciate strictly pure or absolute music with which no associative ideas are implied or related. That is to say, the "Carnival of the Animals" or the "Witches Dance" are generally more easily understood than, for example, Bach's "Brandenburg Concerto No. 6."

6. The teacher should be enthusiastic about music and in particular about the selections she brings to the class. The teacher by her own interest, enthusiasm, and desire to share her interest with children, sets up in the classroom an atmosphere which is conducive to good listening. This is of first importance.

WHAT STEPS MAY BE TAKEN TO INTRODUCE RECORDINGS IN THE CLASSROOM?

Among the readily available and certainly the most pertinent recordings are those provided with series texts. Approximately one quarter to one half of the songs contained in series texts are recorded and contained in albums accompanying texts. (Thirty of the songs and selections included in this text are recorded. See p. 368 for list of titles.) The wise teacher will draw upon these resources at every opportunity.

Next, in order of suitability, are recordings closely related to, or integrated with, a particular song or selection. Information as to titles, composers, etc., is generously provided along with many of the songs in series texts, thus making them readily available for extended listening. The text Music Near and Far, for example, lists two related recordings for "First Signs of Spring." They are "Spring Song" by Mendelssohn, and "To Spring" by Grieg. (See p. 244 in this text.) Again, in the Birchard Music Series Book 2 (see p. 173 in this text) are two appropriate recordings as a follow-up to learning "Cradle Song." They are: Jarnefelt's "Berceuse" and Brahm's "Little Sandman." Such preselected listening suggestions are invaluable aids toward a heightened experience.

Another source for suitable and appropriate recordings can be found in the educational record collections published by many firms. (See p. 160 for a partial listing.) From these collections, the teacher is able to select for herself numerous appropriate examples to illustrate a particular feeling or mood. At least one of these collections should be readily available in all schools.

Additional recordings of greater variety, generally categorized under "program" and "absolute" music, are readily available from record companies and music dealers. These together with those listed above will challenge the most sophisticated ear and provide for listening excursions of almost unlimited scope.

IS TRAINING IN LISTENING IMPORTANT?

One has only to reflect upon the influence of commercial radio, and the promulgation of a vulgarized jazz idiom to arrive at one answer. There can be little question but that "these after four-o'clock teachers . . . pouring a ceaseless stream of noise over mankind"* are undermining much of what the school is trying to do. Radio's beat-pushing impresarios, whose products are listened to most avidly by the young, seem utterly unaware of any other sound but last week's particular rage. A continuous upheaval is evidently intended by much of this industry, its sponsors, and promoters.

The schools must be prepared to offer stimulating and invigorating countermeasures. In the recordings now generally available in most schools, the teacher has the necessary resources. By wise use of these resources, coupled with good planning and patience, the teacher can soon hope to see changes for the better. Although a reassessment of critical values may not always emerge as planned, or be as encouraging in some pupils as in others, the ultimate objectives are eminently worthwhile.

---

*Arthur Honegger, "Artists in Modern Society," International Conference of Artists, Venice 22-28 September 1952. Published by UNESCO, Paris, 1954, p. 32.

Musical recordings are valuable in general education as well.* In the study of geography, history, or social studies of a certain country, for example, the use of recordings indigenous to the people of that country can be most profitable. The joys and sorrows, fears and hopes of mankind everywhere are often revealed through music.

Recent years have shown a marked increase in the production and distribution of recordings of all kinds. Coupled with this has been a resurgence of interest in the reproduction of the older forms of music, folk as well as art forms, stemming from the earliest times of printed or engraved symbols, to the present day. This applies to the whole world, Africa and Asia as well as Europe and the Americas. The historical panorama of the music of all peoples now increasingly available, and of a quality undreamed of a few short years ago, is of great importance in present-day education.

An understanding of music history for its own values, the evolvement of its forms and designs over the centuries should, of course, be a part of anyone's cultural heritage. A knowledge of music from the different periods of music history—e.g., the Renaissance, Baroque, Classical, Romantic, and Modern, to name but the main streams of Western musical history—is normally as relevant to a cultural education as is a knowledge of different styles of literature, painting, or social customs or even fashions of dress.

Finally, training in listening is needed for postschool living. As has been mentioned earlier, few persons will be actively engaged in the performance of music once they leave school. All, however, will have contact with listening. Whatever a teacher can do to advance, sustain, and deepen the musical interests of her pupils will not only serve them well now, but will also have rewards for the future. Certainly one would be averse to a championing of procedures (or a negating of opportunities) which might jeopardize such a rich and challenging prospect. One objective to which most teachers would subscribe is that when the student leaves school he will be on friendly terms with some great tonal literature, to which he can turn to find satisfaction and pleasure.

REFERENCES

Lillian Baldwin, Music For Young Listeners, published in three volumes (The Green Book, The Crimson Book, The Blue Book) by Silver Burdett Co., Morristown, N. J. (Toronto: W. J. Gage and Co.).

Marian Cotton and Adelaide Bradburn, Music Throughout the World and Harriot Barbour and Warren S. Freeman, A Story of Music, both published by Summy-Birchard Co., Evanston, Ill. (Toronto: The House of Grant, Ltd.).

Hugh M. Miller, History of Music, College Outline Series, (New York: Barnes and Noble, 1953).

---

*Tooze and Krone, Literature and Music (Englewood Cliffs, N.J.: Prentice-Hall, Inc., 1955).

POINTERS AND PRACTICE—
CHAPTER 6

I. Transpose the following phrase to the keys shown below:

II. Compare the last melody note and the key note of the first twelve selections of the elementary songbook you are now using or this book. What conclusions can you draw?

III. Compare the first melody note of the first twelve songs in the songbook with the notes found in Chord I for that key. What conclusions can you draw?

IV. Play the following melody on the piano, songbells, or recorder flute:

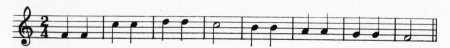

Which sound feels incorrect?

Why?

V. Write and label, as shown in the example given, the primary chords for the following scales:

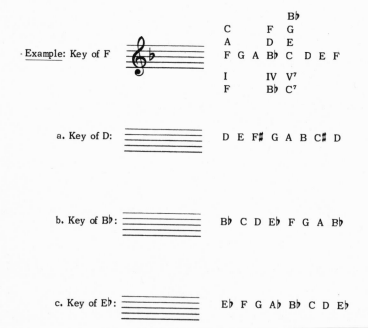

Example: Key of F

```
                              Bb
            C         F   G
            A         D   E
            F G A Bb  C   D E F

            I         IV  V⁷
            F         Bb  C⁷
```

a. Key of D: D E F♯ G A B C♯ D

b. Key of Bb: Bb C D Eb F G A Bb

c. Key of Eb: Eb F G Ab Bb C D Eb

VI. In addition to the primary chords, what additional minor chords are found with melodies in a major key?

148

VII. Write and label correctly the two most common minor chords for the major keys shown below. Insert correct key signature.

a. Key of C: C D E F G A B C

b. Key of E: E F♯ G♯ A B C♯ D♯ E

VIII. Write the primary chords for the following minor keys. (Label as shown in No. V.):

a. Key of E$_m$:   E F♯ G A B C D E

b. Key of A$_m$:   A B C D E F G A

What alteration must be made to one of the chords? Why?

Old MacDonald Had a Farm

Traditional

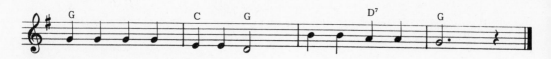

IX. Identify like and unlike phrases in the melody shown above.

How many phrases are there?

Is it binary or ternary form?

What abbreviation is used for this form?

What different chords are used? What are they called?

Graph the harmonic pattern.

If you are playing the autoharp accompaniment, what advantage is there in memorizing this pattern?

X. One method of extending a composition is to repeat the same phrase or melody over and over again, but each time treating it differently. The form indicated is Variation Form and is designated A_1, A_2, A_3, etc., depending on the length and ingenuity of the composer. A simple example of this form, using the first phrase of "Mary Had a Little Lamb," is on the following page.

Original melody (A)

1st variation (A₁)

2nd variation (A₂)

On the staff provided write still another version of this phrase, but this time in 4/4 time.

3rd variation (A₃)

XI. Is "music appreciation" realized only through record listening? Comment on your answer.

XII. Examine the "Listening Program" albums of the RCA Victor Basic Record Library for Elementary Schools or other prescribed recordings for suggestions as to how they may be used. List these as they may apply to a particular grade.

XIII. What period in music history parallels (a) the French Revolution (b) the Industrial Revolution (c) the Second World War?

What are some typical composers and compositions of these periods?

List some of the characteristics of the music of these periods. (For reference, see Hugh M. Miller, History of Music [New York: Barnes and Noble, 1953] or other music history texts.)

XIV. Outline a record-listening period for the upper elementary grades in such a way that music is "studied as a process of inquiry into its nature, meaning, and structure, rather than as the accumulation of predetermined facts about it"*

---

*William C. Hartshorn, "The Study of Music as an Academic Discipline," Music Educators Journal, Vol. 49, No. 3 (Jan., 1963), p. 26.

7

LEARNING AND TEACHING NEW SONGS

The beginning teacher must sooner or later face the practical issues of learning and teaching new and unfamiliar songs. One suggested approach may be stated in question form as follows:

What theoretical or notational concepts are applicable to songs? In what different ways may songs be learned? What additional activities may be incorporated to make the experience more memorable?

To ensure a thorough grasp of this procedure, these questions are applied to each of the following three examples:

Song Example 1

Tell Me, Little Maiden*

Polish Folk Melody

---

*M. Krone (ed.), Music through the Year (Chicago: Follett Publishing Co., 1959), p. 35. Used by permission of the publisher.

What Theoretical or Notational Concepts Are Applicable?
Answer:

1. The key is G, confirmed by the sharp sign (♯) on top line and last note G.

2. The scale (raw materials) from which the melody has been constructed is represented by G A B C D E F♯ G.

3. The range is suitable for young voices and extends from:

4. The primary chords for this key are: G (GBD), C (CEG), and D^7 (DF♯AC), $_{1\ 3\ 5}$ also abbreviated I, IV, and V^7. In this particular selection, only two of the three chords are needed: I and V^7.

5. The harmonic pattern revealed by the given chordal notation (notated under the melody line) is:

<u>1st line</u>: I V^7 V^7 I
<u>2nd line</u>: I V^7 V^7 I
<u>3rd line</u>: I V^7 V^7 I
<u>4th line</u>: I V^7 V^7 I

Each line has the same harmonic pattern although the melody is different for each. This means that the accompaniment can easily be memorized. The chords may be played on the autoharp or piano while the melody is sung or played. (Chord I [GBD] should be played immediately before singing the song as this will establish the tonal center and provide the starting note which is D.)

6. The rhythmic motive pertinent particularly to the first two lines is ♪ ♪ ♩, as it is used at the beginning of alternate measures, and the phrase to which it belongs is two measures long. These patterns for the first two lines are identical, and are two measures in length: | ♪· ♪ ♩ ♩| ♩ ♩| . The rhythmic pattern used for the last two lines is of a contrasting nature, and with one exception, reduces to: | ♩ ♩ ♩| ♫♫ ♩| .

7. The melodic pattern for the first phrase: "Tell me little maiden," and the third phrase: "Are you fond of dancing," are identical, and the patterns revealed in the second phrases: "Waiting there so lonely," and the fourth phrase: "Are you waiting only," are similar. The first two phrases of lines three and four are identical, and the last two phrases of each line are similar.

8. In all, the song seems to divide into two sections; the first, consisting of the first two lines; the second, of the last two lines. A convenient formula for the whole would be AA$_1$BB$_1$ or binary form.

In What Different Ways May Songs Be Learned?
Answer:

1. <u>Class Sight-reads and Sings Song.</u>* Through appropriate questioning the

---

*The suggestions for developing sight reading abilities refer primarily to the middle and upper elementary grades. For initial efforts (reading-readiness principles), and more specifically for the primary grades, see pp. 312-314.

teacher might first encourage the class to identify and classify rhythmic and melodic patterns, noting any special skips or leaps which might offer some difficulty. Next, the class might tap or chant the words to the rhythm of the melody. Finally, the teacher (or a student) should sound the tonic chord, here GBD, the
1 3 5
starting note D, and proceed to sing the song either with a neutral syllable or with the text. Pupils should be advised to carry through to the end despite errors so that they maintain the rhythmic flow. There will be many false attempts and halting efforts; with persistence, however, considerable progress can be made. Any particularly difficult section may be isolated and practiced separately before the whole song is attempted. One physical aid which stimulates alertness is to ask pupils to follow notes and words by pointing to them as they sing. Any procedure which will cause the eye to attend meaningfully to the undulations of the melodic line on the page should be encouraged.

It is also advisable that the chordal accompaniment, here chords I and V⁷, be included with the vocal reading. This increases confidence and accuracy in pitch and rhythm, and also adds to the total quality-effect of the song. It would normally be difficult, for example, for children to sing other sounds but those shown while the G-chord is sounding in the accompaniment:

For a more unified attempt at sight-singing a new song, the melody may occasionally be copied on the blackboard and either the pupil or the teacher follow the notes with a pointer. Whatever is done, the tonic chord G (GBD) and the first note
1 3 5
D should be sounded immediately before the reading is to begin. The tonality must first be heard and felt.

For success in sight-reading, two things are desirable: First, provision for practice, whether daily or weekly, for a few minutes each time, should be made. It is of little use to attempt it merely once or twice and then forget it. Even five minutes, twice weekly, devoted to this problem will prove helpful. Second, any approach to vocal reading should at first be confined to one key. Only in this way will familiarity with skips, patterns, and range be established. One of the reasons why music reading is difficult for children is that the eye has to cope with continual changing of keys. The pupil one day encounters certain patterns; on another day, another set of patterns and skips. The adjustment is not easy. By using one key only for a time, the pupil soon notices certain common factors. In the key of G, for example, some of the more constant factors are:

The first note is usually one of G, B, or D:

The last note is almost always G:

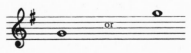

155

The range is usually about one octave:

to

Melodies may be said to consist of a mixture of scale or "step" sounds:

repeated sounds:

and skips:

with occasional use of chromatic sounds. Of these, skips offer probably more of a challenge than other kinds. However, these too are parts of definite patterns, at least in the majority of elementary songs. Most skips are found to be between notes of the I and V^7-chords. Skips such as the following are common occurrences in songs in the key of G:

Chord I skips:

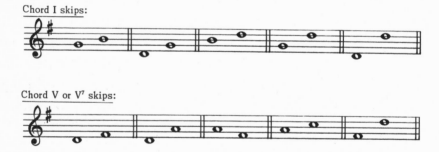

Chord V or V^7 skips:

From the song, p. 153, how many skips are found (a) from the I-chord? (b) from the V^7-chord? Choose other songs in the key of G, and note similar results.

The G and F keys are probably the most suitable for initial sight-reading purposes as (a) numerous examples of songs in these keys are found, and (b) they lend themselves to relatively simple accompaniment whether with autoharp or with piano (see pp. 186-190).

Class reading of new songs is generally recommended beginning about Grade Three.* Considerable success may be achieved, provided: (a) opportunities for reading are regularly given, (b) the reading be confined, at least for a considerable time, to a certain key, (c) chordal accompaniment is used where appro-

---

*See sections entitled "Reading Music," Growing with Music, Books 2-5 (Englewood Cliffs, N.J.: Prentice-Hall, 1963).

priate, and (d) some attempts at grading the songs be considered. Songs of the I- and V-chord variety are as a rule easier to read than those featuring more chords, other factors excluded.

Apart from visual reading problems, many children also have hearing or tone-sensing problems. Even though a class as a whole may appear to do quite well in singing a new song, there will be some who seem to drone along at an indefinite pitch, and others who follow somewhat more accurately but several pitches lower. A sense of pitch, particularly the pitch of others, is, for many, not easily felt. The terms "highness" and "lowness" as applied to the visual symbols are not necessarily felt as such in an auditory or tonal sense. Abilities differ depending usually upon experience, interest, age, and ability. Many uncertain singers* simply lack sufficient practice, not only in singing per se, but in involvement with sound through playing, experimenting, listening, moving, etc. In the same way that children absorb and refine their concepts of "hot" and "cold" by concrete and meaningful experiences with a measuring instrument, (thermometer) so too with "high" and "low," the prescribing of meaningful and appropriate musical instruments are needed. Imitating sounds from the immediate environment, the use of tone-matching calls, dialogue or question-and-answer songs and chants, attempting to find a particular vocal pitch on the song-bells or the piano, are some examples of approaches that may be made (see also p. 29). The use of direct, and often embarrassing, individual drill for singing on pitch seldom accomplishes musically what it destroys psychologically.

In general, the teacher should strive first to find the tones which are successfully sung by these children and proceed from there through remedial exercises to discover new ones. Any teacher who reveals skill in isolating and defining the particular vocal problem, and who shows patience, ingenuity, and good humor in applying remedial measures, will soon find that most if not all problem cases will disappear.

Finally it must be remembered that the beneficial psychological effect of confidence and assurance derived from the adopting of a systematic and cohesive note-reading method, such as was suggested earlier in this section, will also improve results.

The steps which may be taken in teaching a new song to a class have been discussed at some length (pp. 154-160). For the Primary grades particularly, the onus falls directly on the teacher; for older children, a sharing of responsibility in learning new songs is quite in order. Older children generally take considerable pride in solving their own problems. Actually, there is no more reason why teachers of music should "give away all the answers" in showing how a song goes than there is for teachers of other subjects so to do. However, best results will most often occur when the teacher is also knowledgeable about musical symbols, at ease with the skills required for its execution, and interested in the literature to be learned. Only then will she be free for an imaginative handling of the subject.

2. Teacher Sings Song. Many teachers feel diffident about singing for others. This feeling is often a result of their own childhood disappointments in home or school. It is not unusual for adults to complain of insensitive treatment by teachers in their early singing experiences, many going so far as to say they were deliber-

---

* The terms "nonsinger" and "monotone" are avoided because of their inaccurate and derogatory meanings. Other appropriate terms perhaps are "delayed" or "different" singers.

ately told they had no singing ability. Experiences of this kind reflect a voice-production emphasis, or a conservatory-type vocal training, rather than one devoted to involvement in interesting and challenging song literature.

The lack of practice in singing songs is another factor contributing to a feeling of diffidence or shyness. Where the early years of growing up physically should also provide many and varied opportunities for growing up tonally through singing, humming, and even whistling, this, for many, has been denied. It is only by making a determined effort to catch up, as it were, that a reawakened interest and competence will gradually take place. There are few if any nonsingers (see p. 157), apart from those with injured or handicapped vocal mechanisms, but there are many potential singers who only need confidence and practice.

The experience of singing in front of a class should be thought of as an objective undertaking. That is, it is the mood and feeling of the song that is significant, not the personal singing aptitude and competence of the teacher. Singing happens when there is a mood, a feeling, or a thought in a song deserving to be shared in the same way that a certain speaking happens when a mood or thought is to be captured in a poem or story. It is nothing more and nothing less. Children are interested in the story suggested by the text, the rhythmic or melodic beauty of the tune. They are not particularly concerned whether or not the teacher's voice is "pretty," rich, or even absolutely true. Any shyness or hesitation the teacher may have, therefore, is unwarranted.

How to learn a song is for many a considerable problem. Obviously, the teacher must first know it. Lacking adequate music-reading ability, the teacher should perhaps play on the piano in one-finger fashion if necessary, or on a set of song-bells, the notes of the song several days before the event, at the same time chanting the words until a more or less accurate hearing and singing is developed. A little effort expended in learning to play the plastic flute or recorder (see Appendix A, p. 331) may also provide a means to sound out the melody. Persistence and repetition will increase the ability to sing more and more correctly. The important thing is to keep trying.

When the time comes to sing the song for the class, the teacher should first sound the tonic chord G (I), or GBD, on the autoharp or piano, and the beginning
$$\underset{1\;3\;5}{}$$
note $\underset{5}{D}$, in order to ensure a comfortable range and to establish tonality (key center). After she has sung the song once or twice and commented perhaps upon some interest feature of the song, the children should open their books to the appropriate page and be encouraged to participate in subsequent repetitions. They might also follow notes and words by pointing to them as they sing.

For additional practice in singing, the teacher's participation in less formal singing activities such as those offered in assembly gatherings, church, or home and school meetings cannot be overemphasized. Songs included on such occasions are often familiar tunes of which at least texts and rhythms are well known. A concerted effort to follow the less familiar melodic undulations would help to single out the particular problem for further practice.

3. <u>Teacher Plays Melody on Piano or Songbells</u>. The playing of the melody on the piano or songbells has already been suggested. The notes, in themselves, are not difficult to find. The playing of them in a relaxed, sensitive, and rhythmic fashion is not an immediate accomplishment, at least for the beginner. Such playing requires a near-memorization of the piece. At first glance, this may appear to be quite difficult. This is not the case, however, if one first scans the music

for rhythmic and melodic patterns (see pp. 138-139).

There are sixteen measures in the song. The rhythm pattern in measures one and two, | ♪. ♪ ♩ ♩| ♩ ♩|, is repeated four times, and the rhythm pattern in measures nine and ten, | ♩ ♩ ♩ | ♫♫ ♩ | , is repeated three times. With the exception of the last two measures, fifteen and sixteen, there are only two different rhythm patterns in the whole song!

The melodic patterns are also relatively easy to grasp. In the first two lines, measures one and two, five and six are identical, and three and four are similar. They indicate further that if, on the piano, the thumb of the right hand is placed on the lowest note D, and the fifth finger is allowed to fall on the third-space C, all eight measures may be played without moving the hand position. Only finger movement is required.

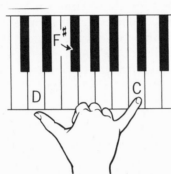

Similarly, the last two lines reveal that measures nine and ten, thirteen and fourteen are identical, and eleven and twelve, fifteen and sixteen are similar. Again, no hand movement is needed.

It is worth pointing out once more that the scanning of melodies to determine melodic and rhythmic groupings is always worthwhile. Notes of melodies individually considered, like letters of the alphabet in words, complicate and add to the time necessary for understanding, whereas grouping of notes in significant, unified patterns, like grouping of letters in words and phrases, reduces the time required for comprehension.

4. Teacher Plays Melody on Recorder-type Instrument. This is a simple, inexpensive instrument, the playing of which all teachers should be able to master. For a fuller treatment of this topic, see Appendix A, p. 331.

It will be sufficient to point out that as there are only six different sounds used in the melody, certainly the position for the fingers is simple. With some practice, a fair rendition of the melody is not beyond the teacher.

5. Class Plays Recorder-type Instrument. Beginning about Grade Three many teachers instruct their pupils in the playing of these instruments. Class playing provides a change from singing, and also stimulates and advances the ability to read more effectively. It will be quite in order, therefore, to ask pupils to play the song through a few times on their own. Once played, heard, and felt, the singing of the song offers little difficulty.

6. Child Plays Melody. There may be one or more pupils in the class with piano or other instrumental background who can be called upon to play the melody. This kind of participation should be encouraged because it provides opportunity

for further practice, recognizes and provides practical outlets for the skill, and encourages others to begin the study of an instrument.

7. Child Prepares at Home (to play or sing). Pupils like to be given the opportunity to show what they can learn. Teachers may profitably assign different melodies to different children, asking them to prepare them at home several days before they are to be used in school. For example, if there are several sets of songbells, or other melodic instruments in the classroom, some may be reserved for home study, and brought back when the selection is mastered. In homes with pianos this, of course, is not essential. Conceivably, this practice will no doubt find much favor with parents as well, most of whom are more than anxious for their children to express themselves musically.

8. Teacher Uses Recording (if available) of Song. As was mentioned earlier, many of the series-text songs are recorded and contained in albums for the particular grade.* (Some of these are listed, p. 369.) It is quite a simple matter therefore, to play the selection through a few times, allowing the children to follow the notes and text in their books. Upon hearing it once or twice, children will normally follow the recorded voice on the third attempt. Children respond with considerable interest to these recordings not only for the sake of learning new songs, but because of the richer instrumentation and excellence of the singers.

A teacher using a tape recorder, could also record the song beforehand. Any acquaintance, friend, fellow teacher, or student, who is not too self-conscious in singing or playing the song could act as the recording artist. Thus, a recording of any song or selection is relatively easily obtained.

Note: Related to recordings accompanying series texts are innumerable titles pressed and distributed through local music stores everywhere by many record companies. Apart from general sources such as is provided in Schwann's Long-Playing Record Catalogue, issued monthly and listing recordings of all companies, teachers will find much of value in school collections such as the following (see also Chap. 6 p. 141 and Chap. 10 p. 287): Adventures in Music Series, RCA Victor, Camden, N.J.; Bowmar Orchestral Library, Bowmar Records, 4921 Santa Monica Blvd., Los Angeles, Calif.; RCA Victor Basic Record Library for Elementary Schools, RCA Victor, Camden, N.J.; Musical Sound Books, The Sound Press Society, Box 222, Scarsdale, N.Y.; Folkway Records, Folkways Records, 177 W. 46th St., New York 36, N.Y.; Children's Record Guild and Young People's Records, The Greystone Corporation, 100-6th Ave., New York 13, N.Y.; Recordings for Education, Columbia Records Educational Dept., 799-7th Ave.; New York 19, N.Y.

---

*The songs in Growing with Music series, published by Prentice-Hall, Englewood Cliffs, N.J., are all recorded.

What Additional Activities May Be Incorporated to Make the Experience More Memorable?

Answer:

Rhythmic Activity. The song is strongly rhythmic. Sung with some feeling, a decided stress on the first beat of measures 2, 4, 6, and 8 in particular is apparent. The text suggests bodily activity of some kind. This may take the form of a patterned dance routine or a freely interpreted action (see pp. 175-186).

An alternate possibility may include a rhythmic accompaniment using one or two large drums or tom-toms, the players either improvising a pattern spontaneously or playing a prescribed pattern such as the following:

For the next eight measures, which are less strongly rhythmic, the use of a pair of woodblocks playing a pattern such as the following:

will heighten the contrast between the two sections.

Pupils will take a keen interest in trying different media and patterns. Pupil participation in experimenting, discussing and critically appraising results should at all times be encouraged.

Song Example 2

Hawaiian Boat Song*

From the Hawaiian

G   D⁷   G   Our boat   is

Our boat   is   glid - ing, glid - ing,   glid - ing,   Our boat   is

D⁷   G   G   D⁷

glid - ing   o'er   the   wa - ter.   Our boat   is   glid - ing, glid - ing,

G   D⁷   G

glid - ing,   Our boat is   glid - ing   o'er   the   sea.

D⁷   G

The uk - u - le - les,   the uk - u - le - les,   are sound - ing

D⁷   G   G

gent - ly   o'er   the   wa - ter,   sea.

What Theoretical and Notational Concepts Are Applicable?

Answer:

1. The key is G. This is confirmed by the sharp sign ($\sharp$) on the F-line, and the final note G. The range of this song is somewhat lower than many though not out of reach for elementary school children:

It is not suitable for recorder-type instruments as the lowest note, B, is below the range of these instruments. To be applicable, it would have to be transposed one step higher to the key of A, which would fix the range at:

2. The scale (raw material) for this song is: G A B C D E F$\sharp$ G. No other sound is used in the melody of this song.

3. The primary chords for this key are: I or G (GBD), IV or C (CEG), and
V⁷ or D⁷ (DF$\sharp$AC) of which only I and V⁷ are needed. The harmonic pattern, given by the chordal notation is:

    Measures 1-4   (omitting first three notes): |I   V⁷|I I|V⁷ V⁷|I I|
    Measures 5-8: |I   V⁷|I I|V⁷ V⁷|I I|
    Measures 9-12 (omitting first three notes): |V⁷ V⁷|I I|V⁷ V⁷|I I|
    Measures 13-16 (repeat of 9-12): |V⁷ V⁷|I I|V⁷ V⁷|I I||

Both lines of the verse have the same harmonic pattern, though the melodies are slightly different, and both lines of the chorus have the same harmony. The harmonic pattern is simple and may be easily memorized for accompaniment purposes.

The first note of the "Hawaiian Boat Song" is sound 3 (B), again one of the notes of the I-chord. The appropriate chord to sound therefore immediately before singing the song is the G- or I-chord with perhaps an emphasis given to sound 3, the first note.

4. The rhythmic motive accentuated in this selection is a <u>syncopated</u> or off-

beat figure: ♪♪♪ . This figure is repeated ten times throughout the selection. The patterns to which it belongs are each two measures long in the verse. There are four, of which two are identical and two are similar. In the chorus, the pattern is broken to allow for 1-measure units and 2-measure units:

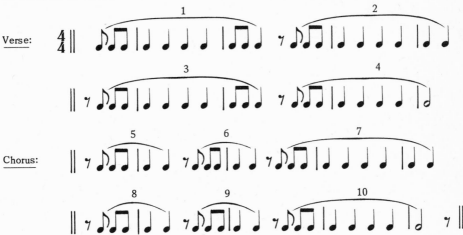

5. The melodic pattern, using the numbering shown above, is as follows: 1 and 3 are identical; 2, 4, 7 and 10 are almost identical, 6 and 9 are similar to 5 and 8.

6. The song divides into two sections, two lines in each. The form is AA₁BB₁, similar to the form of "Tell Me, Little Maiden," p. 153.

In What Different Ways May the Song Be Learned?
<u>Answer:</u>
1. The teacher sings it for the class.
2. The teacher plays the melody on piano or songbells.
3. The use of recorder-type instrument is not appropriate unless song is transposed.
4. The teacher asks one of the pupils to play it for her.
5. The teacher assigns the melody to a particular pupil for home study.
6. The teacher may use the recording which is provided for this song. (Children should be helped to discover the treatment given recording, the use of ukulele, etc.)
7. The class may sight-read the song. The intervals may offer some difficulty in this case as some of the skips are large and the melody moves along quickly. For sight-reading, establish a system: (a) note rhythmic and melodic patterns— identical, similar, etc.; (b) rehearse briefly some of the more difficult skips;

(c) clap or tap the rhythm of the song so that its rhythmic swing may be felt as a whole; (d) sound the G-chord and starting note B and immediately begin song. For detailed account of the above factors review pp. 154-157.

What Additional Activities May Be Incorporated to Make the Song More Memorable?

Answer:

1. Playing Ukulele and Guitar. One feature of this particular selection is the suggested ukulele accompaniment. This instrument is particularly appropriate here, as the song is from Hawaii, and the text makes reference to the instrument.

The open strings of a ukulele are generally tuned to the following sounds:

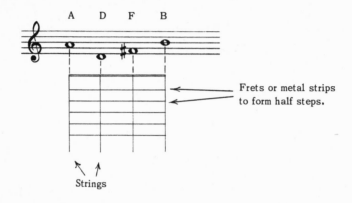

In order to find the chord of G, the strings A and F♯ would have to be shortened to produce the higher tones of B and G respectively. One finger placed on the second fret of the A-string would provide for the B sound, while another finger on the first fret of the F♯ string gives sound G. Thus, the fingering for the G-chord is:

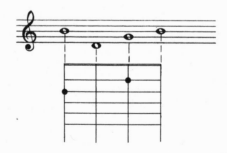

or as given with the song.

For the V^7-chord, only the B-string needs altering. The nearest chord sound above B is C, hence the fingering for the V^7-chord is:

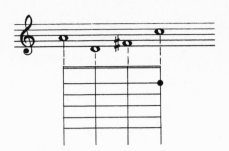

Question: What is the fingering position for the C-chord? E$_m$-chord?

For those interested in guitar chords, it is appropriate to indicate its tuning:

In order to play the G-chord on this instrument the fingering position is as follows:

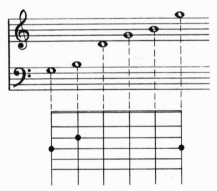

Question: Can you find the correct position for the D^7-chord? the C-chord?

2. Exploring Related Recordings. Listening activities may be extended with the recording of "Hawaiian Boat Song" which is provided in the album accompanying the text, followed by related recordings such as "Barcarolle" by Offenbach, "The Beautiful Blue Danube" by Johann Strauss*, or other suitable choices.

*For an account of Johann Strauss and his music, see Lillian Baldwin, Music for Young Listeners, "The Crimson Book" (Morristown, N.J.: Silver Burdett Co., 1951), pp. 10-13.

Each of these recordings reflect the quiet mood of waves rising and falling, or of a boat rocking gently up and down.

The class may wish also to explore and learn about boat songs such as "Come Rowing With Me" (p. 137 in this text) or others listed in the classified index of the particular music text used. The enterprising teacher will seek out and allow the class to explore any worthwhile activity suggested by either text or melody of a song.

Song Example 3

Wind through the Olive Trees*

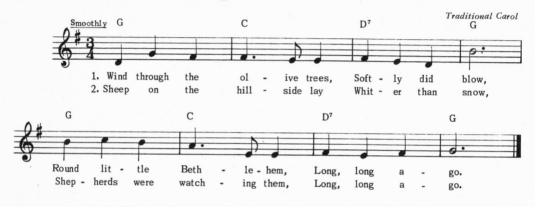

3. Then from the starry skies
   Angels bent low,
   Singing their songs of joy,
   Long, long ago.

4. For in a manger bed
   Long, long ago,
   Christ came to Bethlehem,
   Long, long ago.

What Theoretical or Notational Concepts Are Applicable?
Answer:
1. The key is G, confirmed by the sharp sign (♯) on F-line and last note G.
2. The range is moderate:

It is within the range of recorder-type instruments.
   3. The scale for this song is: G A B C D E F♯ G, and all scale sounds are used.
   4. The primary chords for this key are: I or G (GBD), IV or C (CEG), and V⁷
   $$\underset{1\ 3\ 5}{}$$
or D⁷ (DF♯AC), and all are notated on the score.
   The harmonic pattern, indicated by the chordal notation is:

> 1st line: I IV V⁷ I
> 2nd line: I IV V⁷ I

*Book 3, <u>Birchard Music Series</u>. Copyright © 1962, Summy-Birchard Co., Evanston, Ill. Used by permission. (See also Harry R. Wilson, Walter Ehret, Alice M. Snyder, Edward J. Hermann, <u>Growing with Music</u>, Book 2 [Englewood Cliffs, N.J., Prentice-Hall, 1963], for descant version).

Both lines have the same harmonic pattern, though the melody changes. The pattern is simple and easily memorized for accompaniment purposes.

The first note of the song is sound 5 (D), one of the notes of the I-chord. Chord I and note D should be played immediately before singing the song in order to establish the first note and key feeling.

5. Phrase rhythms are identical for both lines:

There is no perceptible rhythmic figure.

6. The melodic pattern of the two lines are slightly similar. Note measures 2, 3 and 6, 7.

7. The form indicates A B structure.

In What Different Ways May the Song Be Learned?
<u>Answer</u>:
See suggestions for previous two examples.

What Additional Activities May Be Incorporated to Make the Song More Memorable?
<u>Answer</u>:
1. <u>Chordal Accompaniment</u>. This song is in striking contrast to the first example and less so to the second in rhythmic emphasis. The reverse is true in harmonic implications. The melody of "Wind through the Olive Trees" is enriched considerably by chordal accompaniment as suggested. Note particularly the chords for measures 2 and 6. The first-beat notes are foreign to the C-chord given, thus creating a tension (<u>dissonance</u>) which otherwise might not be felt. An autoharp or piano accompaniment sensitively played will heighten the mood of this song and make it more enjoyable. (One may add here that if an autoharp accompaniment is contemplated, use a soft felt pick and strum slowly across the strings.)

2. <u>Playing Recorder-type Instrument</u>. This song, with its slow, evenly spaced quarter notes and limited range, is well within the capacity of beginners on the recorder-type instrument.* Apart from instruction books specifically designed for the recorder-type instrument, teachers should take advantage of similar suitable and appropriate song literature as found in their song texts. Many of these, if not already within the range of these instruments as given, may often be adapted to the appropriate range (see p. 162). The experience of playing not only provides variety and interest in the classroom activities, but adds new skills as well.

To conclude this chapter, two observations are made: (1) songs are as different and as meaningful as it is within our capacity to see and understand; (2) the learning of a new song, regardless of how simple it may appear to be, may yet involve all our resources—physical, emotional, mental and imaginative.

---

*For detailed information on learning to play the recorder-type instrument, see Appendix A.

POINTERS AND PRACTICE—
CHAPTER 7

I. In what way does a group of rhythmic and/or melodic patterns help in playing a new melody on piano or songbells?

II. A teacher has assigned a melody to a certain child for home learning. Comment upon any value(s) this may have.

III. The class use of recorder-type instrument is often begun about Grade Three. What advice do you have about the level of difficulty of music that should be used in early learning stages? (See Appendix A, p. 331)

IV. What chord should be played just prior to singing a song in the key of D? Key E♭? Why?

V. What are likely to be some common skips found in melodies in the key of C? Key of D? Show some on the staff provided:

Key of C   Key of D

VI. From your song text choose a song in the key of C and one in the key of D and compare with above. Are there any similarities?

VII. In what way may a set of songbells help an uncertain singer in pitch awareness? Discuss.

VIII. Find a two-chord song in your song text and chart its harmonic pattern. Do the same with a three-chord song.

First song

Title:

Where found:

Second Song

Title:

Where found:

Of what value are these patterns for a beginner accompanist on the autoharp?

170

IX. Practice tapping out the rhythm of several melodies in your song text. Do they fall into patterns? Are they easily memorized?

X. Indicate (using x's) the notes of the scales for the following major keys:

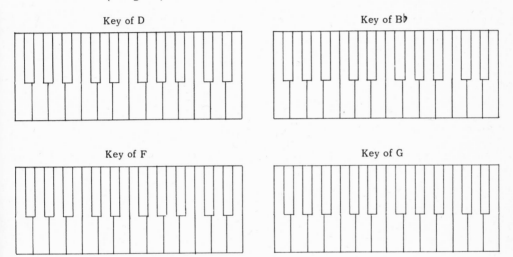

Key of D

Key of B♭

Key of F

Key of G

XI. A. In playing the following phrase in the key of C on the piano, show an appropriate position for the right hand:

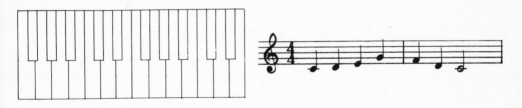

Is this phrase easily memorized?   Do you have to move the hand?

B. Show an appropriate position for this phrase.

XII. The song on the following page is found in one of the textbooks. Give the following information about it:

A.   The key:

B.   The tonic chord:

C.   The first note:

D.   The last note:

E.   Indicate the tonic chord on the keyboard:

F.   When should it be played?

G.   What are the primary chords for this key?

H.   Which is omitted in this song?

I.   Where are these primary chords found on the autoharp?

J.   What is the harmonic pattern?

First line:

Second line:

K.   Of what value is this pattern?

L.   What is the form?

M. Can this melody be played by beginners on recorder-type instruments? Explain.

Cradle Song*

Words: Isaac Watts
Music: Rousseau

Note: Helpful suggestions with respect to suitable recordings other than those provided with series texts are often given in students texts as well as in manuals accompanying each book. Two suggested and related recordings for use with this song are provided: Jarnefelt, "Berceuse" (RCA Victor Listening Activities II); Brahms, "Little Sandman" (MSB-Musical Sound Books).

8

RHYTHMIC
AND HARMONIC
EXPERIENCES

It was suggested, Chapter 7, p. 167, that the three song examples revealed a gradation in rhythmic and harmonic power. Rhythmically, there is a weakening, and harmonically, a strengthening. Graphically, the results may be shown as follows:

Song Title	Rhythmic Strength	Harmonic Strength
Tell Me Little Maiden	Marked	Slight
Hawaiian Boat Song	Average	Average
Wind through the Olive Trees	Slight	Marked

This is by no means to suggest that melodies generally can or should be characterized as to their rhythmic or harmonic tendencies in such a neat fashion, for this is simply not the case. It does mean that some melodies reveal a more marked rhythmic drive than others, and that others again exhibit strong harmonic tendencies. If a teacher is alert to these properties, can sense the promise of each in the song to be taught, and then can prescribe fitting activities to enhance the experience, teaching music will soon become an art as well as a thing of joy.

An indication of the meaning and scope of rhythmic and harmonic properties, with particular emphasis upon various types of activities which may be initiated is, therefore, the subject of study in this chapter.

Selections with Rhythmic Emphasis

In the past, many teachers emphasized the rhythm band as a promising medium for the development of rhythmic independence for young children. Of late years, many have come to feel that for young children, considerable preparatory involvement in freer, creative exercises should precede the more formal, externally imposed notated patterns. Jacques Dalcroze, and more recently Carl Orff* have

---

*For a fuller account of Oriff's ideas on music education see Doreen Hall. <u>Music for Children</u>, published by Associated Music Publishers, Inc. New York, 1960 (Toronto: Leeds Music Co.). See also Chap. 11, pp. 307-317 in this text.

stressed the importance of creative movement and natural speech patterns as bases for the development of rhythmic understanding and development.

It is well known that wide variation in aural aptitudes exists among children. Most children, however, respond readily to jingles, rhymes, and chants. In the development of rhythmic ability, or more broadly, musicianship, it seems wise therefore to begin with these fundamental patterns—to draw upon the resources that are latent <u>within</u> children, and from these to proceed gradually to the more formal aspects of notation and theoretical understanding. Once a genuine feeling for rhythms of speech and movement and the movement of melody against a steady pulse is developed in children, the symbols which represent these rhythms are easily comprehended, interpreted, and expressed. The eye thus helps the ear to clarify what it hears and makes it possible for the child to enjoy even more intricate and complex rhythmic nuances.

A broad, general plan outlining some progressive stages of rhythmic development from preschool through the elementary grades, may be outlined as follows:

1. Speech and movement patterns.
2. Activity songs, singing games.
3. Folk dances.
4. Written or notated patterns with singing or playing.
5. Improvised and created patterns—through movement.
6. Improvised and created rhythms—through rhythm instrument and notation.

The following examples are illustrative of the various stages.

1. SPEECH AND MOVEMENT PATTERNS

Street calls, nonsensical rhymes, and the like have familiarized children with phrases and tones of different strength. For example, children normally have an instinctive feeling for rhymes such as:

One potato, two potato, three potato, four,
Five potato, six potato, seven potato, more.

They will chant it and move to it in perfect time, unhampered by any arithmetical implications it may later appear to have such as:

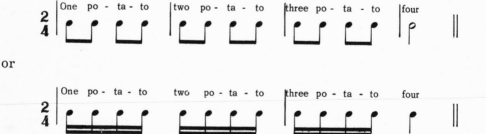

or

To reverse the procedure, to begin with notation unrelated to the feeling implied by them, denies to children the very essence of music, a feeling for it. Many of the chant rhythms can be directly translated into fundamental natural rhythms and "stepped out." Experiencing rhythms in total bodily movement is the best means of developing rhythmic understanding (see pp. 28-29).

Chant	Play Instruments
Chant in a deliberate manner, emphasizing the last word in each line of the following:	Six children, each with a different instrument play in turn the underlying beat, while the class chants:

Bonefish, bluebird, black sheep, CROW	Triangle	$\frac{4}{4}$ | ♩ ♩ ♩ ♩ |
Chickadee. doodlebug, robins in a ROW	Tambourine	| ♩ ♩ ♩ ♩ |
Banty rooster, peep squirrel, caterpillar, FLEA	Sticks	| ♩ ♩ ♩ ♩ |
Muley on the mountain and a BIG BUMBLE BEE	Drum	| ♩ ♩ ♩ ♩ |
Fly in the cream jar, frog in the POOL	Finger Cymbals	| ♩ ♩ ♩ ♩ |
Clap for the children here at SCHOOL	Maracas	| ♩ ♩ ♩ ♩ |

Related Listening: "Little Indian Drum," Young People's Records (YPR) #619.

A wide use of simple chants and jingles for children of preschool and Primary age will provide a sound foundation for subsequent musical experiences. The realization and understanding of note values, time signatures (tone strengths), phrase groupings, and dynamics should be a part of normal learning, arising from pleasant experiences in speech and movement (see p. 119).

2. ACTION SONGS AND SINGING GAMES

Physical activity coupled with imaginative response is required for selections such as the following:

When I Was a Drummer**

Adapted Words
German Folk Tune

Oh - when I was a drum - mer, a drum - mer, a drum - mer

Additional stanzas may be sung about:

When I was a baby (rock baby in arms).
When I was a barber (snip, as with scissors).
When I was a carpenter (hammer nails or saw wood).
When I was a dancer (make up dance steps).

For a birthday song, the children like the following:

Oh, Mary has a birthday, a birthday, a birthday!
Oh, Mary has a birthday, let her choose a song (game);
A birthday for Mary, a birthday for Mary!
Oh, Mary has a birthday, let her choose a song (game).

Theoretical Analysis

1. The key is G. Confirmed by sharp sign on F line, and last note G.
2. The scale is G A B C D E F♯ G, and all sounds are used except F♯.
3. The range is moderate for singing but too high for flute-type instruments, except recorder. In order to accommodate song flutes, tonettes, or flutophones, transpose to key of F, one step below. Thus:

4. Autoharp chord notation is given. Only two chords, G and D⁷ are required.
5. The harmonic pattern is simple and easily memorized:

	1	2
Measures 1-8:	I I V[7] I	I I V[7] I
	3	4
Measures 9-16:	V[7] I V[7] I	I I V[7] I

6. The rhythmic and melodic patterns as well as the harmonic pattern above indicate the form is AA_1BA_1. Each section or phrase is four measures long.

7. Piano accompaniment. As with many texts for kindergarten and Grade One, the piano accompaniment often features the melody for the right hand and accompaniment for the left. Note the pattern given to the left hand. Only chord notes are used with an independent rhythm pattern. Notice also the contrast in accompaniment for the B-section (beginning with ". . . went this way . . ." to ". . . that way . . .," 12th measure).

An appropriate piano introduction for this melody could be the last four measures, beginning with ". . . Oh, when I . . . ." (See also p. 187 or simple accompaniment patterns.)

A singing game with directions, and embodying more advanced patterns of movement, is shown next:

The Elephant*

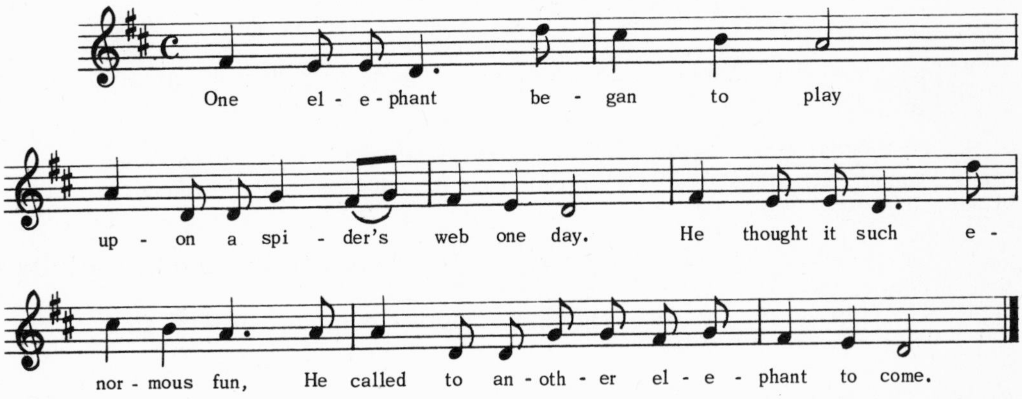
One el - e - phant be - gan to play
up - on a spi - der's web one day. He thought it such e -
nor - mous fun, He called to an - oth - er el - e - phant to come.

Directions:

Formation: One dancer in the middle of the room; the others standing or sitting around the sides.

Figure 1: While all sing, clap, or play rhythm instruments, the dancer in the center, moving in any direction, takes three walking steps forward, starting on the right foot (measure 1, first three beats).

On the fourth beat of measure 1 he stands, and in place points the left foot over the right until the two touch the floor. Still in place, he steps on the left foot on ". . . = gan" and points the right over it on "to," steps the right foot on the first beat of "play" (measure 2). Starting with the left foot, he takes three walking steps forward and repeats the points as above, but starting with the right toe (measures 3-4).

---

*From Learning Music through Rhythm by Hood and Schultz, published by Ginn and Company, owners of the copyright. Used by permission.

Repeat Figure 1 (measures 5-8).

Figure 2: Beckoning to a player, the center dancer performs Figure 1 as outlined above, but is followed by the person he has invited to join him. This new
player places both hands on the hips of his leader and follows his steps closely.
Everyone in the room sings, claps, or plays "two elephants," etc.

Figure 3: The second player now chooses another player, and a third person
places his hands on the hips of the second dancer and follows closely behind
the other two, while all sing "three elephants," etc.

Repeat until the whole group is dancing in line.

Theoretical Analysis

1. The key is D, confirmed by the two sharp signs, and the last note D.
2. The scale is D E F♯ G A B C♯ D.
3. The range is moderate for singing and appropriate for flute-type instruments.
4. The chords for the key of D are not found on the autoharp. Therefore, if
autoharp accompaniment is desired, the melody should be transposed one step
lower, to the key of C. Thus:

The chords and the harmonic pattern can then be determined by ear or by analysis; see Chapter 9.

Related Listening: "The Elephant" from "Carnival of the Animals" by Saint-
Säens; "Jumbo's Lullaby" from "Children's Corner Suite" by Debussy, Musical
Sound Books (MSB) #78037.

5. It is a short song, of form ABAB, or AB, where each letter represents two
measures.
6. The C given for the time signature implies common, or 4/4, time.

3. FOLK DANCES

Broadly speaking, action songs are emphasized in the kindergarten and Primary grades, singing games in Primary and early elementary grades and folk
dances in upper elementary grades. These latter activities are of a more formal
structure. See, for example, the directions provided for the following folk dance.
For additional examples, consult the classified index of your series texts, particularly those for the upper elementary grades. (See also Question 1, p. 195.)

Captain Jinks*

pass your part - ner by the right. Swing your neigh bor

so po - lite, for that's the style in the ar - my.

Stanza

All join hands and cir - cle left, cir - cle left, cir - cle left,

All join hands and cir - cle left, for that's the style in the ar - my.

Dance directions:

Stand in a single circle, boys and girls alternating. All hold hands and face
toward center of circle.

Refrain: All take two steps toward center of circle, then two steps back to place
and drop hands. Partners face and pass each other by the right shoulders, each
boy proceeding to the partner of the boy on his right. Swing new partners.

Stanza: Face in and form a single circle. All join hands and walk or skip around
in a clockwise direction. Repeat dance as many times as desired, ending the
last time at "Fine."

Optional words:

2. Captain Jinks of the Horse Marines;
   I feed my horse on corn and beans,
   And sport young ladies in their teens,
   Though a captain in the army.

3. I teach young ladies how to dance,
   How to dance, how to dance,
   I teach young ladies how to dance,
   For I'm the pet of the army.

4. Captain Jinks of the Horse Marines;
   I feed my horse on corn and beans,
   And often live beyond my means,
   Though a captain in the army.

Note: Opportunities to create and experience musical rhythm through expressive bodily movement should also be given for older boys and girls. Patterns of
movement, sensitively worked out and similar in form to the adult forms of
ballet, modern and interpretive dance, generally reflect the music more adequately than do the stylized and unvarying forms of the square or folk dance.

4. WRITTEN OR NOTATED PATTERNS WITH SINGING OR PLAYING

Beginning about Grade Two or Three, notated rhythm patterns are often provided along with melodies. The primary purpose in indicating these patterns is

181

to emphasize the mood or feeling appropriate to the melody and text. The use of rhythm instruments en masse is therefore not generally recommended. One instrument is often most effective, as in the example given below:

The Waves*

This pattern may be played throughout the song.

Theoretical Analysis

1. The key is G, confirmed by the key signature and last note. The key is also given at the beginning of the song. (This is a feature in this particular music series.)

2. The scale for this key is: G A B C D E F♯ G, of which only five sounds are used: 1 2 3 5 7.

3. The range is moderate and appropriate for both singing and playing.

4. Only the tonic or I-Chord is suggested for accompaniment.

With strongly rhythmic melodies, the use of several different rhythm instruments and patterns may be desired. One example, featuring the use of drums, tambourines, woodblocks, and bells with unique and interesting parts is the following, a popular marching song:

When the Saints Go Marching In**

*Used by permission of Katherine H. Dent. From This is Music, Book 2 (Boston: Allyn and Bacon, 1962).

**William R. Sur, Mary R. Tolbert, William R. Fisher, Gladys Pitcher, This is Music, Book 4 (Boston, p. 23. Copyright © 1961, by Allyn and Bacon, Inc. Used by permission.

saints go march-ing in —— Lord, I want to be in that
num-ber, —— When the saints go march-ing in —

Bells play the melody

Drum:

On the repeat:

Bells:

Tambourine:
Wood blocks:

Drum:

Bells:

Tambourine:
Wood blocks:

Drum:

Theoretical Analysis

1. The key is F, confirmed by the flat sign, third line, and last note F. The key and time signature are both inserted, upper left-hand corner.

2. The scale for this key is F G A Bb C D E F.

3. The range is limited to five sounds, from F to C and is appropriate for both singing and playing.

4. The three primary chords: F, Bb, and C⁷, or I, IV and V⁷, are all used. An interesting feature of this song is the dancelike, syncopated (offbeat) rhythm. Note that the parts for the tambourine and woodblocks emphasize weak rather than strong beats (beat 2 rather than beat 1).

5. IMPROVISED AND CREATED RHYTHMS—THROUGH MOVEMENT

Values in musical responsiveness and in personality development come through expressive bodily movement, especially when the child improvises his own rhythmic movement to music he hears or feels. In Primary and even older grades this is often accomplished by having children seated on the gymnasium floor listening, eyes closed, to music on the phonograph. One by one, two to six children may use the open floor space to explore their interpretations in movement. Returning to their places on a signal from the teacher, other children then move to the music. Many self-conscious children have found themselves able to grow in confidence and skill through such experience. Having explored their ideas without the whole class watching they are often willing to volunteer to repeat what they did for their friends.

For older children there is often a resistance to expressive bodily movement, due in part to lack of opportunity to enjoy and become skillful in such activity in Primary grades. Teachers commonly bypass this freer movement in favor of the stereotype patterns of square and western folk dance. One stimulating and exciting compromise is found in the stick dances of the Polynesians.

Participants have a piece of bamboo or a dowell, 14 to 16 inches long (rhythm sticks will do), in each hand. In time to the music they work out movement and tapping patterns involving striking sticks on the floor ahead, behind, or at their sides, striking sticks together overhead, in front, at sides, or near the floor, or striking partner's sticks in rhythm. The Polynesians become as expert as some of our baton twirlers, tossing sticks in air, passing to partners, etc., never missing a beat. A simple illustration with the "Kookabura Song" (see pp. 86-88) will show this:

1. Partners face each other (music sung quite slowly).
2. On first word each strikes his own sticks together to his left.
3. Moving sticks parallel to the right at face height, each contacts partner's sticks three times directly in front.
4. Each strikes own sticks together to his right. (Opposite of 2.)
5. Moving sticks parallel to the left at face height, each contacts his partner's sticks three times directly in front.
6. Turn body a quarter turn left; strike floor with both sticks.
7. Turn another quarter turn left; strike sticks together.
8. Turn another quarter turn left; strike floor with both sticks.
9. Turn another quarter turn left; resuming original position; strike sticks together.
10. Repeat 2 through 9 throughout the singing of the song.

184

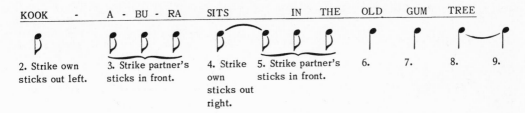

KOOK - A - BU - RA SITS IN THE OLD GUM TREE

2. Strike own sticks out left.

3. Strike partner's sticks in front.

4. Strike own sticks out right.

5. Strike partner's sticks in front.

6. 7. 8. 9.

Thus a stick dance may be created. This activity might, like folk dancing, be criticized as a rote-learned stereotype pattern of movement unrelated to music. Its value as a creative activity depends entirely on its being approached on the basis of improvisation. The children must listen to the music, become familiar with it, then improvise stick and movement patterns to express the music. Its special merit lies in the fact that older beginners enter into this type of movement exploration more readily than into a completely free interpretive dance.

6. IMPROVISED AND CREATED RHYTHMS—THROUGH RHYTHM INSTRUMENT AND NOTATION

Rhythmic additions to songs should be considered for many songs. The criteria might well be: (1) Is the spirit of the song such that rhythmic emphasis will contribute to a fuller appreciation of the particular selection? (2) Is the mood of the melody or text such that a particular quality of rhythmic sound would be effective in enhancing this mood? If the answers are "Yes," interpretation in the actual playing of the particular rhythm instrument should generally be given free reign. Often, the resulting pattern is one of three types. These are shown below.

1. Strong-beat Patterns: Instrument is playing on strong beat only.

2. Melody Patterns: In such patterns the rhythm part is the same as the melody rhythm.

3. Independent Rhythm Patterns: These patterns are distinct from either the melody or strong-beat patterns and have a shape or phrase of their own. Note, for example, the drum part for "When the Saints Go Marching In."

Changing both the pattern and the instrument in longer selections to accentuate a new or different theme within it, is also effective. In the familiar "Old MacDonald Had a Farm," for example, it would be appropriate to change both pattern and instrument, beginning at ". . . with a chick, chick here . . ." then reverting, at the end of this portion, to the original instrument and pattern for the remainder. (See Chapter 10, pp. 273-274.)

Opportunity to experiment with rhythmic color—to discard one rhythmic sound in favor of another, or to change from one pattern to another, and later to learn how to notate these in notebooks or on the blackboard—should be commonplace in the classroom.

Selections with Harmonic Emphasis

PLAYING CHORD ACCOMPANIMENTS ON AUTOHARP AND PIANO

The use of autoharp chords and simple piano accompaniment patterns along with singing or playing melodies has already been suggested. Chord-notations and suggested patterns are frequently given in most music texts for elementary grades. This is a promising innovation. The effect, of course, is a thickened, tonal sound, rather than the lean, melodic sound where chords or accompaniments are not played. This is not to suggest that the playing of chords or piano accompaniments are mandatory. Far from it. Certain melodies lend themselves to harmonic enrichment, and others do not. Where this form of enrichment does apply, however, it adds variety and interest to the classroom music program, and contributes <u>considerably</u> to an awareness of pitch and tonal security. An ability to play chords on autoharp or piano, particularly the primary chords as they so frequently apply to songs, is obviously a desirable ability.

On the autoharp this is relatively simple as only one button needs to be depressed for any particular chord. For the first two examples studied in Chapter 7, pp. 153, 161, the chords required were two: G and D^7. For the third, three chords were shown: G, C, and D^7. Notice from the diagram below, that all three chords are conveniently placed to the right of the instrument.

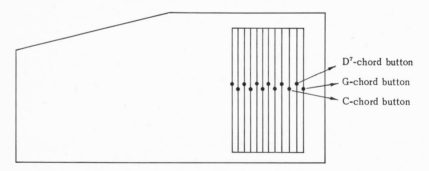

On the piano three fingers are needed to play a chord such as the G-chord, and four fingers for a four-note chord such as the D^7 chord:

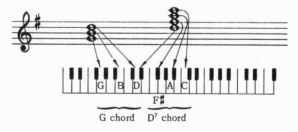

In moving the right hand from one chord position to another, i.e., from I to V^7, it is necessary to move the hand five degrees (notes) to the right as shown above, and one must also remember to press down the proper notes at the same time. This is somewhat awkward, and the beginner has to search for the right notes.

A simpler solution is to rearrange the notes of the chords, first to a lower position so that the sounds of the chords more adequately <u>support</u> the singing of the melody, and second to a more convenient position so that they are <u>closer</u> to each other, thus minimizing hand movement. The following illustration will suffice:

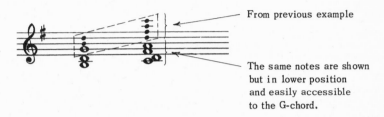

From previous example

The same notes are shown but in lower position and easily accessible to the G-chord.

By omitting the A-note* in the D^7-chord an even simpler pattern can be shown:

G   to D^7

Now both chords are found within a reduced space on the keyboard, and only finger movement is necessary in order to move freely from one chord to the other:

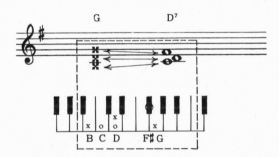

A convenient rule to use for changing from one chord to the other with the right hand on the keyboard is stated as follows:

In order to change from I to V^7 (G to D^7), move the B and G fingers inward to C and F♯ respectively, leaving the other finger where it is. In changing from V^7 to I, reverse the procedure.

An easily found hand position for both chords is desirable when the accompaniment calls for rapid changes of chord.

The piano (right-hand) accompaniment for the first line of "Hawaiian Boat Song" may now be written as shown:

---

* It is not essential that all notes of a chord be sounded.

Once these positions are memorized chords do not need to be written out in full, as they may be read from the chord symbols shown with the melody.

The manner in which the chords are played is important. The accompaniment should reflect the mood and feeling of the melody. A more appropriate accompaniment to this particular song is indicated by the following broken-chord (arpeggio) version:

The placing of the chord notes is unaltered; the notes are merely spread out to effect a smoother and more appropriate accompaniment.

Similarly, the accompaniment for "Tell Me, Little Maiden" (p. 153) may be written as follows:

or, as shown below:

The type of accompaniment used depends on the effect desired. For added support add roots of chords (left hand), thus:

The sound is thickened and enriched, and an opportunity to learn the bass-staff notation is provided in a natural learning situation. Note that quite young children can be shown how to play left-hand accompaniments in their first keyboard experiences, as only two or three single notes are required.

A right-hand pattern appropriate for a three-chord song such as "Wind through the Olive Trees," p. 166, is shown below. Again because of the position chosen for the IV-chord, hand movement is minimized, and only finger movement is necessary. The roots for the left hand are shown on the bass staff:

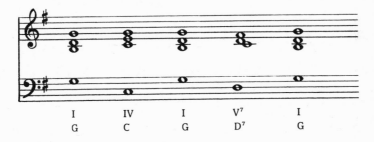

I	IV	I	V⁷	I
G	C	G	D⁷	G

Try using this pattern while humming the melodies of well-known songs as "Old MacDonald Had a Farm" or "Home on the Range."

Once fluency is gained in playing simple accompaniments in the key of G, the patterns may be applied to other keys. For the key of F, for example, transpose all notes down one step, thus:

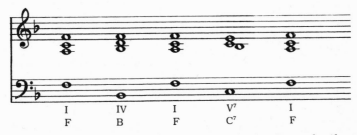

I	IV	I	V⁷	I
F	B	F	C⁷	F

Some modifications in the pattern are advisable for keys further removed. In the key of C, and using the same pattern, the right-hand chord-I position would be either:

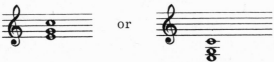

189

The first is too high for general use, and the second, too low. For the key of C, and other nearby keys, a modification to positions adopted for the keys of G or F above would be more appropriate:

Every opportunity should be taken to practice chord patterns in many different ways. The ability to play chord accompaniments is probably of more value to the teacher than the ability to play melodies. Since these chords are applicable to hundreds of tunes, they can be used over and over again.* Within a school year all children of elementary grade age, at least, should be able to master the simpler position as discussed herein.

For quicker results, especially for class-teaching purposes, the use of cardboard, wooden, or plastic**keyboards are a distinct aid to keyboard understanding. The teacher might institute, on a weekly basis, five-minute drills with these keyboards until all can move fluently from one chord position to the next.

Although many songs, particularly folk songs, nursery tunes, and the like, require only primary-chord accompaniments, many other melodies call for a greater variety of harmonic color. Among chords most frequently encountered along with I, IV, and V are II_m and VI_m. An example, featuring I, V^7, II_m and VI_m chords, is shown next:

Long Ago†

Author unknown
Music: Lilla Belle Pitts

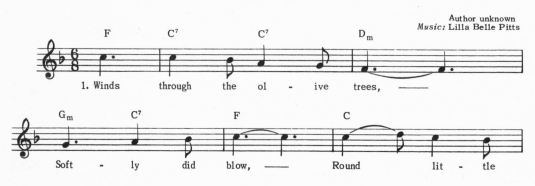

---

*For further piano study, and particularly for the adult beginner, see: R. Pace, Piano for Classroom Music (Englewood Cliffs, N.J.: Prentice-Hall, 1956). Frackenpohl, Harmonization at the Piano (Dubuque, Iowa: Wm. C. Brown, 1962).

**See the "Vandre" Interlocking Plastic Keyboard. Mills Music, Inc., 1619 Broadway, New York 19, N.Y.

†From Singing on Our Way of "Our Singing World Series" published by Ginn and Co., owners of the copyright. Used with permission.

Beth - le hem, Long, long a - go.

2. Sheep on the hillside lay, whiter than snow,
   Shepherds were watching them, long, long ago.

3. Then from the happy sky, angels bent low,
   Singing their songs of joy, long, long ago.

4. For in a manger bed cradled, we know
   Christ came to Bethlehem, long, long ago.

Theoretical Analysis

1. The key is F major, confirmed by the flat sign on the third line, and the last note F.
2. The scale is represented by the sounds F G A B♭ C D E F.
3. The range is suitable for both singing or playing.
4. Of special interest is the inclusion of the chords G_m (GB♭D) and D_m (DFA), or II_m and VI_m. (See also pp. 136-138.)

		B♭			
C D		F	G	A	
A B♭		D	E	F	
F G	A B♭	C	D	E F
I	II_m	IV	V^7	VI_m	

They provide a contrast to the brighter, more positive qualities of the I-, IV-, or V^7-chords. Sing the song several times with autoharp or piano accompaniment as shown, then compare the result with an accompaniment which features only the primary chords:

Which best suits the mood of the song? The beginnings of ear-training, appreciation, and musicianship come from experiments of this kind.

A suitable piano pattern which might apply to the first line of "Long Ago," p. 190, is

Note that all chords, including II$_m$ and VI$_m$, have been placed within easy reach of each other.

An accompaniment better suited to the mood of this particular melody may be indicated as follows:

The use of primary chords is also feasible and appropriate to melodies in minor keys. On the autoharp, two minor keys are permissible: D-minor, and A-minor. The primary chords for these are:

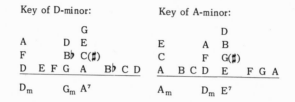

The chords are labeled on the autoharp as above.

In the following selection, the three primary chords for the key of D-minor are all featured:

Quiet Is the Night*

Old Rhyme
Music: Henry H. Halvorsen
Adapted by L. H. S.

---

*From <u>Singing on Our Way</u> of "Our Singing World Series" published by Ginn and Co., owners of the copyright. Used with permission.

Note the addition of another minor chord—A_m, last measure, second line.

Theoretical Analysis

1. The key is D-minor, confirmed by the key signature and the final note D (two below its relative major—F, see p. 132).
2. The scale is represented by D E F G A B♭ C D.
3. The range is appropriate for both singing and playing.
4. Note that although no C♯ appears in the melody (C does), the C♯ is essential in the A^7 chord:

```
                    G
A           D   E
F           B♭  C(♯)
D   E F G   A       B♭ C D
─────────────────────────
Dm          Gm  A⁷
```

Otherwise, the V^7-chord would not sound very convincing. Try it on the piano and compare.

Question: Can you devise a right-hand piano accompaniment suitable for this song?

The playing of autoharp and piano patterns from a given chordal notation is only one aspect of interesting harmonic experiences open to teachers and pupils in the classroom. The use of chord notations for the purpose of determining parts for singing or playing, and <u>composing</u> and <u>arranging</u> chords or parts appropriate to a particular song or selection, are dealt with in the following chapter.

POINTERS AND PRACTICE—

CHAPTER 8

I. It was suggested, p. 180, that folk dances are generally introduced following experiences with action songs and singing games in the Primary grades. Thus they are usually emphasized in the upper elementary grades.

Some authorities question the educational values, musically speaking, of folk and square dances on the grounds that they are too formalized, too patterned in a mathematical sense, and that the music becomes merely an adjunct to the activities prescribed. One authority says that "if we let ourselves think for one moment that they really bring children's rhythmic responses to greater maturity, more precision, more subtlety, I am convinced that we are fooling ourselves."*

Comment fully upon this, first noting opinions such as are expressed in:

1. Robert E. and Vernice T. Nye, Music in Elementary School (Englewood Cliffs, N.J.: Prentice-Hall, rev. ed., 1964), Chapter 2.
2. Parks Grant, Music for Elementary Teachers (New York: Appleton-Century-Crofts, 1960), Chapter 23.
3. James L. Mursell, Music Education, Principles and Programs, Chapter 9.
4. Emil Jacques Dalcroze, Eurthythmics, Art and Education (New York: A. S. Barnes, 1935).
5. Paul W. Matthews, You Can Teach Music (New York: A. S. Barnes 1935, E. P. Dutton 1953), Chapter 5.

---

*James L. Mursell, Music Education, Principles and Programs (Morristown, N.J.: Silver Bl Co., 1956), p. 271.

II. From your song text how many songs can you find which feature:
Introductions:

Codas:

What form do some of them take?

What should determine the kinds of instrument(s) prescribed for an introduction or coda?

III. Complete the piano accompaniment for the "Cradle Song," in the manner suggested in the first measure (see also pp. 188, 189):

IV. Complete, as shown below. Which do you prefer? _____ .

V. Transpose melody and accompaniments to the key of F, and repeat above. Add key signature.

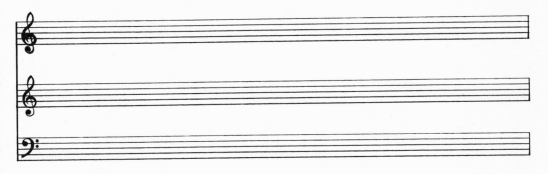

VI. The harmonic pattern for "When I Was A Drummer" (p. 177) is:

I I V⁷ I
I I V⁷ I
V⁷ I V⁷ I
I I V⁷ I

While whistling or humming this well-known melody, apply the following type of accompaniment to it:

All you need is the harmonic pattern shown above. It is a kind of shorthand or formula most useful for accompaniment. The pattern is easily memorized, thereby permitting full attention to the keyboard.

If you find it more comfortable to hum or sing it in a lower key, adjust your accompaniment to the key of F, for example, and proceed as before.

VII. Is there any advantage in transposing this melody to the key of F as far as the recorder-type instruments are concerned? Explain.

197

VIII. Using the two chords F and C^7, construct an appropriate piano accompaniment for the following song:

Dairy Maids*

*Book 3, Birchard Music Series. Copyright © 1962, Summy-Birchard Co., Evanston, Ill. Used by permission.

pails in hand, Ma - ry, Mol - ly and I. ____

IX. If you wish to include both melody and chords for the right hand, adjust the chord notes so they lie relatively close under the melody. The chord notes are generally played on the strong beats. Note the following example:

Complete in the manner shown above. Try it without notation.

X. In Pointers and Practice, Chapters 3 and 4, you experimented with chord accompaniment. Now try the I-chord songs listed on p. 71; the I- and V^7-chord songs on pp. 72-73.

Practice singing and playing simple accompaniments to as many songs as you know apart from those suggested above. You will find that your ear will soon tell you when to change from one chord to another.

XI.

The Huron Carol*

Words: Dr. J. E. Middleton
Arranged by Dr. Healy Willan
Jesuit-Canadian Song

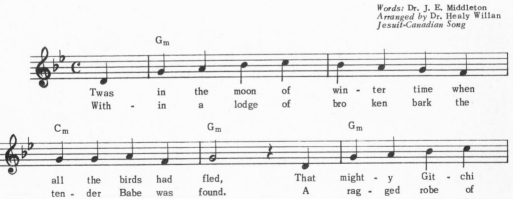

Twas in the moon of win - ter time when
With - in a lodge of bro - ken bark the

all the birds had fled, That might - y Git - chi
ten - der Babe was found. A rag - ged robe of

---

*Published by permission of the copyright owner, The Frederick Harris Music Co., Limited, Oakville, Ont., Canada.

A. Write the scale for this key:

B. What are the primary chords?

C. What alteration must be made to one of the chords?

D. Is this chord used in the song?

E. What additional chords are found?

F. Do the chordal sounds add to the mood of the song?

G. If you are strumming an autoharp for accompaniment, what kind of pick (plectrum) would be most suitable? Plastic or felt?

H. If you want to play both melody and right-hand chords on the keyboard, how would you write the first line?

XII. If chord I_m key of D_m is as shown below, find "easy-to-reach" right-hand piano positions for chords IV_m and V^7. Compare, for example, with the pattern suggested for the key of C, p. 190.

I_m　　　　IV_m　　　I_m　　　V^7　　　I_m

XIII. Translate your answer to Question XII to the keyboards below. The I-chord is indicated:

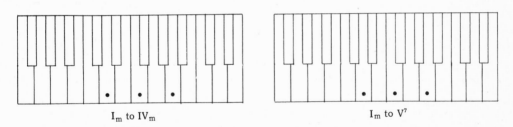

I_m to IV_m　　　　　　　　　I_m to V^7

XIV. Apply these chords in these positions to "Quiet Is the Night," p. 192, and play an accompaniment to it. Add roots for the left hand. Write and memorize the harmonic pattern for the song so that you can play the accompaniment without the music.

XV. If the I-chord, key of F (inverted), is as shown below, find "easy-to-reach" right-hand piano positions for chords IV and V^7:

I　　　　IV　　　I　　　V^7　　　I

XVI. Translate your IV and V⁷-chord answers to the keyboards provided below:

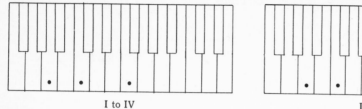

I to IV

Show corresponding IV-chord

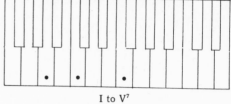

I to V⁷

Show corresponding V⁷-chord

XVII. Using these chords in these positions and with the addition of a root-bass for the left hand, fashion an appropriate accompaniment to the song "When the Saints Go Marching In," p. 182. You can concentrate on the keyboard if you first memorize the harmonic pattern. Write harmonic pattern:

XVIII. Of what advantage are relatively low piano positions for right hand chords when playing accompaniments?

XIX. For a review of piano chords in "easy-to-reach" positions for the three keys C, F, and G, complete the following patterns:

Key of C:

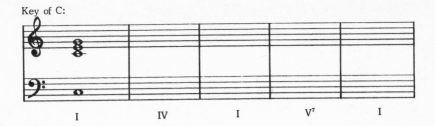

$$\text{I} \qquad \text{IV} \qquad \text{I} \qquad \text{V}^7 \qquad \text{I}$$

Key of F (insert key signature):

$$\text{I} \qquad \text{IV} \qquad \text{I} \qquad \text{V}^7 \qquad \text{I}$$

Key of G (insert key signature):

$$\text{I} \qquad \text{IV} \qquad \text{I} \qquad \text{V}^7 \qquad \text{I}$$

XX. On p. 187, the right-hand piano positions for the I–V^7 chords in the key of G are shown as:

What would they be for the key of F, one step lower?

What would they be for the key of E$^\flat$, two steps lower?

What roots would now be pertinent for the left hand in the:

Key of F? Key of E$^\flat$?

203

9
ENRICHING THE
MELODY – I

Finding and Arranging Chordal Accompaniments

Many melodies in school songbooks have a strong attraction for, and are intimately bound to, certain common harmonies or chords. These chords can be determined from the melody notes and, when found, may provide a ready means for accompaniment. The procedure suggested is as follows. From the melody:

1. Determine the strong-beat pulse.
2. Match the notes falling on strong-beat pulses with the appropriate primary chord.
3. Indicate that chord with the melody, and play accompaniment on autoharp, piano, or other suitable instrument.

Applying this procedure to the first two lines of the melody "Noah's Ark" shown below, gives the following result:

Noah's Ark*

Traditional Words
American Song

Old Noah he built him - self an ark, There's
He built it out of hick' - ry bark,

one more ri - ver to cross. There's one more

---

*William R. Sur, Mary R. Tolbert, William R. Fisher, Gladys Pitcher, <u>This is Music</u>, Book 4 (Boston), p. 23. Copyright © 1961, by Allyn and Bacon, Inc. Used by permission.
Note: For different version of "One More River" see p. 25, <u>Singing Together</u> from "Our Singing World Series," published by Ginn and Co.

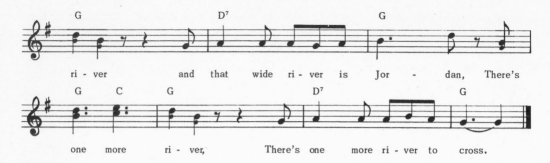

ri - ver   and   that   wide   ri - ver   is   Jor - dan,   There's

one   more   ri - ver,   There's one   more ri - ver to   cross.

1. In 6/8 time or $\left(\begin{smallmatrix}2\\ \bullet\cdot\end{smallmatrix}\right)$, as shown in upper left-hand corner above the melody, the strong beats are two per measure. These pulses may be felt by rhythmic reading of the pattern:

First line: -ty   skip - ty   skip - ty   skip - ty   skip - ty

Second line: skip - ty   tri - ple - it   walk   -ty   walk walk

The emphasized notes are therefore:

> First line: (| G   B | G   B |)
>
> Second line: (| A   A | G   – | D   E |)
> From large notes shown

2. Matching these notes with the notes of the primary chords for this key:

			C				
D			G	A			
B			E	F♯			
G	A	B	C	D	E	F♯	G
1	2	3	4	5	6	7	8
I			IV	V⁷			
or							
G			C	D⁷			

The appropriate chords would therefore appear to be:

> First line: | G   G | G   G |
>
> Second line: | D⁷   D⁷| G   –| G   C |

or, as given on original score, p. 205.

Note that with the three sounds G, C, and D, there is a choice of chord as these sounds are each present in two chords. In such cases both chords should first be tried, thereupon eliminating the one which sounds less satisfying.

Piano or autoharp accompaniments for many songs may be extracted in this way, thence used for accompaniment.

Finding and Arranging Parts for Singing or Playing

After finding the chords for a particular melody, notes from these chords may be used in a variety of ways to provide the following kinds of arrangements:

1. Root-bass parts.
2. Chord-endings (Partial harmony parts).
3. Simple chants and harmony parts.
4. Melodic or descant parts, combination songs.
5. Rounds, Canons and Fugues.

Each of these will be discussed in turn.

1. ROOT-BASS PARTS

One of the simplest arrangements available is a root-bass part found from the lowest note (root) of the chord, or from the chord-name:

This root part may be written on the treble staff as shown here:

It may be sung or played to the rhythm of the melody. Alternately, it may be written on the bass staff for left-hand piano accompaniment, or as a part for changing or changed voices:

The root part may also be sounded by plucking the strings on 'cello or guitar:

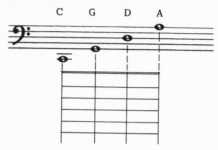

The 'cello particularly (and string bass an octave lower) lends itself to such parts because in this key G and D are both <u>open-string</u> positions. The 'cello is tuned as follows:

The guitar* is tuned as follows:

Three keys which provide open-string tonic and dominant positions are the keys of C, G, and D.

The guitar* is tuned as follows:

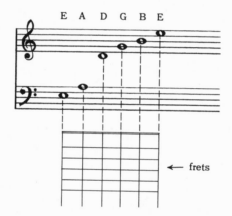

On the guitar and for this key, only the C note needs to be fingered. G and D are both open-string positions.

Of the two C's shown below, possibly the first or lowest C is more appropriate:

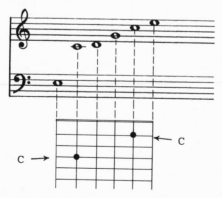

---

*See fn., p. 93, for other ways to use guitar for chord roots. See also p. 165.

The writing and reading of such parts, for playing or for singing, have the added effect of facilitating the learning of the bass-clef lines and spaces.

Many examples of simple root parts, for voices or instruments, are found in school music texts. The one shown next is typical:

The Darby Ram*

American Folk Song

The bass part is given as follows (note melodic rhythm):

Bass part for piano or 'cello. Voices may sing an octave higher.

It will be observed that only roots of the two chords G and D⁷ are used in this arrangement.

2. CHORD ENDINGS (partial harmony parts)

In the elementary grades one should avoid, at least in the earlier grades, any prolonged attempts at part-singing. It is too much to expect half a class of Grade Four pupils, for example, to sit quietly for a long time while the teacher is rehearsing a harmony part with the other half. It is possible, however, to cultivate and further an interest in part-singing if the rehearsals are not too long for any

*William R. Sur, Robert E. Nye, William R. Fisher, Mary R. Tolbert, <u>This Is Music</u>, Book 5 (Boston), p. 64. Copyright © 1962, by Allyn and Bacon, Inc. Used by permission.

one group, and especially if the students also have an insight into the principles and techniques involved.

Look, for example, at the small-sized notes in the last two measures of the second line, p. 205. The harmonic portion is short and relatively simple. Such arrangements are typical of the kind teachers and students can fashion and later perform. The chords have already been found; the addition of some simple chord-note part to the melody is relatively easily determined. This has been done in the arrangement shown on p. 205. A portion of it is analyzed as follows:

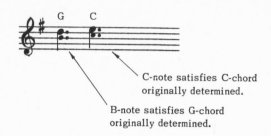

C-note satisfies C-chord originally determined.

B-note satisfies G-chord originally determined.

A harmony part is most effective near the end of a melody. Here, the two contrasting chord-colors, I and V or V⁷, are often found, and almost invariably the chordal pattern is V to I, as it is in "Noah's Ark," p. 206, last two measures.

The following parts are readily available for early experiences in part-singing:

Part 1
Melody
Part 2
Part 3

Note that the 3rd of the chord, the B-note, is added at the end. In this connection, it may be stated that if a choice is to be made between adding a 3rd or a 5th, it is generally better to include the 3rd. Any one of three possible and easily felt parts is permissible, thus allowing four-part singing passages (three plus the melody).

In the following song the harmony part is added to the refrain. Note again the D⁷ to G-chord ending. Add a third part ending for the last two measures.

Careless Shepherd*

English words: Margaret Marks
French Folk Song

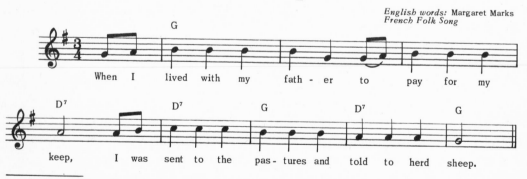

When I lived with my fath - er to pay for my

keep, I was sent to the pas - tures and told to herd sheep.

*James L. Mursell et al., Music Near and Far (Morristown, N.J.), p. 45. Copyright © 1962, by Silver Burdett Co. Used by permission.

Refrain

Poor sheep, poor sheep! I had – hard - ly an - y one.

Opportunities for constructing and participating in simple part-singing activities should not be overlooked in the elementary grades. Early experience with hearing sounds in their fuller context sharpens the ear and reduces careless singing habits. The singing of melodies alone is not necessarily an assurance that pitch-accuracy will follow. First, the sounds of a melody often change more rapidly than sounds of a chordal part; the child does not have time to center the one sound before it moves to another pitch. Second, the chord-quality associated with many pitches in a melody is missing in a unison song (except where provided by accompaniment) so that its place within a group of sounds is not felt. For these reasons, opportunity should early be provided for harmonic sounding, hearing, and evaluating. If, at the same time, the pupil is theoretically and physically involved in the construction of such harmonic parts there will generally be a greater interest in the sound resulting, hence an improvement in pitch accuracy.

3. SIMPLE CHANTS AND HARMONY PARTS

The chordal notation given or found with a melody may also provide a chant-like part. In the selection shown next the second part, or chant, consists of contrasting note-values. The melody consists almost entirely of quarter notes ($\quarternote$) and the chant of half notes ($\halfnote$). Only the two chords F and C^7 are needed to satisfy the melodic line. Observe that the notes of the chant agree with or match these chords.

Rainy Day*

Words and Music: Daniel Hooley

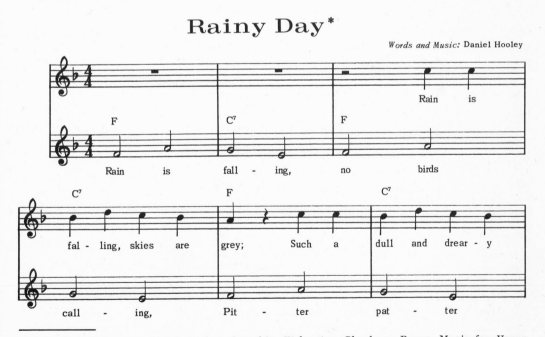

Rain is
Rain is fall - ing, no birds

fal - ling, skies are grey; Such a dull and drear - y
call - ing, Pit - ter pat - ter

---

*Richard C. Berg, Daniel S. Hooley, Josephine Wolverton, Claudeane Burns, Music for Young Americans, Book 4 (New York: American Book Co., 1960). Used by permission of the publisher.

211

The F and A notes of the chant are taken from the F-chord notated with the melody, and the E and G notes from the C^7-chord (see below).

```
                      Bb
           C      F   G
           A      D   E
           F G A Bb C D E F
           I          V7
              or
           F          C7
```

For this next song, written in the key of G, a simple chant for a set of melody or songbells is found. Only three different notes, chosen from the G- and D^7- chords, are used to make up the chant. It is written below the melody. Note, also, the bell introduction:

Dancing with Rosa*

Flemish Folk Dance
English words: M. F.

Introduction for bells

*M. Krone (ed.), <u>Music Round the Town</u> (Chicago: Follett Publishing Co., 1959), p. 99. Used by permission of the publisher.

An interesting arrangement featuring <u>three</u> simple chants for voices or instruments is "Ifca's Castle" shown below. The melody is based on the harmonic pattern |I V⁷|I −| so the chants are constructed accordingly. Note their ingenious use in the introduction.

Ifca's Castle*

Czechoslovakian Folk Song
Arranged by A. Hewson

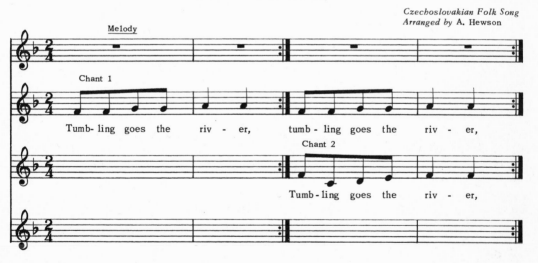

*A. Hewson, <u>Breakthrough in Music Reading</u> (New Westminster, B.C., Canada). Copyright © 1961, by Empire Music Publishers Limited. Used by permission.

(continue to end of melody)

tumb - ling goes the riv - er,   (continue to end of melody)

Chant 3

Tumb - ling goes the riv - er,_____

Melody

1. A - bove the val - ley fresh and green, a
2. But no 'tis not a fig - ure head, 'Tis

(continue to end of melody)

Melody

fig - ure head is plain - ly seen;
If - ca's Cas - tle there in - stead.

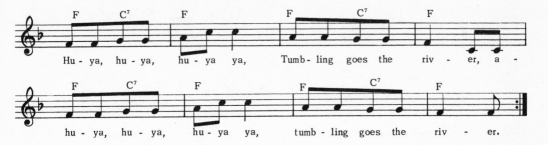

The steps suggested for constructing simple chants or harmony parts are as follows:

First, scan the given melody for appropriate chords:

The procedure for determining the chords was given on p. 206. The steps taken may be summarized as follows: (a) determine strong beats; (b) match strong beat notes with appropriate chord; (c) insert chord notation with melody.

For the melody shown above, the strong beats, for 4/4 time, are 1 and 3. The notes found on these beats are:

First line: | E G | F A |
Second line:| G B | G C ||

Matching these with the primary chords for this key:

```
                F
G      C  D
E      A  B
C D E F  G  A B C

I      IV V⁷

or
C      F  G⁷
```

the chords are then found to be:

First line: C C | F F|
Second line: G⁷ G⁷| C C |

and are written with the melody as shown:

Second, use the chords to construct chant or harmony part. In this, a choice has to be made whether the added part should go above or below the melody. As chants are usually lower than the tune, the choice here will be for the lower part. In order that the part should not lie too low for singing, a chant such as is shown below would be one solution:

Animal Song*

Folk Song from Michigan

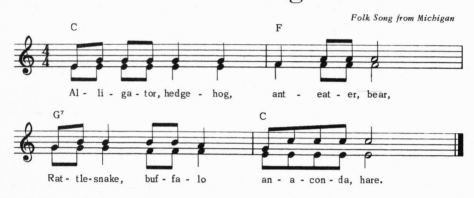

Al - li - ga - tor, hedge - hog, ant - eat - er, bear,

Rat - tle - snake, buf - fa - lo an - a - con - da, hare.

Related Listening: "Carnival of the Animals" by Saint-Saëns.

This particular arrangement is found, as you will note, in one of the series texts. In this arrangement the E notes (1st measure) are taken from the C-chord; the F notes (2nd measure) from the F-chord; the G and F notes (3rd measure) from the G⁷-chord; and the E notes again (last measure) from the C-chord.

For additional parts of this kind, any chord note may be used. Three possible chants similar to those described in Chapter 4, pp. 87-91, for a primary chord melody such as "Animal Song" are:

Other chants may be derived by crossing over as shown here:

---

*James L. Mursell et al., Music Near and Far (Morristown, N.J.), p. 21. Copyright © 1962, by Silver Burdett Co. Used by permission.

In two-part arrangements, however, not all will sound equally acceptable. For example, if the C note instead of the E note had been chosen for the first measure

the effect would be "empty" or "barren." Apparently the interval of the 3rd, rather than the 5th as shown above, is more appropriate for the particular melody given, hence the treatment on p. 216 Note also that in "Rainy Day," p. 211, all intervals on strong beats are 3rds and 6ths.

If a parallel may be used to describe interval qualities, the following order may be observed (the C-chord is used as an example):

The remaining two intervals in a major scale, the 2nd and 7th, may be described as having a "harsh" or "dissonant" quality.

An interesting example of the appropriateness of the interval of a 5th is shown by this next arrangement. Note also the effectiveness of the root-note "F" (key of F_m), for left hand.

Indian Chant

Arapahoe (Traditional)

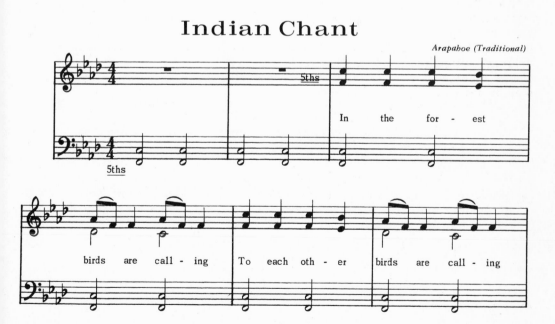

Related Listening: "Little Indian Drum" (Young People's Records).

Note: Encourage children to compose an effective drum accompaniment for this song.

It is evident, therefore, that considerable variation in mood or feeling is permissible, depending upon the particular interval emphasized in any chosen selection. An interesting example featuring several different strong-beat intervals (cold and warm) is the following:

Night Herding Song*

Traditional American Cowboy Song
Adapted by L.H.S.

Intervals of the 6th, 4th, 2nd, and 8th (octave) predominate on strong beat pulse (1 and 4) in this arrangement.

Related Listening: "Cowboy Rhapsody" by Morton Gould; "All Day on the Prairie" by David Guion; "Songs of the West" sung by Norman Luboff Choir, Capital Records.

Note the effectiveness of the two-note chant for the following melody:

*James L. Mursell et al., Music in Our Country (Morristown, N.J.). Copyright © 1962, by Silver Burdett Co. Used by permission.

Texas Cowboy's Song*

Chords: I = F Maj.; IV = B♭ Maj.; V⁷ = C⁷

Note: F-chord—first four notes of melody.

In some cases, and the preceding two songs are examples, the relation of the notes of the chant to the predominant chord or harmony is less obvious. This is particularly noticeable in melodies that lend themselves to either major or minor chords, or to a mixture of both.

*M. Krone (ed.), <u>Music across Our Country</u> (Chicago: Follett Publishing Co., 1959). Used by permission of the publisher.

With two evenly tuned autoharps try this experiment: On chord I let one person play the F-chord and the other the D_m chord; on chord-V^7 let one play the C^7-chord and the other the G_m-chord. Apply this coloring to the "Texas Cowboy Song" and the first half of "Roving Cowboy" and notice the difference. Note the simple chant below:

Roving Cowboy*

American Cowboy Song
Chant by L.H.S.

Note: Coconut Shell:** One shell turned from side to side on table top.
Play coconut shells on table top for sound of bronco's hoofs.

Although the use of all intervals as shown earlier is permissible, 3rds and 6ths predominate. This is evident in texts of the middle and upper elementary grades. It seems justifiable not only for the "warmer" qualities but also because such parts are common with I, IV, and V^7-chord structures. It may be shown, for example, that all 3rds or 6ths for all notes of a scale may be indi-

*James L. Mursell et al., Music Now and Long Ago (Morristown, N.J.). Copyright © 1962, by Silver Burdett Co. Used by permission.
** Another device which is often used to give a lighter, hollow sound is a pair of walnut-halves attached to thumb and forefinger by means of rubber bands (see p. 17).

cated as belonging to chord I, IV, or V^7. Note examples below as applied to the key of F major:

	I	V⁷	I	IV	V	IV	V	I		I	IV	V	IV	V	I	V⁷	I
		B♭														B♭	
Full triad	C	G	C	F	G	F	G	C		C	F	G	F	G	C	G	C
notes	A	E	A	D	E	D	E	A		A	D	E	D	E	A	E	A
	F	C	F	B♭	C	B♭	C	F		F	B♭	C	B♭	C	F	C	F

As these intervals are appropriate to primary-chord melodies, many song arrangements like "Rainy Day," p. 211, "Animal Song," p. 216, and those following, are found in most texts beginning about Grade-Four level.

The harmony part given with "The Darby Ram," p. 209, is shown as follows (note that the melody, shown in small-sized notes, has been added below the harmony part to show the relationship between them).

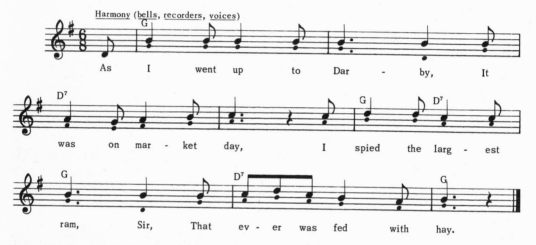

Only intervals of the 3rd and 6th are used, and the new part agrees also with notes of the chords.

In the following example the harmony part is written below the melody. Intervals of the 3rd and 6th are featured. Try the piano accompaniment provided.

Comin' through the Rye*

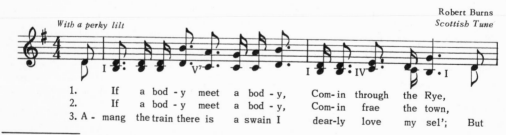

---

*M. Krone (ed.), <u>Voices of America</u> (Chicago: Follett Publishing Co., 1960), p. 146. Used by permission of the publisher.

If   a bod - y   kiss   a bod - y,   Need   a bod - y   cry?
If   a bod - y   greet   a bod - y,   Need   a bod - y   frown?
what's his name, or where's his hame, I   din - na choose to   tell.

Ev - 'ry las - sie has her lad - die,   Nane they say, hae I;   Yet

a' the lads they smile on   me,   When   com - in' through the Rye.

Chords: I = G Maj.; I⁷ = G⁷; IV = C Maj.; V⁷ = D⁷

Acc. by Ray Henderson

The next song, in a minor key, features the second part below the melody. It consists of 3rds and 6ths almost exclusively.

This song comes from the Swedish province of Värmeland, and is a song of praise and devotion to it.

Oh, Varmeland*

*For an account of this famous folksong see pp. 26, 27, Chapter 5, <u>Music for Young Listeners</u>, "The Crimson Book," by Lillian Baldwin (Morristown, N.J.: Silver Burdett Co., 1951).

Note the similarity to Greig's "Solveig's Song,"** a portion of which is shown:

Related Listening: "Greensleeves Fantasy" by Ralph Vaughan Williams; "Oh, Vermiland" (Hamburg Symphony Orchestra); MSB, #JM223.

---

*On the Da Capo (D.C.), sing the second line of the text only.

**"Solveig's Song" is found in Harry R. Wilson, Walter Ehret, Alice M. Snyder, Edward J. Hermann, Albert A. Renna, Growing with Music, Book 4 (Englewood Cliffs, N.J.: Prentice-Hall, 1963).

An interesting contrast to "Oh Värmeland" is another folk song, this time from Indonesia. A portion of it, here arranged predominantly in 3rds, is shown next.

Suliram*

(Excerpt)

Words: Marc Merson
Indonesian Folk Song
(Traditional Melody)

Note the three-part harmonic ending in this next arrangement:

Springtime**

Ludwig van Beethoven
Arranged by Don Krause

* Words from <u>Music Around the World</u>, © 1962, Silver Burdett Company.

**From <u>Basic Goals in Music</u>, Book 5, Lloyd H. Slind and Frank E. Churchley, Toronto: McGraw-Hill Company of Canada Limited, 1964. Used by permission.

4. Melodic or Descant Parts and Combination Songs

Chord notes may be arranged to provide a more tunelike part, called a <u>descant</u>. Because of the altered rhythm, new words must generally be composed for it.

Sandy Land*

*The American Play-Party Song, with a Collection of Oklahoma Texts and Tunes (University of Nebraska Studies, Lincoln, Neb.) Copyright ©1937, by B. A. Botkin. Used by permission. Arrangement from James L. Mursell et al., Music Near and Far (Morristown, N.J.). Copyright ©1962, by Silver Burdett Co. Used by permission.

2. Raise sweet potatoes in Sandy Land.

3. Right and left in Sandy Land.

Note: An interesting and appropriate embellishment for "Sandy Land" might include a rhythmic, root-'cello part, and perhaps a contrasting tone-block part, a four-part orchestration.

On Top of Old Smoky

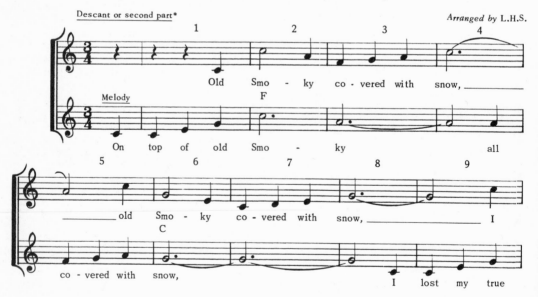

*For changed voices, transpose one octave lower.

Another example showing how chord notes have been used to create a descant part is shown above. Note that the strong-beat notes are determining factors in "solving" the second part.* For smoother effects passing notes, or notes joining two different chord notes, have occasionally been added. See measures 3, 7, 10, 11, 12, and 13. These help to keep the second part in character with the original melody, which also consists of a mixture of chord notes and passing notes. Similar construction is found in the following selection:

Down in the Valley**

Kentucky Folk Song

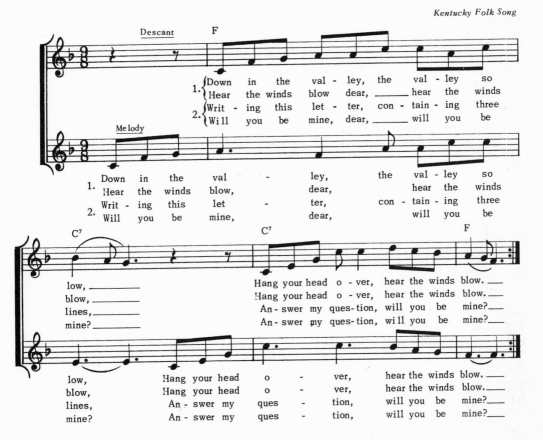

---

*This is not invariably true. See p. 234.

**From The Singin' Gatherin' by Jean Thomas, the Traipsin' Woman, and Joseph A. Leeder, published by Silver Burdett Company, © 1962. Reprinted by permission.

3. Build me a castle forty feet high,
So's I can see him as he goes by.
As he goes by, dear,
As he goes by,
So's I can see him as he goes by.

How many passing notes are there in the descant part? What makes it relatively easy to read?

Note the contrast with the following arrangement where 3rds and 6ths predominate:

Down in the Valley*

Southern Folk Song
Arranged by I.W.

Smoothly, with an easy swing

1. Down in the val - ley, the val - ley so low, Hang your head
2. Ros - es love sun - shine, vio - lets love dew, An - gels in
3. Build me a cas - tle, for - ty feet high, So I can

o - ver, hear the wind blow. Hear the wind blow, dear, hear the wind
heav - en know I love you; Know I love you, dear, know I love
see him as he rides by; As he rides by, dear, as he rides

blow,____ Hang your head o - ver, hear the wind blow.____
you,____ An - gels in heav - en know I love you.____
by; ____ So I can see him as he rides by.____

CHORDS: I = G Maj.; II = A min.; V⁷ = D⁷

The 4ths, 5ths, and 7ths occur as a result of "smoothing out" a phrase, or in order to make a part more tuneful.

A descant easily memorized and easily sung is shown next. Notice that only one passing note is used. Which is it?

*M. Krone (ed.), Voices of America (Chicago: Follett Publishing Co., 1960). Used by permission of the publisher.

Hayride*

Rhythmically
Descant

Words and Music: Richard C. Berg

We are go - ing

Come on a - long, we're go - ing for a hay - ride,

for a hay - ride,

Fill up the wa - gon with a load of hay;

Au - tumn days are

Come on a - long, we're go - ing for a hay ride,

on their way.

Frost's on the pump - kin, au - tumn's on its way.

*Richard C. Berg, Daniel S. Hooley, Josephine Wolverton, Claudeane Burns, <u>Music for Young Americans</u>, Book 6 (New York: American Book Co., 1960). Used by permission of the publisher.

For an accompaniment, play this rhythm on wood blocks:

The descant in this song consists of the descending and ascending C-major scale.

An interesting two-part arrangement, where the second part is actually another well-known melody, is the following:

The Lone Star Trail*

American Cowboy Song

*William R. Sur, Robert E. Nye, William R. Fisher, Mary R. Tolbert, This is Music, Book Five (Boston). Copyright © 1962, by Allyn and Bacon, Inc. Used by permission.

Other well-known combinations songs are:*

1. "Ten Little Indians" and "Skip to My Lou."
2. "Solomon Levi" and "A Spanish Cavalier."
3. "Keep the Home Fires Burning" and "There's a Long, Long Trail."
4. "Humoresque" and "Old Folks at Home."
5. "Ring the Banjo" and "The Girl I Left behind Me."

Note: Although chords are often chosen from the strong-beat sounds, this is not always the case. Sometimes the following beat or beats are more indicative, in which case the preceding or beat-note may be called a "leaning note." See, for example, the chord suggested for the 2nd and 6th measure below:

Wind through the Olive Trees**

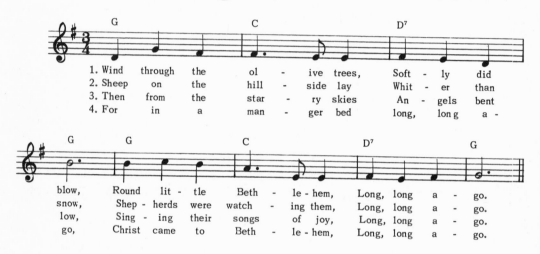

1. Wind through the ol - ive trees, Soft - ly did blow, Round lit - tle Beth - le - hem, Long, long a - go.
2. Sheep on the hill - side lay Whit - er than snow, Shep - herds were watch - ing them, Long, long a - go.
3. Then from the star - ry skies An - gels bent low, Sing - ing their songs of joy, Long, long a - go.
4. For in a man - ger bed long, long a - go, Christ came to Beth - le - hem, Long, long a - go.

5. ROUNDS, CANONS, AND FUGUES

We have seen how portions of a melody may be used to create descants (p. 213). When all of the melody is used for a second part the arrangement is called a round or canon. Such arrangements are possible only when the entry of one part is delayed. In "Scotland's Burning," shown here, the second voice begins when the first has reached the 3rd measure (2):

---

*For additional combination songs see Partner Songs and More Partner Songs, selected and arranged by Frederick Beckman (Boston: Ginn and Co., 1958, 1962).

**Book 3, Birchard Music Series, Copyright © 1962, Summy-Birchard Co., Evanston, Ill. Used by permission. For a different harmonization of this song, see Growing with Music, Book 2 (Englewood Cliffs, N.J.: Prentice-Hall, 1963)

Scotland's Burning*

Traditional

Scot-land's burn-ing, Scot-land's burn-ing, Fetch the en-gine,

Fetch the en-gine Fire, fire, fire, fire, Pour on wa-ter, Pour on wa-ter.

The melody entitled "Leavin' Old Texas" was shown, p. 233, as a descant. Here, now called "Old Texas," it is shown as a round:

Old Texas*

Oklahoma Cowboy Song
Traditional Melody

1. I'm goin' to leave _____ old Tex-as now, _____

I'm goin' to leave old Tex-as

They've got no use _____ for the long-horn cow. _____

now, _____ They've got no use _____ for the long-horn cow.

2. They've plowed and fenced my cattle range,
   And the people there are all so strange.

3. I'll take my horse, I'll take my rope,
   And hit the trail upon a lope.

4. Say adios to the Alamo
   And turn my head toward Mexico.

*Arrangement from James L. Mursell et al., <u>Music in Our Country</u> (Morristown, N.J.: Silver Burdett Co., 1962).

The following round is written in two different ways so that you may see the relationship between the parts:

The Brass Band*

*Richard C. Berg, Daniel S. Hooley, Josephine Wolverton, Claudeane Burns, <u>Music for Young Americans</u>, Book 4 (New York: American Book Co., 1960). Used by permission of the publisher.

236

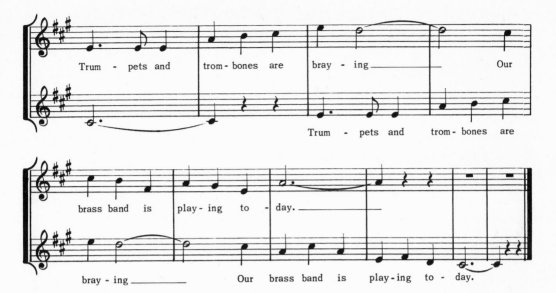

Related Listening: "Round and Round," Young People's Records (YPR), #431 (features the round, canon, and fugue).

Two delightful French rounds for the Christmas season are shown next:

Carol of the Birds*

This eighteenth-century legend carol came from Bas-Quercy, at one time a province in southern France. It tells how the birds flocked to Bethlehem to sing their own songs of joy and love to the Christ Child. Like many French noels, this one borrows its tune from a church melody.

Traditional
Bas-Quercy Noel
Arranged by Mary Elizabeth Whitner

237

wings a - far, No - el star?
birds of sky, God doth lie.

Fol - low - ing straight the No - el star? Birds from the woods in
Come where the Son of God doth lie; Christ on the earth with

Birds from the woods in won - drous flight,
Christ on the earth with men doth dwell,

won - drous flight, Beth - le - hem seek this
men doth dwell, Join in the shout, "No -

f

rit.

Beth - le - hem seek this Ho - ly night
Join in the shout, "No - *rit.* el, No - el!"

Ho - ly night.
el, No - el!"

rit.

Noel, Noel*

(Canon)

Old French Carol
Translated and Arranged by Robert E. Nye

In the example shown above note that the two voices end at the same time. The second part has been altered so that both voices may end together.

Related Listening: "Let's Sing a Round," collected and edited by James R. Clemens, Bowmar Records.

*William R. Sur, Robert E. Nye, William R. Fisher, Mary R. Tolbert, This Is Music, Book Five (Boston). Copyright © 1962, by Allyn and Bacon, Inc., Used by permission.

239

In rounds and canons, because of the more melodic qualities, 3rds and 6ths are less prominent. Other intervals are also found, as has been noted in preceding examples. In compositions of this kind melodic properties take precedence over harmonic properties. Also, there is generally more movement in all parts. While one part is stationary for a moment the other moves about; consequently the ear is not given much time to "feel" the harmony.

Numerous examples of rounds and canons are to be found in most school songbooks. Older children will delight in testing their ability to hold such parts against other parts.

Somewhat similar in construction is the fugue, a form or style of writing most popular during the seventeenth and eighteenth centuries. A short fugue for two voices, and written in the seventeenth century, is shown next:

Little Fugue

Traditional
Johann Joseph Fux (1660)

240

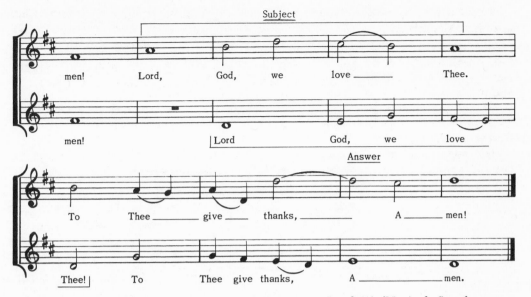

Related Listening: "Cat's Fugue" by Domenico Scarlatti (Musical Sound Books: MSB). (See also Lillian Baldwin, "The Blue Book," Music for Young Listeners [Morristown, N.J., Silver Burdett Co.] pp. 7-15, for a full account of this composition.) "Eight Little Fugues" by J. S. Bach (Columbia Records, #ML-5078).

In contrast to the "second" voice of the canon, the "answer" in a fugue is always written either a 5th below or a 4th above the "subject." The answer is in the dominant key.

Probably the greatest composer of fugues was Johann Sebastian Bach (1685-1750). One of the more popular of his three-voice keyboard fugues begins in the following manner:

Fugue in Three Voices

From The Well-Tempered Clavier

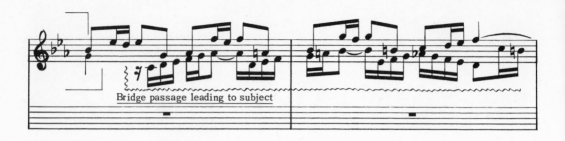

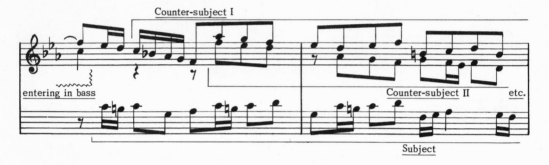

The plan of the fugue form is graphically shown as follows:

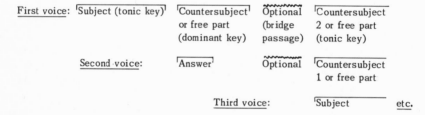

Many compositions, similar in style and in technical demands as the one just shown, are also found for the recorder family—soprano, alto, tenor, and bass. Sixteenth- and seventeenth-century composers were prolific in writing for these instruments. Through recorder playing (and recorders are now to be found in schools everywhere), many people are rediscovering much of this music which had been forgotten for a century and more. Turn to Appendix A, p. 331, for some examples of this music for recorder players.

In this chapter attention has been given to different kinds of two-part arrangements, from simple chants to rounds and fugues. Emphasis was also placed on some of the principles underlying part-arranging. This was attempted because (1) teachers and pupils are normally inquisitive and interested in such endeavors and (2) an ability to adapt, change, or to arrange music to suit local classroom situations is practical and rewarding. A similar course, applied to more ambitious and diversified arrangements, follows in the next chapter.

POINTERS AND PRACTICE—
CHAPTER 9

I. From the primary chords associated with the key of F:

```
              B♭
    C    F   G
    A    D   E
    F G A B♭ C D E F
    I    IV  V⁷
```

determine the chords, two per measure, for the following melody:

The Hunter's Horn*

German Folk Tune
Words by Florence Martin

The hun＿＿ters horn at ear＿＿ly morn Re-

sounds a-cross the plain,＿＿＿ Re-sounds a-cross the

plain,＿＿＿ Its sharp, crisp call a-wak-ens all to

join the hunt a-gain,＿＿＿ to join the hunt a-gain.＿＿＿

Using the **autoharp** or piano, test your answer, and correct it if necessary. Write
the chord accompaniment you have devised above the words of the song.

Write two versions of a three-part harmonic ending (two parts and melody).
Begin with the next to the last measure. Which sounds better?

---

*From Book 5 of <u>Growing with Music</u> by Wilson, Ehret, Snyder, Hermann, and Renna. Copy-
right 1963, Prentice-Hall, Inc. Used by permission of the publisher.

On the staff provided below write (1) a simple chant to first line after manner of p. 216, and (2) a root-bass part (use bass clef):

1. Chant

2. Bass roots

<u>Note</u>: See Chapter 10, p. 254 for different version.

II.

First Signs of Green*

English words: Ruth and Thomas Martin
Robert Schumann

How glad I am this time of year when
How glad I am when I have seen those

those first signs of spring ap - pear! Gone is the win - ter's
ten - der leaves of ___ gen - tle green, They warm my heart and

gloom and grey, Now love - ly spring is on her way.
make it sing, For now I know at last its spring.

<u>Note</u>: Two recordings given for related listening are: "Spring Song" by Mendelssohn and "To Spring" by Grieg. Another suitable selection is "On Hearing the First Cuckoo in Spring" by Frederick Delius.

*James L. Mursell et al., <u>Music Near and Far</u> (Morristown, N.J.). Copyright ©1962, by Silver Burdett Co. Used by permission.

This lovely little song is enhanced by the addition of the I-V^7-chords sensitively played on piano or autoharp.

From the key signature, find (1) the scale, (2) the I-V^7-chords, and by matching first-beat notes with I-V^7-chord notes find (3) the chords then (4) insert them above melody line.

Is the range appropriate for recorder-type instrument?

What is the form?

III. Compute the chords (I, IV, V^7) for the following melody. (In some places you may find that you will require two different chords per measure):

Wait for the Wagon

Traditional

Test your answer by using the autoharp or piano. Compare your results with those shown in James L. Mursell et al., Music Near and Far (Silver Burdett Co., Morristown, N.J., 1962), p. 121.

Christmas Is Coming

1. Christ - mas is com - ing, the goose is get - ting fat.

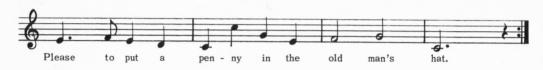

Please to put a pen - ny in the old man's___ hat.

Please to put a pen - ny in the old man's hat.

Traditional English Round

2. If you have no penny, a ha'-penny will do,
   If you have no ha'-penny, then God bless you.
   If you have no ha'-penny, then God bless you.

In the round shown above, where does the second voice come in? The third voice, if there is one?

<u>Related Listening</u>: Album of Christmas carols sung by Robert Shaw Corale.

V This Land Is Your Land*

Words and music: Woody Guthrie

1. As I was walk - ing___ that rib - bon of high - way___
___ I saw a - bove me ___ that end - less sky - way___

Omitting the first given chord (G) above, chart the harmonic pattern:

After memorizing the pattern and noting the chord positions suggested by this key, add a crisp and syncopated (offbeat) accompaniment as suggested below:

Two may play the piano accompaniment if it is at first too difficult for one person, one for the left-hand and one for the right-hand patterns.

VI. From the song "Springtime," p. 226, answer the following:

A.   What is the key?

B.   What is the scale?

C.   What are the primary chords?

D.   Using similar piano positions to those given for primary chords, key of G or F, complete a suitable pattern for the primary chords in this key. Show pattern for both hands.

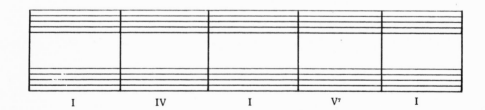

I   IV   I   V⁷   I

E.   Determine the chords for the song and enter above melody.

VII. Compute the chords (I, IV, V) for the following folk song, enter results above the melody, then test your answer by ear:

The Monoshee Range*

Words: George E. Winkler
Music: P. J. Thomas

There's a strike at Mis - ty Moon lake, ___
And I'm set and read - y to go, ___
For there's ground that a fel - low can stake, ___
But its cov - ered at pres - ent with snow. ___

Chorus

'Way up in the Mon - o - shee Range. ___

Note: The Monoshee Range is a mountain range lying in a southerly direction in the interior of British Columbia, east of the Okanagan valley.

Write a chant or harmony part for the chorus and enter above.

VIII. Where two different songs can be sung at the same time (combination songs), are the harmonic patterns generally different, similar, or identical? Explain.

*From Basic Goals in Music, Book 5 Lloyd H. Slind and Frank E. Churchley, Toronto: McGraw-Hill Company of Canada Limited, 1964. Used by permission.

IX.

Duck of the Meadow *

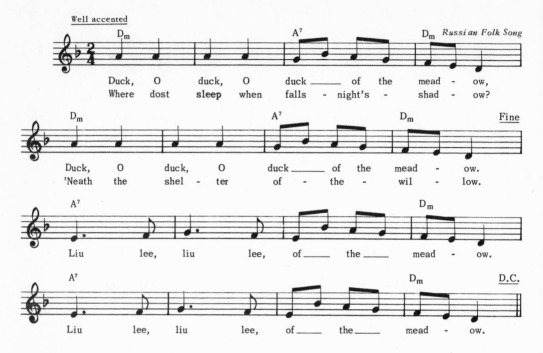

Well accented

Russian Folk Song

Duck, O duck, O duck ____ of the mead - ow,
Where dost sleep when falls - night's - shad - ow?

Duck, O duck, O duck ____ of the mead - ow.
'Neath the shel - ter of - the - wil - low.

Liu lee, liu lee, of ____ the ____ mead - ow.

Liu lee, liu lee, of ____ the ____ mead - ow.

Listen to the recording of another Russian dance that is well accented and gay: Tchaikovsky's "Trepak" from <u>Nutcracker Suite</u> (MSB). "Duck of the Meadow" is slower, but in a similar style. Try to sing it that way.

<u>Note</u>: An interesting feature of this music series is additional student's books and charts. One of these books for this grade is called an <u>Instrumental Easel</u> and contains instrumental descants, melodies, and obligatos for bells, keyboard instruments, and orchestral instruments. The bell part for "Duck of the Meadow," shown below, is taken from this <u>Easel</u>.

Justify, from the chord notation above, the notes used for the bell part. Why is C♯ used instead of C?

* From <u>Skip to My Lou</u>, published by Girl Scouts of the United States of America. Arrangement from Book 4, <u>Birchard Music Series</u> (Evanston, Ill.: Summy-Birchard Co., 1962). Used by permission.

Write an appropriate piano accompaniment pattern:

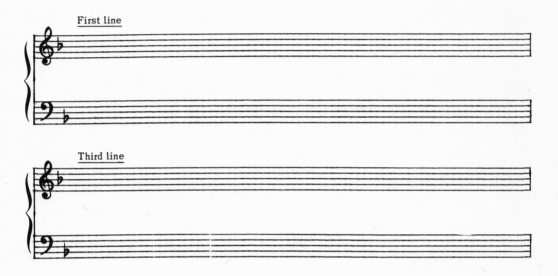

First line

Third line

10

ENRICHING THE MELODY-II

Arranging and performing music (singing and playing) in two, three, and more parts are feasible and appropriate activities for boys and girls in upper elementary and junior high grades. Authorities generally prescribe the following sequence of musical training in elementary grades:

1. For Primary grades—unison singing.
2. For intermediate elementary grades—unison and two-part singing and playing.
3. For upper elementary and junior high grades—unison, two- and three-part singing and playing.

An examination of (1) three-part vocal arrangements, (2) combined vocal-instrumental selections, and (3) instrumental music (continuing the discussion begun in Chapter 9) is, therefore, the purpose of this chapter.

Three-Part Vocal Arrangements

Three-part vocal arrangements may be conveniently considered under the following headings:

1. Two-part with root-bass part.
2. Two-part with descant.
3. Three-part harmonic arrangements.
4. Open-score arrangements.

1. TWO-PART WITH ROOT-BASS PART

One of the simplest kinds of arrangements is the two-part arrangement discussed in Chapter 9, but with added root-bass part (see pp. 207-209). Consider the following arrangement, for example:

253

Bugle Note*

Bb Trumpets play this introduction

German Folk Song

1. The wood - lands sleep in si - lence deep; Not
2. From camp re - mote, a bu - gle note Comes
3. The woods re - peat the ech - oes sweet O'er

e'en a leaf is stirred. *Not e'en a leaf is*
through the night so still. *Comes through the night so*
lake, from glen and hill. *O'er lake from glen and*

stirred. The bird's at rest with - in its nest, And not a sound is
still. And all a - round the ech - oes sound O'er field and for - est
hill. The soft re - frain comes back a - gain And then the night is

heard. *And not a sound is heard.*
hill. *O'er field and for - est hill.*
still. *And then the night is still.*

A simple three-part vocal arrangement can be obtained by adding a root part from the given chord signature, the first line of which is shown below:

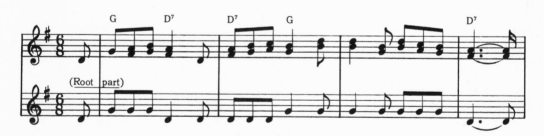

(Root part)

For changed voices, it is written as follows:

---

*From A World of Song. Used by permission. Arrangement from Music in Our Country (Morristown, N.J.: Silver Burdett Co., 1962). Reprinted by permission of the publisher.

254

The addition of a root part is particularly appropriate to the primary-chord-type melody, as only two or three additional sounds are needed. Furthermore, this part may be read directly from the chord signature without further change, hence is readily available (see Chapter 8, pp. 186-193). Opportunities for singing root parts should be initiated beginning about Grade Three or Four. Written examples, such as the following two solutions, are found in most upper books:

Three White Doves*

Translated by Christine Turner Curtis
Italian Folk Song

---

* From <u>Singing in Harmony</u> of "Our Singing World Series," published by Ginn and Co., owners of the copyright. Used with permission.

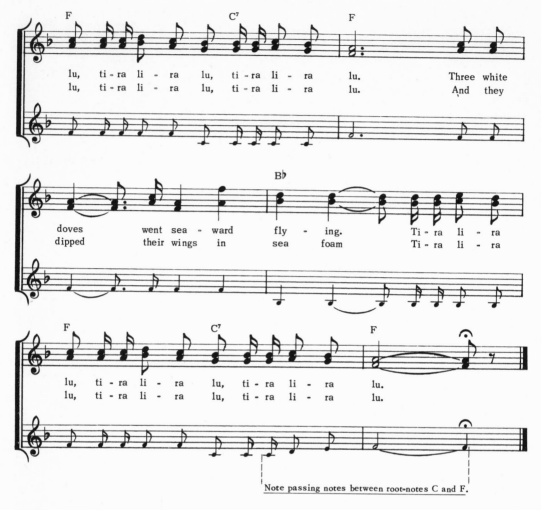

lu, ti-ra li-ra lu, ti-ra li-ra lu. Three white
lu, ti-ra li-ra lu, ti-ra li-ra lu. And they

doves went sea-ward fly-ing. Ti-ra li-ra
dipped their wings in sea foam Ti-ra li-ra

lu, ti-ra li-ra lu, ti-ra li-ra lu.
lu, ti-ra li-ra lu, ti-ra li-ra lu.

Note passing notes between root-notes C and F.

The addition of the root of the chord adds solidity and accuracy to the other parts.

The Papaya Tree*

(Pronounced pa PYE ya)

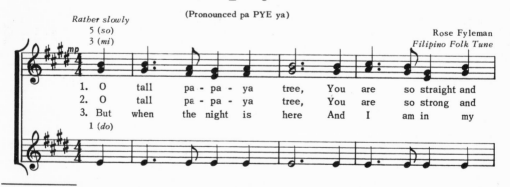

1. O tall pa-pa-ya tree, You are so straight and
2. O tall pa-pa-ya tree, You are so strong and
3. But when the night is here And I am in my

* From Singing in Harmony of "Our Singing World Series," published by Ginn and Co., owners of the copyright. Used with permission.

Except for the two passing notes (7th measure), the third part consists entirely of I-, IV-, and V-chord roots.

2. TWO-PART WITH DESCANT

These arrangements generally feature a distinctive melodic part in addition to the melody and harmony parts. It is usually added above the melody:

257

Battle Hymn of the Republic*

(Chorus)

Words: Julia Ward Howe
Music: William Steffe

Related Listening: Recordings from ''Growing with Music'' series by Beatrice and Max Krone (Bowmar Educational Records, Los Angeles, Calif.). ''Pomp and Circumstance'' by Elgar; ''Marche Militare'' by Schubert.

Note the exclusive use of 3rds and 6ths between the melody and the harmony part. The descant part is constructed from chord notes with added passing notes. It is melodic in character and features rhythmic motives taken from the melody.

The descant shown next for ''The Ash Grove'' is of similar construction. In both cases altered texts are necessary as the rhythmic structure (rhythm patterns) is different.

The Ash Grove *

(Chorus)

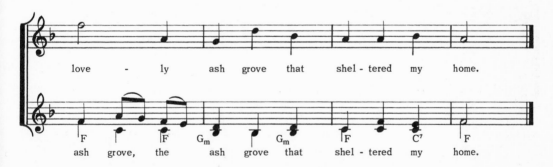

From the example above, note that both descant and harmony parts are constructed almost entirely from chord notes. In the first two measures, for example, the notes

are all taken from the F-chord common to those two measures.

* M. Krone (ed.), Voices of the World (Chicago: Follett Publishing Co., 1959). p. 18. Used by permission of the publisher.

<u>Note</u>: In the elementary grades, voice parts should not generally be written lower than

or higher than

and these but sparingly and for those children who can sing them without strain. The ranges above for descant and lower part are moderate and within both extremes.

3. THREE-PART HARMONIC ARRANGEMENTS

In this type of arrangement the melody is usually written above the harmony parts.

Silent Night *

---

* From <u>Singing in Harmony</u> of "Our Singing World Series," published by Ginn and Co., owners of the copyright. Used with permission.

			peace,	Sleep	in	heav - en - ly	peace.
			born!	Christ,	the	Sav - iour, is	born!
			birth!	Je -	sus,	Lord, at Thy	birth!

Note that circled chords (chords on strong-weak beats) contain notes from primary chords for this key:

			G					
A			D	E				
F♯			B	C♯				
D	E	F♯	G	A	B	C♯	D	
I			IV	V⁷				

Of special interest is the string quartet arrangement (three violins and 'cello) provided. Note the open-string, root 'cello part.

Silent Night

(Arranged for string quartet: three violins and cello)

Parts are often constructed from other chords, II and VI for example, besides I, IV, and V. Such is the case in the next arrangement. An analysis of the first two measures reveals six different chords, including the chord G^7 which here belongs to the key of C. Can you identify them?

How Brightly Shines the Morning Star*

Adopted from the German by I. W.
Phillip Nicolai, 1556-1608
Harmonized by J. S. Bach

1. How   bright - ly shines the   morn - ing   star, The   heav'n - ly mess - en -
Thou   son   of__ Dav - id's   roy - al - line, Be - lov - ed Lord   and

---

* M. Krone (ed.), <u>Voices of the World</u> (Chicago: Follett Publishing Co., 1959), p. 79. Used by permission of the publisher.

ger   a - far   of   Thine   e - ter - nal   bless - ing!
Mas - ter mine, My   heart   and   soul   pos - sess - ing!

Lov - ing   Sav - iour,   Ev - er lov - ing,   and for - giv - ing,

Rich - ly bless - ing. High en - throned a - bove for   ev - er.

Three-part vocal arrangements written upon the treble staff are specifically for unchanged voices or voices of similar quality. They are generally unsuitable for use in mixed choruses with changed voices, particularly where the lowest part is for boys with changed voices. If changed voices are included and treble-staff arrangements used, these voices should generally sing the middle or upper parts, or preferably a more appropriate arrangement.

Often, the third or lowest part is written upon the bass staff. This practice should be encouraged even for unchanged voices. Although they will sound an octave higher, familiarity in reading from the bass staff is advisable since later they will normally be required to read from it. For boys with changing or changed voices, of course, it is normally written as shown in this next arrangement:

Rise Now, Oh Shepherds*

Adapted by M. F.
Bohemian Folk Carol

Angels: Rise,   now   oh,   shep - herds,   to   Beth - le - hem   go;
Shepherds: Come, let   us   find Him,   come, fol - low the   light
All: Sing,   all   ye   peo - ple,   your   voi - ces pro - claim

* M. Krone (ed.), <u>Voices of the World</u> (Chicago: Follett Publishing Co., 1959), p. 110. Used by permission of the publisher.

CHORDS: I = F Maj.; IV = B♭ Maj.; V⁷ = C⁷; VI = Dₘ

Voice parts may be played by violins or flutes, octave higher; small notes of accompaniment by 'cello.

4. OPEN-SCORE ARRANGEMENTS

The open-score arrangement shown next is not generally found in elementary grade textbooks, but is more common in choral arrangements associated with junior or senior high school. A separate staff for each part is necessary for independently treated (contrapuntal) parts with their independent texts and rhythms. Where such arrangements are products of the ingenuity of teacher and class, teachers or pupils often transcribe them upon large wall charts (wrapping-paper rolls) which may be hung on the wall and used again and again. In transcribing parts for this purpose different colored felt pens are used so that parts are easily distinguished.

On Top of Old Smoky*

American Folk Song
Arranged by L.H.S.

265

Sweet Nightingale*

Old English Tune

* From Slind, <u>More Melody, Rhythm and Harmony</u> (1956). Used by permission of the copyright owner, Mills Music, Inc., New York City.

gale as she sings in the val-ley be-low, ___

___ as she sings in the val-ley be-low, ___ as she

___ as she

___ As she sings in the val-ley be-low. ___

sings in the val-ley be-low, be-low, in the val-ley be-low.

sings in the val-ley be-low; as she sings in the val-ley be-low.

An unusual but interesting three-part arrangement is the following:

Fruits and Vegetables*

Translation by Clara L. Seiler
Folk Song from India

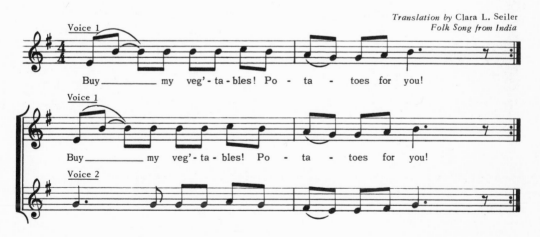

Voice 1
Buy___ my veg'-ta-bles! Po-ta-toes for you!

Voice 1
Buy___ my veg'-ta-bles! Po-ta-toes for you!

Voice 2

Each of these market calls may be sung independently and then combined in any way the singers plan. When they have been sung any number of times, end with the coda.

Combined Vocal-Instrumental Arrangements

Although some reference has been made in previous chapters to the use of instruments in the classroom, the emphasis thus far has been on the vocal. In subsequent pages instrumental applications, particularly those of a more varied as well as of a more selective kind, will be emphasized.

For convenience, two general types of instruments may be used:

<u>Classroom instruments</u>: including various flute-type instruments, tonettes, recorders, flutophones, etc.; autoharps, harmolins; tone bars, melody bells, glockenspiels, metalophones, xylophones; 'cellos or adaptations of the 'cello such as the gamba; percussion instruments. Often associated with these are ukuleles, guitars, and piano.

<u>Orchestral or band instruments</u>: those particularly applicable to classroom music are clarinets, violins, 'cellos, basses, trombones, trumpets, flutes; percussion and piano.

1. CLASSROOM INSTRUMENTS WITH CLASS SINGING

Arrangements featuring classroom instruments along with singing are now commonly found in elementary grade songbooks. This is a relatively new trend, as a glance at texts in use some fifteen years ago will show.

Although many of the simpler classroom instruments are used in the earlier elementary grades, their continued use in upper elementary and junior high general-music classes is also warranted. The contrasting tone quality of certain instruments often adds interest to otherwise routine songs as well as building skill and dexterity and improving music-reading ability.

The arrangements shown on subsequent pages are by no means the only appropriate solutions. Pupils and teacher, through experimentation, observation, and discussion, may create equally interesting scores.

One of the simpler combined arrangements, similar to some already noted in earlier chapters and featuring two drum parts, melody and autoharp parts, is shown below:

Driving Steel*

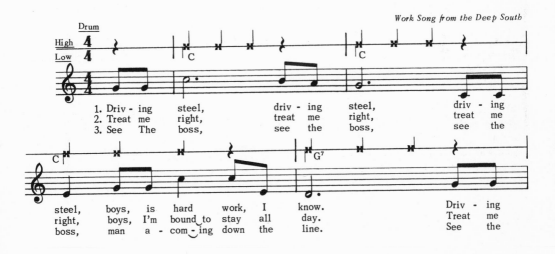

Work Song from the Deep South

* From <u>Music in Our Country</u>, copyright © 1961, Silver Burdett Co. Used by permission.

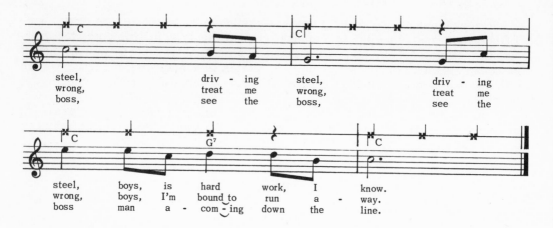

steel, driv - ing steel, driv - ing
wrong, treat me wrong, treat me
boss, see the boss, see the

steel, boys, is hard work, I know.
wrong, boys, I'm bound to run a - way.
boss man a - com - ing down the line.

A song of the work gang on the early railroad whose job it was to drive the huge steel or iron spikes through the rail bottoms into the railroad ties. Men hammered in rhythm as they sang.

Note the effectiveness of the drum parts with their slow, heavy, and steady sounds. The addition of even the simplest rhythm instrument may, with certain songs, contribute considerably to the mood and atmosphere intended by text and melody (see also pp. 181-184).

An arrangement which features a rhythm part for pencils, a unison melody-bell part, and a piano and/or autoharp part is shown next:

I Can't Do That Sum*

From Babes in Toyland

Music: Victor Herbert
Words: Glen MacDonough

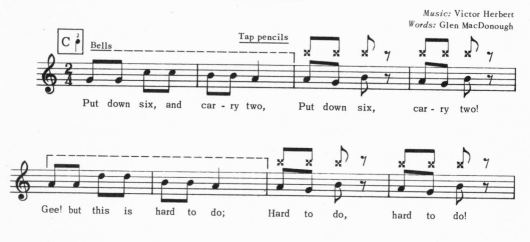

Put down six, and car - ry two, Put down six, car - ry two!

Gee! but this is hard to do; Hard to do, hard to do!

You can think and think and think Till your brains are numb!

I don't care what teach - er says, I can't do that sum.

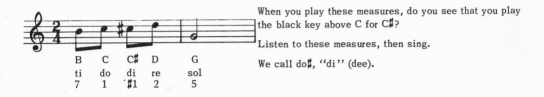

B C C♯ D G
ti do di re sol
7 1 ♯1 2 5

When you play these measures, do you see that you play the black key above C for C♯?

Listen to these measures, then sing.

We call do♯, "di" (dee).

Can you play these chords on the piano or autoharp while you sing the song?
The notes with the stems turned down are to be played with the left hand

R.H. C C G⁷ G⁷ G⁷ G⁷ C C C F G⁷ C F C F C G⁷ C

L.H.

Note that the right-hand piano pattern shown is or should be identical to answer given Question XIX, Chapter 8, p. 203. For added depth, play root notes as well.

An instrumental arrangement for recorders, autoharp or piano, and percussion instruments follows:

Minuet*

Wolfgang Amadeus Mozart

Wood Blocks:

Drum:

Recorder or other wind instrument

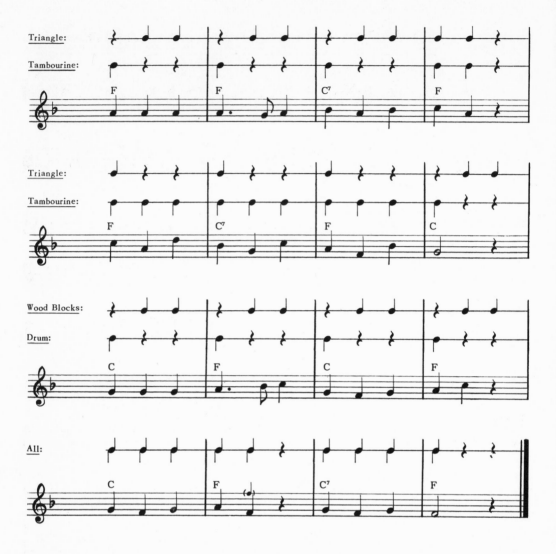

Many well-known instrumental themes are to be found in most school-music texts, some of which lend themselves to similar treatment. The playing of a particular theme, arranged or not, prior to hearing a recording of the selection, establishes a meaningful point of contact and is to be encouraged.

Ensemble treatment of many songs becomes an interesting possibility for classrooms, as may be seen from the example shown next. With such instruments the class may perform as an orchestra, a chorus, or as a combined ensemble, some singing, and some playing.

Old MacDonald Had a Farm*

D.C. al fine

here a chick, there a chick, ev-ery-where a chick, chick

An effective melody-bell trio, or song with song-bell accompaniment is this next arrangement. Note the introduction and coda (ending):

Lark in the Morn*

(Bell accompaniment)

Folk Song from Somersetshire
Arranged by Frederick Beckman

1. As I _____ was a -
2. The lark _____ in the

walk - ing one morn - ing in the spring,   I
morn,   she will rise up from her nest   And

* From <u>Singing Together</u> of "Our Singing World Series," published by Ginn and Co., owners of the copyright. Used with permission.

met a pret - ty dam ____ sel, so sweet - ly did she
mount up in the air ____ with the dew all on her

sing; And as we were a - walk - ing these ___
breast; And like the pret - ty plough - boy she will

words ___ she did say, ___ "There is no life like the
whis ___ tle and sing, ___ And at night she will re -

plough - boy's all in the month of May."
turn to her own nest back a - gain.

rit.

pp

275

2. ORCHESTRAL INSTRUMENTS WITH CLASS SINGING

By the time pupils have reached the upper elementary and junior high grades, many have had one or more years as members of bands or orchestras. Among the most often used instruments are clarinets, cornets or trumpets, trombones, violins, and 'cellos. Many students are proficient on more than one of these instruments.

Those with some technical skill on an instrument should occasionally be allowed to play a descant, or second part, to a song the class is singing.

An example featuring a violin arrangement with rhythm instruments follows:

Tum Balalaika*

*From Growing With Music, Book 5, by Wilson, Ehret, Snyder, Hermann and Renna. Copyright 1963 by Prentice-Hall Inc. Used by permission of the publisher.

A three-part arrangement for girls' chorus (Soprano, Soprano, Alto) with violin or flute obligato is shown here:

Somewhere a Child is Singing*

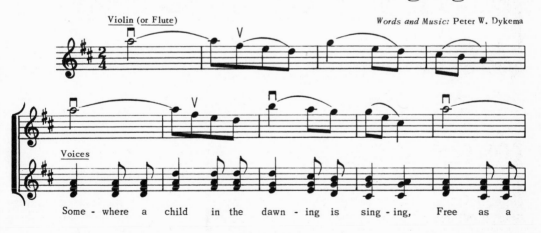

Words and Music: Peter W. Dykema

*Used by permission of copyright owner, Summy-Birchard Co., Evanston, Ill., and reprinted from Basic <u>Music for Classroom Teachers</u>, by Robert E. Nye and Bjornar Bergethon, Prentice-Hall, Inc. (Englewood Cliffs, N.J., 1954).

bird when it wel - comes the day. Ris - ing and fall - ing

on goes the song, Ring - ing with joy and with hope that is

strong. We, too, need mu - sic to lift us and

cheer us, Come then, and sing all our cares a - way.

Somewhere a child in the twilight is singing,
  Living a-new all the joys of the day.
Song brings contentment, song brings release,
  Sorrow is banished, the heart's filled with peace.
We, too, need music to lift us and cheer us;
  Come then, and sing all our cares away.

In most folk songs the melody and the accompaniment (if there is one) is the same for all verses. In an art song, however, both the melody and accompaniment often change from verse to verse. The reason for this is the desire on the part of composers of art songs to reflect as sensitively as possible the moods, feelings, or thoughts, as they may vary from verse to verse.

Probably the greatest writer of art songs was Franz Schubert (1797-1828). In the short time that he lived—he died in his thirty-first year—he composed over six hundred art songs, many of which are performed today.

The song shown below features a descant, or obligato, for violin.

278

Woodland Song*

English words: C.T.C.
Franz Schubert

1. Down the hills and val - leys green walks the smi - ling

sum - mer sprea - ding trea - sures like a queen

For the ear - liest com - er. Buds as red as

sun - set skies, Love - ly flow'rs with bright blue eyes,

Gol - den bursts of wood - land song, charm the list - 'ner

all day long. Gol - den bursts of wood - land song

charm   the list - 'ner   all   day long.

Piano all alone

Piano and 'cello

The next arrangement features the autoharp, psaltery, 'cello, and piano. Note that the psaltery part may also be played on the autoharp (by plucking respective strings) or on the guitar. The 'cello part has only two notes which must be fingered:

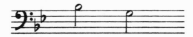

The other notes are open positions (see p. 208):

Note the poem and added comments provided for an introduction or as a follow-up commentary on the song.

There was neither man nor hero
Neither ancient dame nor maiden,
Whom he did not touch to weeping.
Wept the young and wept the aged,
Wept the mothers, wept the daughters,
Wept the warriors and the heroes,
At the music of his making,
At the songs of the magician.

From the <u>Kalevala</u>

The Kalevala is the greatest epic poem of Finland. Vainamoinen was the famous
legendary singer of its stories. The rhythm of the words of this song is like the
rhythm of the Kalevala. Longfellow was inspired by his reading of the Kalevala to
write the poem "Hiawatha" in the same rhythm.

Vainamoinen's Gift*

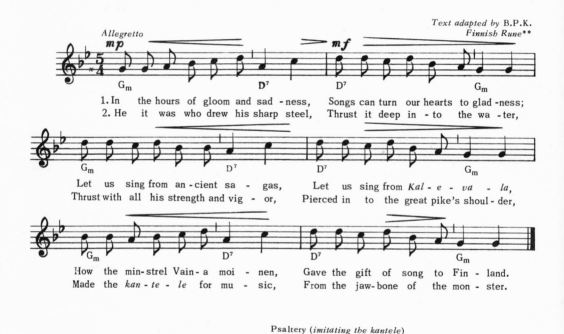

The psaltery and 'cello parts, played
three times will accompany the entire song.
They may be used also as an introduction,
and as a coda.

---

* M. Krone (ed.), <u>Voices of the World</u> (Chicago: Follett Publishing Co., 1959). Used with permission of the publisher.
** Rune: Ancient Finnish song.

Many varied possibilities are indicated by the arrangement shown next. It may be used for small ensembles—duets, trios, quartets, or for large groups:

Send Down Thy Truth*

Words: Edward Rowland Sill (1876)
Music: Aaron Williams (1763)

1. Send down Thy truth, O ____ God! Too ____ long the shad - ows frown; Too long the dark - ened way we've trod: Thy truth O ____ Lord, send down!
2. Send down Thy peace, O ____ Lord! Earth's ____ bit - ter voic - es drown In one deep o - cean of ac - cord: Thy peace, O ____ God, send down!

---

*William R. Sur, Robert E. Nye, William R. Fisher, Mary R. Tolbert, This is Music, Book 5 (Boston). Copyright © 1962, by Allyn and Bacon, Inc. Used with permission.

283

Clarinet or Cornet (add this part to make a trio)

Orchestration for Send Down Thy Truth

Duet for Violin or bells

Violin or Bells (add this part to make a trio)

'Cello or Trombone (add this part to make a quartet)

Try singing the violin parts.

Occasionally in series books, particularly for the upper elementary and junior high grades, orchestral arrangements of the kind shown next are provided. Although bands and orchestras do not exist as such in the individual classroom, it is often possible to feature a small group of instrumentalists chosen from one or more grades for purposes of illustrating the fuller and more varied orchestral sound. This is particularly appropriate preceding a discussion or a series of lessons devoted to instrumental literature (see pp. 286-287).

The following arrangement would be effective as an assembly exercise. One class could be the chorus (on unison melody), accompanied by a small group of instrumentalists.

Faith of Our Fathers*

Frederick W. Faber
Henri F. Hemy

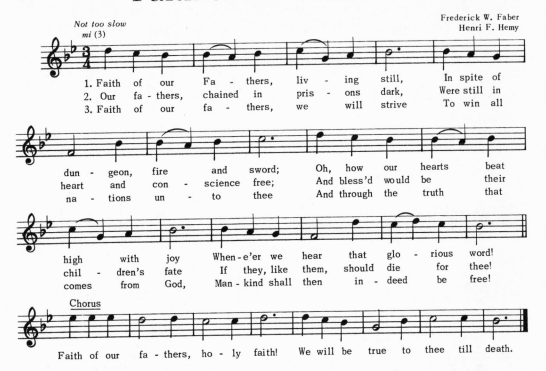

1. Faith of our Fa - thers, liv - ing still, In spite of
2. Our fa - thers, chained in pris - ons dark, Were still in
3. Faith of our fa - thers, we will strive To win all

dun - geon, fire and sword; Oh, how our hearts beat
heart and con - science free; And bless'd would be their
na - tions un - to thee And through the truth that

high with joy When-e'er we hear that glo - rious word!
chil - dren's fate If they, like them, should die for thee!
comes from God, Man - kind shall then in - deed be free!

Chorus

Faith of our fa - thers, ho - ly faith! We will be true to thee till death.

Orchestration for <u>Faith of Our Fathers</u>: violins and flutes play the voice part.

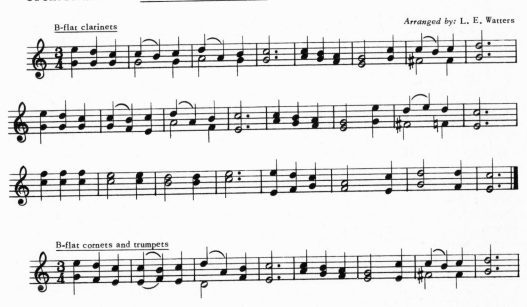

Arranged by: L. E. Watters

B-flat clarinets

B-flat cornets and trumpets

E-flat altos (mellophones) and E-flat saxophones

'Cellos, trombones and baritones

Instrumental Music

A discussion of "serious" instrumental music is beyond the scope of this book. However, in an effort to further musical interest beyond the song-singing stage, the wise teacher will draw upon experiences gained through the use of recordings, films, personal membership in performing groups, concert attendances, studies in music literature, history, and upon other relevant sources.* It is gratifying to note that, more and more, authors of series textbooks are making increased use of the literature of the adult concert world.

---

*Two books containing program notes for standard orchestral literature are Charles O'Connell, Victor Book of Overtures, Tone Poems, and Other Orchestral Works (New York: Simon and Schuster, 1950); Aaron Copland, What to Listen for in Music, rev. ed. (New York: McGraw-Hill Book Company, Inc. 1957).

Musical learning and understanding is a cumulative process, depending not only upon instruction, but also upon age and experience of the participant. To attempt too soon a recording of a Beethoven string quartet is apt to be courting disaster. To move toward it through vocal and instrumental involvement appears to be a more promising approach. Recordings should be used to augment and extend musical insights and understandings which lie beyond the student's own capacity to explore. This assumes an adequate library of recordings,* a selection of recordings pertinent to the area of study, and a presentation which draws upon related experiences gained through active participation.

This chapter began with a consideration of the harmonic structure of three-part selections. It became evident that for many songs and instrumental selections, additional parts for harmonic or color purposes contribute considerably toward the total apprehension of the meaning. Skill and discrimination in arranging melodies in different ways can be of direct value in the classroom. A teacher with this ability is in a position to fashion the music to the particular situation at hand. The best textbook may yet be the one which the teacher and class compile together.

---

* Partial Bibliography of Instrumental Recordings (see also Chap. 6 p. 141 and Chap. 7 p. 160).

Introductory: A Young Person's Guide to the Symphony Orchestra by Benjamin Britten (Mercury record #MG 50055); Meet the Instruments of the Symphony Orchestra with film strips and large color charts of instruments (Bowmar Educational Records, Los Angeles, Calif.); The Wonderful Violin (Young People's Records #311); Instruments of the Orchestra with Teaching Guide (RCA Victor); Instruments of the Orchestra, Introduction Series (Columbia Recording Corp.); The Complete Orchestra by Beckett (Music Education Record Corp., Englewood, N.J.).

A listing of recordings from all record companies is found in Schwann's Long-Playing Record Catalogue, issued monthly and available at most music stores.

For films, kinescopes, and film strips, a new and complete listing is found in Film Guide for Music Educators by Shetler, published by Music Educators National Conference, 1201-16th St., N.W. Washington, D.C.

POINTERS AND PRACTICE-
CHAPTER 10

I. Transpose the first line of "The Papaya Tree," p. 256, to the nearest primary key (C, F, or G). Write all three parts.

From your answer deduce the autoharp or piano chords for the whole song and enter notation above the melody line, p. 256.
What is the over-all harmonic pattern?

Transcribe the first line of the third part in Question I above upon the bass staff:

II. Is there any advantage in using the bass staff in the upper elementary grades? Explain.

III. Determine the chords (2 per measure) for the first four measures of Schubert's "Woodland Song," p. 279. Comment briefly on the style of the piano accompaniment.

IV. From the chords notated with "The Ash Grove," p. 259, justify the notes used in the descant. Combined with the other two parts, do you feel that it is an effective and interesting part? Why?

V. Determine the chords on strong-weak pulses for the last two lines of "Silent Night," p. 260. (Note example.) Enter the chords above the staff and use for auto-harp or piano accompaniment.

VI. Construct a descant (above the melody) for "Wind through the Olive Trees," p. 234. Adjust the text as necessary.

If a clarinet is to be used for the descant, in what key must it be written? Write your answer on the staff provided:

It is noted with "Wind through the Olive Trees" that the strong beat is not always a determining factor in finding appropriate chords. In your song text find other examples of this. List them.

VII. Among the simplest of three-part song arrangements are often those that are limited to I-, IV-, and V-chord harmony. Accuracy in hearing and reproducing the sounds of harmony (ear-training) is most important for a proper performance of any particular selection. Short, appropriate chord drills are therefore of value in focusing attention on the chord qualities of I, IV, V, or V[7].

Choosing part A, B, or C, and then exchanging parts, practice singing the following suggested patterns (other keys may also be used):

Type I (one-chord drills):

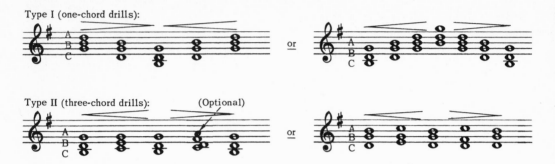

Type II (three-chord drills):   (Optional)

VIII. Comment briefly on the value(s) of vocal-instrumental arrangements as shown, pp. 268-286.

IX. A boy in Grade Five or Six is proficient in playing the clarinet. You have indicated that you would like him to play his clarinet while the **class sings** "Vainamoinen's Gift," p. 282. On the staff below, write the first line of the melody for him.

X. Comment on the value(s) of playing (using the simple recorder-type instruments) notable themes from standard orchestral and other extended works.

XI. On p. 262, the first phrase of the three-part song entitled "How Brightly Shines the Morning Star" is harmonized as follows:

A variety of chord-colors are used including **minor** chords II_m, III_m, and VI_m. From the table below, identify all the chords with the exception of the next to last chord.

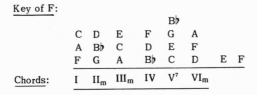

Key of F:

				B♭			
C	D	E	F	G	A		
A	B♭	C	D	E	F		
F	G	A	B♭	C	D	E	F
I	II_m	III_m	IV	V^7	VI_m		

Chords:

Write your answer, using roman numerals, under the chords above.

Note: The B♮ in the next to last chord is foreign to the key of F. Often composers will indicate a preference, even momentarily and for the sake of contrast, for the added color associated with the substitution of another key system. In considering the new key to be used, that chosen is very often the key of the dominant. In this case, as the initial key is F, the key of the dominant would be the key of C. The new dominant chord, an important chord in asserting the new key, would therefore be the G or G^7 chord:

The chord in question then should be written V of V (V⁷ of V), or G or G⁷, the dominant chord of the dominant key.

Complete the analysis of the next two phrases of this song:

Notice the delayed C-chord at *. On what beat is it resolved?

Come, Let Us All This Day

J. S. Bach

M.Metr. ♪ = 92

mf

Come let — us all — this day — with ho — ly songs be
Let him — whom God in - spires — by ho — ly word and

prais ___ ing; Tell out the works of God, ___ once
spi ___ rit, To whom is given to share ___ the

more our voi_____ces rais_____ing. This day the Ho_____ly
Sa - viour's grace and mer_____it, U - nite with us, _____and

cresc.

Ghost _____ He ro____ic hearts has fired, _____ So
praise_____ our God for ev - er true, _____ Whose

cresc.

let us pray that ours_____ by Him may be____ in - spired.____
mer - cies are this day,____ and ev'____ ry morn____ ing new.____

XII. One of the reasons Bach's music is highly regarded is because of the careful workmanship and organization which most of his music reveals. In the selection here given, though it is a short one, Bach introduces two additional keys. Note particularly measures 3-4, 7-8, and 9-10. What keys are established?

In measures 8-11, several E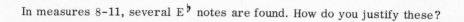 notes are found. How do you justify these?

Name the chords on strong-weak pulses (counts 1 and 4) in the first two measures. (Ignore first note.)

The song "Come, Let Us All This Day" is appropriate as a soprano or tenor solo. Capable and interested pupils in upper elementary or junior high grades should be encouraged to learn and perform art songs of good quality. From your song text or other sources learn to play or to sing some of these compositions. Listen to recordings of famous singers of art songs.

11

CREATING MUSIC

Creating a musical composition should not be any more unusual than writing a paragraph or a story. Although people are generally more at home with words, this is not necessarily true for the young. Witness, for example, the infant's banging of pots and pans or the sing-song chants of the six-year-old while playing. The young child's world is as much sound-centered as word-centered, but this tonal dimension diminishes as the child grows older. Certainly the lack of emphasis on tonal arts in the school curriculum is a contributing factor. And the quality or kind of instruction is the most significant aspect of the problem. The practice of merely reproducing the tunes of others at the expense of one's own creation is all too common. The teaching of music should be like that of other subjects, with stress on thought-provoking problems and individual experimentation. Audio-visual aids, a spirit of inquiry and investigation, questions and discussions, paper and pencil should be just as much in evidence in the music class as in a social studies, science, or mathematics class.

The creative approach has been emphasized throughout this book. The first four or five chapters were devoted to the fundamental, preliminary aspects of tone-consciousness and its development—the less formal aspects of music learning—and subsequent chapters dealt with the more formal ideas. In Chapters 8, 9, and 10, for example, emphasis was placed upon various ways of treating songs, of enriching and embellishing them. Sometimes a rhythmic emphasis was apparent, at other times a melodic or harmonic one. In this chapter suggestions with regard to the creating of music will be the focal point.

Creating Music Using the Major Scale

Harmonic patterns, noted with many of the songs earlier in this book, provide a useful guide for creating melodies. Suppose, for example, the following harmonic pattern for a four-measure phrase, is observed:

<u>Key of C</u>: 4/4 | I   IV | I   I | IV   V⁷ | I   - |

297

It should be possible, at least in a mathematical sense, for a pupil to construct a linear series of notes based on the above pattern to give some such result as the following:

I   IV   I   I   IV   V⁷   I

It will be seen that the melody notes are all taken from the primary chords:

```
                    F
     G        C   D
     E        A   B
     C  D  E  F  G  A  B  C
     ──────────────────────
     I        IV V⁷
     ──────────────────────
```

A modification to include some passing notes and altered rhythms may result in melodies such as the following:

Innumerable variations are apparent. Some guiding principles are suggested as follows:

1. Indicate the shape or design of the desired melody. In the example above, it is sloping downward in scale fashion from C1 to Middle C. Other visual shapes are:

2. If a complete melody (statement) is contemplated, the first note is usually 1, 3, or 5, and the last note 1. This is confirmed by observation of most songs.

3. Limit initial experiments to two- or four-measure phrases, later extending them to eight or sixteen.

4. In first attempts use I-V patterns as found with other songs for harmonic outlines, followed later with observable I-IV-V patterns. For example, from a certain song as found in one of the texts, the following pattern is taken:

Key of F: 3/4 ‖I |I |IV |IV |V⁷ | V⁷ |I |I |
                |V⁷ |I |V |I |I |I |V⁷ I ‖

One melodic version based on the above pattern may result somewhat as follows:

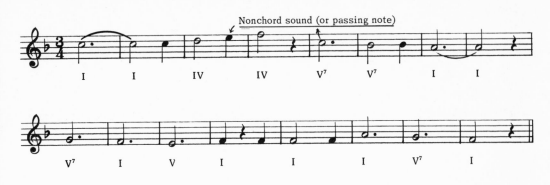

Another might be:

Note that where a nonchord sound has been included, it has been approached and quitted by step, not by skip. Nonchord sounds, or passing notes, are often used to produce a smoother effect.

The melody for this particular harmonic pattern (large notes), and adapted to the text, is found as follows in one of the textbooks:

Spin, Spin, My Darling Daughter*

(Answer Song)

*Pennsylvania Dutch Version
of an Old German Song*

1. Spin, spin, my dar-ling daugh-ter I'll buy you a shawl! Yes, yes, my dar-ling moth-er, And that not too small!
2. Spin, spin, my dar-ling daugh-ter, I'll buy you some shoes! Yes, yes, my dar-ling moth-er, The best ones I choose!

* Used by permission of Pennsylvania Folklife Society. Reprinted from William R. Sur, Robert E. Nye, William R. Fisher, Mary R. Tolbert, This is Music, Book 5 (Boston: Allyn and Bacon, Inc., 1962).

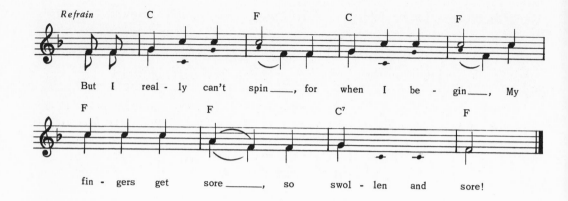

Refrain

But I real-ly can't spin____, for when I be-gin____, My

fin-gers get sore_____, so swol-len and sore!

3. Spin, spin, my darling daughter,
   I'll buy you a gown!
   Yes, yes, my darling mother,
   Have them send it right down!
   <u>Refrain.</u>

4. Spin, spin my darling daughter,
   I'll buy you a hat!
   Yes, yes, my darling mother,
   But why stop at that?
   <u>Refrain.</u>

5. Spin, spin my darling daughter,
   I'll buy you a man!
   Yes, yes, my darling mother,
   I'll spin if I can!
   Now watch me spin!
   Just let me begin.
   My finger's not sore,
   My finger's not sore!

(Note the piano patterns proposed for accompaniment—a variant of those given in Chapter 7.)

5. Consider the mood or feeling desired. A "happy" tonal idea is generally more rhythmic (uses shorter notes) than one of more somber nature. If a march-like melody is intended, Example 1 (below) is better than Example 2, and certainly more appropriate than Example 3, though all have the same harmonic formula:

Example 1:

I   I   IV   I   IV   I   V⁷   I

Example 2:

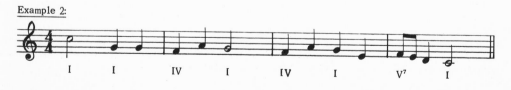

I   I   IV   I   IV   I   V⁷   I

Example 3:

6. If a poem is to be set to music, study its rhythm and mood. It is likely that a genuine folk melody like the following originated more from the text and its flavor rather than from any harmonic base. The words not only fit the tune but in themselves "roll well on the tongue," and hence suggest a tune:

Blow, Ye Winds*

Forecastle Song from New Bedford, Mass.

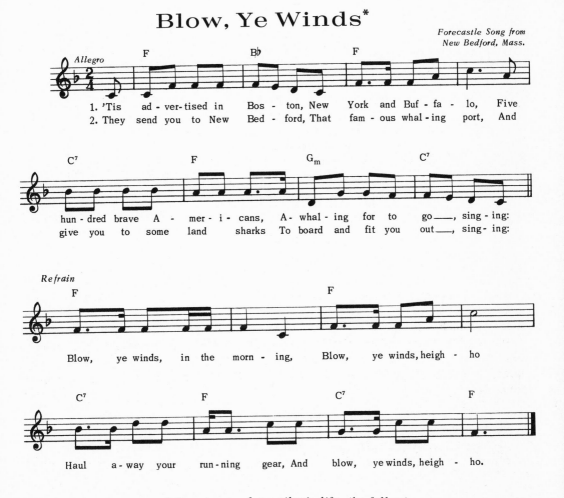

1. 'Tis ad-ver-tised in Bos-ton, New York and Buf-fa-lo, Five
2. They send you to New Bed-ford, That fam-ous whal-ing port, And

hun-dred brave A - mer-i-cans, A-whal-ing for to go——, sing-ing:
give you to some land sharks To board and fit you out——, sing-ing:

Refrain

Blow, ye winds, in the morn-ing, Blow, ye winds, heigh - ho

Haul a-way your run-ning gear, And blow, ye winds, heigh - ho.

For a full account of the rigors of a sailor's life, the following verses are provided:

---

*William R. Sur, Robert E. Nye, William R. Fisher, Mary R. Tolbert, This is Music, Book 5 (Boston). Copyright © 1962, by Allyn and Bacon, Inc. Used by permission.

3. They send you to a boarding house, there for a time to dwell,
   The thieves are there much thicker than the other side of hell, singing,
           Blow, etc.

4. They tell you of the clipper-ships, a-going in and out,
   And say you'll take five hundred whales before you're six months out, singing,
           Blow, etc.

5. It's now we're out to sea, my boys, the wind comes on to blow,
   One half the watch is sick on deck, the other half's below, singing
           Blow, etc.

6. But as for the provisions, boys, we don't get half enough,
   A little piece of stinking beef and a damned small bag of duff, singing,
           Blow, etc.

7. The skipper's on the quarter-deck a-squintin' at the sails,
   When up aloft the lookout sights a heaving school of whales, singing,
           Blow, etc.

8. Now clear away the boats my boys, and after him you'll go,
   And if you get too near his fluke, he'll kick you to the devil, singing,
           Blow, etc.

9. When we get home, our ship made fast, and we get through our sail,
   A winding glass around we'll pass and damn this blubber whalin', singing,
           Blow, etc.

Related Listening: "Sea Chanteys" sung by Leonard Warren (RCA Victor record LM-1168); "Song of the Sea" by Burl Ives (RCA Victor record KK-710).

7. Sometimes the creation of a song may arise out of studies in other subjects as is the case in the true story quoted below from Miss Kathe Peters:

This little song originated in our school after a social studies lesson in Grade Five, although the pupils of Grade Four participated too. After we had discussed the Maritime Provinces, their fishing and boat building industries, the children brought cut-outs of all kinds of boats to school, which were mounted on a frieze. Two models came in, one of them being that of the "Cutty Sark," a trading tea-boat.

At first, one of my young artists together with some helpers, drew a picture of her in colored chalk on the blackboard. This gave me an opportunity to introduce scale drawing. The children were very proud of their lovely boat. Sailing words and boat words were inserted in columns around the "Cutty Sark."

One day she had to come off the blackboard which caused sorrow to the whole classroom. We decided to make up a poem about the boat. In a language hour while we were just discussing "Enjoying Poetry" the poem was created, crudely as you might imagine. We kept changing words until the children thought it was good enough. Then, in a few music periods, the tune was made up. The children love it.

The Cutty Sark*

By the pupils and teacher,
Kathe Peters, *of Denman Island School*

The Cut-ty Sark was a tra-ding boat, and a gal-lant boat was sail-ing

she; On man-y a voy-age a-cross the sea, her car-go was Black

Tea. A nor-thern gale a-rose one day and drove the Cut-ty Sark a-stray. She

ran u-pon a cor-ral reef, that fin-ished her sto-ry in sor-row and grief.

8. Provide frequent opportunities to hear, discuss and subsequently to alter results if need be. Initial efforts, for many, will reveal little coherence or phraselike unity; however, by repeated hearings and comparisons with other fine examples, results should gradually improve.

However the composer proceeds—whether he "picks the melody out of the air," so to speak, or whether he fashions it from text or chords, or more likely both, he often succeeds in creating noteworthy products of his life and times which, for generations later, are significant and rewarding. The two examples shown next are typical.

Little Man in the Woods**

(Jack-in-the-pulpit)
(From <u>Hansel and Gretel</u>)

Translated
Humperdinck

so (5) *do* (1)

1. There stands a lit-tle man in the deep, dark wood; He
2. He stands there on one leg bend-ing to and fro; And

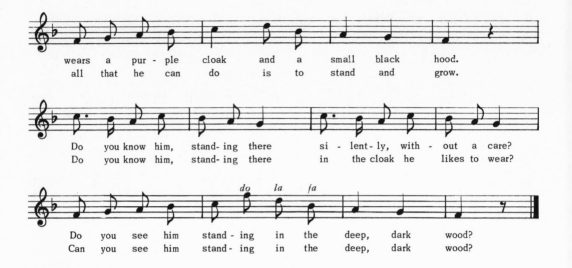

wears	a	pur - ple	cloak	and	a	small	black	hood.
all	that	he	can	do	is	to	stand	and	grow.

Do	you know	him,	stand- ing	there	si - lent- ly,	with - out	a	care?
Do	you know	him,	stand- ing	there	in	the cloak	he	likes to wear?

do la fa

Do	you	see	him	stand - ing	in	the	deep,	dark	wood?
Can	you	see	him	stand - ing	in	the	deep,	dark	wood?

Related Listening: Hansel and Gretel by Humperdinck (Victor Listening Album 4).

Features that may be singled out for study are:

1. The gentle rise and fall of lines 1, 2, and 4.
2. The simple harmonic outline.
3. The change in rhythm and melodic shape of line (phrase) 3.
4. The sense of climax achieved in the last line with the use of the high F-note.
5. The unity of the whole song, though the last line is slightly different from the first two.

Can you suggest some reasons why the following song is notable?

Oh, Rest in the Lord*

(From Elijah)

Felix Mendelssohn

Slowly, with deep feeling
do (1)

Oh, rest	in	the	Lord,	wait	pa - tient - ly	for
Him,	And	He	shall —	give thee	thy heart's	de —

---

* From Singing in Harmony of "Our Singing World Series," published by Ginn and Co., owners of the copyright. Used with permission.

sires. —— Oh, rest —— in the Lord, wait pa - tient - ly for

Him, And He — shall — give thee thy heart's — de —

sires; —— And He shall give thee thy heart's de - sires.

<u>Related Listening</u>: A recording of "Oh, Rest in the Lord."

Examples of many fine art songs are found in most school songbooks. A detailed study of their construction will prove worthwhile in extending one's own knowledge of melodic properties and in understanding and appreciating the works of others.

Creating Music Using the Minor Scale

The procedure for creating melodies in minor keys is similar to that suggested for major keys. Suppose, for example, that a melody is to be composed for a given harmonic pattern in the key of D_m:

$$4/4 \mid D_m \quad D_m \mid G_m \quad D_m \mid A^7 \quad D_m \mid A^7 \quad D_m \mid D_m \quad D_m \mid G_m \quad D_m \mid A^7 \quad A^7 \mid D_m \; - \;\|$$

Using the primary chords for this key,

```
                    G
A          D   E
F          B♭  C(♯)- - - - - - - - Note altered C
D  E  F  G  A   B♭  C  D
─────────────────────────
I_m        IV_m V⁷
```

one version might be:

$D_m \quad D_m \quad\quad G_m \quad D_m \quad\quad A^7 \quad D_m \quad\quad A^7 \quad D_m \quad\quad D_m \quad D_m \quad\quad G_m \quad D_m \quad\quad A^7 \quad A^7 \quad\quad D_m \; -$

Adjusted to include some rhythmic variation, the following may result:

The shape of the first four measures is ⌒ , and of the last four
⌣ . Note the B♮, measure 7. B♭ to C♯ is called an augmented second, an awkward interval to sing. An easier interval is obtained by using B♮ just
before the C♯.

Sometimes a question-answer form of melody may be appropriate. A harmonic
pattern such as the following, for example,

Key: D_m

4/4 |I_m IV_m | I_m I_m | I_m IV_m | V^7 - | I_m IV_m | I_m I_m | IV_m V^7 | I_m - ||

with the V^7 in the fourth measure, is definitely unresolved and unstable, hence
like a question mark. The ending on chord I_m indicates finality, hence the answer. The melodic result may therefore appear somewhat as follows:

The shape of both phrases is the same: ⌒ and ⌒ .

Composers often turn to the minor scale when a melancholy mood is desired.
Though the composer of this next song is unknown, note how the mood of the text
is reflected by the melody.

Far, Far Away*

*From Basic Goals in Music, Book 6, Lloyd H. Slind and Frank E. Churchley, Toronto: McGraw-
Hill Company of Canada Limited, 1964. Used with permission.

Come back to me, lit - tle bird of the for - est, ___

Leave me not a - lone, leave me not a - lone.

Creating Music Using the Pentatonic Scale

A predecessor of the minor scale, the pentatonic,* is somewhat easier to use because only five sounds are permissible. The five black notes on the piano, beginning on F♯ constitute one such scale:

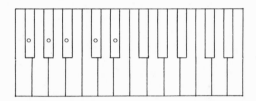

The familiar tune "Auld Lang Syne," consisting of an arrangement of these five sounds, begins in the following manner:

Another "black-note" melody is:

Old Mother Hubbard**

Mother Goose Rhyme
Donald J. Grout

Old Moth - er Hub - bard, She went to the cup - board to

---

* See also Chap. 4, pp. 84, 103-104.
** Book 2, <u>Birchard Music Series</u>. Copyright © 1962, Summy-Birchard Co., Evanston, Ill. Used by permission.

get her poor dog-gie a bone,_____ But when she got there, the

cup-board was bare, and so the poor dog-gie got none.

Transposing this melody from the key of F♯ a half step lower to the key of F, it is written as follows:

Another example limited to this five-note scale is the "Texas Cowboy Song," shown on p. 220.

The pentatonic scale is formed by omitting the fourth and seventh notes of the major scale. In the key of F, the scale is as follows:

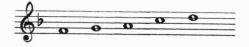

Note that in the preceding song samples the fourth and seventh notes of the scale are absent.

Although I-, IV- and V^7-chords may be associated with such melodies, occasionally additional chords, particularly minor chords II$_m$ and VI$_m$, are also found. This is true of the following:

Lullaby*

Words: Christina Rossetti
Music: Alys Bentley

Gently rocking

F   Dm   F   Dm   Gm   Dm
Lul - la - by, oh, lul - la - by, Flow'rs are closed and

Gm   C⁷   F   Dm   F   Dm
lambs are sleep - ing; Stars are up, the moon is peep - ing,

Gm   Dm   Gm   C⁷   F   Am   F   Am
Lul - la- by, oh, lul - la- by. While the birds are si - lence keep - ing,

Gm   Dm   Gm   C⁷   F   Dm
Sleep my ba - by, fall a -sleep - ing, Lul - la - by, oh,

F   Dm   Gm   Dm   C⁷   F
lul - la - by,_____ Lul - la - by, oh, lul - la - by.

For some pentatonic melodies, the chord structure is often indefinite. In others, a combination of major and minor chords seem to be effective. Try, for example, the effect of combining chords as was suggested in Chapter 9, p. 221. Use two autoharps as directed:

Autoharp 1		Autoharp 2
F	with	Dm
C⁷	with	Gm

Apply this chord structure to "Lullaby" in the manner shown below and note the effect:

F and Dm _ _ _ _ _ _ _ _ _ _ _ _ _ _ _C⁷ and Gm _ _ _ _ _ _ _ _ _ _ _ _ _ _

---

*M. Krone (ed.), <u>Music Across Our Country</u> (Chicago: Follett Publishing Co., 1959). Used by permission of the publisher.

One reason why the primary chords do not generally apply to pentatonic melodies is due to the elimination of the fourth and seventh notes in the major scale:

$$
\begin{array}{lllllll}
 & & & ? & & & \\
C & & F & G & & & \\
A & & D & ? & & & \\
F & G & A & ? & C & D & ? & F \\
\hline
I & & & IV & V^7 & & \\
\end{array}
$$

There is no longer any IV- or V-chord. The only complete primary chord is I. The five remaining sounds, with the exception perhaps of sound 1, have no particular allegiance to normal chord groupings, at least of the primary-chord type. By eliminating the strong fourth sound, and the unstable, dependent seventh, the most individualistic of scale sounds, one is left with five sounds of relatively equal stress or emphasis; consequently, they may be used with more abandon. Given some measure of rhythmic unity in the phrase line it does not matter, at least in experimental stages, which tone follows which (note examples):

Example 1:

Key signature: C

Example 2:

Key signature: G

Sometimes the results are not particularly successful but with practice and persistence better results normally follow:

Example 3:

The following pentatonic melody has endured for many years:

Toodala*

Adapted

Might - y pret - ty   mo - tion too,
Rock old Sam - uel   too - da - la,
   Too - da-la,   Too - da - la,

Might - y pret - ty   mo - tion too,
Rock old Sam - uel   too - da - la
Too - da-la - la   la - dy.

<u>Related Listening</u>: "Folk Dances for all Ages" (RCA Victor record #LPM-1622); "Festival Folk Dances" (RCA Victor record #LPM-1621).

It is possible to construct freely, without recourse to a chordal base or outline, a new and interesting type of melody.

Many modern composers reflect a renewed interest in some of the ancient scale-forms. One example, illustrating in this case not a pentatonic but a similar melody derived from another ancient scale, is:

Our History Sings**

Words: Catherine Cate Coblentz
Music: Norman Dello Joio

Our   his - tory sings of   cen - tu - ries, Such   var - y - ing songs it

sings!   It   starts with winds,   slow - mov- ing sails, It   ends with skies and wings.

Though it begins and ends as though it were in the key of C, the B♭ instead of the B gives it a distinctly different flavor. Substitute the B for the B♭ and note the difference.

---

*It is an old Texas dance tune. Words were frequently improvised depending upon the occasion. Often, entire families, from babes in arms to old people, took part. See Ruth Crawford Seeger, <u>American Folk Songs for Children</u> (Garden City, N.Y.: Doubleday & Co., Inc., 1948) for other suitable folk songs.

**Words used by permission of L. Huntley Cate. Music used by permission of Silver Burdett Co. Reprinted from James L. Mursell et al., <u>Music Near and Far</u> (Morristown, N.J.: Silver Burdett Co., 1962).

THE PENTATONIC SCALE AND SIGHT-READING (Primary Grades)

A separation of the elements of text, rhythm or movement, and melody must be considered in a systematic approach to music reading. Combined, these elements (as they apply to songs) are too difficult for the beginner.

The concept of rhythm, first felt through bodily movement and later refined and extended to include the symbols of rhythm, is the first element to receive attention. In Preschool and Primary grades, as was suggested in Part I of this book, developmental experiences should be provided.

The development of the melodic concept should parallel and follow rhythmic development. The pentatonic scale has certain properties that make it significant for first experiences in melody reading. An account of some of these properties as they pertain to what may be termed a reading-readiness program for the Primary grades is therefore discussed here. This will serve to augment suggestions presented in the section entitled "Reading by Note—Intermediate and Upper Elementary Grades," pp. 154-157, as well as in Part I of this book.

The prospect of melody, relatively easily realized through the use of the pentatonic scale, makes it eminently suitable for use in early sight-reading experiences. First, even the shortest of melodic phrases appear to be meaningful and significant. Note, for example, the following melodic units:

The sounds of the pentatonic, even though only two different notes are used, are quite complete tonal ideas and particularly so when improvised or traditional texts are sung to them.

Second, only five different sounds are used as compared with seven for the major or minor scale. The range, therefore, can be such as to apply even to those most limited in ability. With the key of C signature, for example, the range span for a melody could be:

Third, the choice of sounds in the composing of a melody, as was indicated earlier, is much freer. Melodies may be composed even by random choice of sounds. Exercises can therefore be designed to meet individual limitations of range and pitch more adequately.

Fourth, a short melodic phrase may be joined to other phrases to form longer and more varied selections. A pentatonic phrase, not being bound to cadential requirements associated with traditional harmony of the major and minor scale and not being a finite entity in itself, may therefore be repeated and extended at will.

A sequential procedure which a teacher may use to develop music reading skills is shown as follows:

1. Two-note (minor 3rd) exercises with improvised or nursery-rhyme texts:

One,   two,   here we   go

2. Three-note units:

Ring   a - round   the   ro -   sy

3. Four-note units:

Rain,   rain,   oh   go   a - way,   Come a - gain some oth - er   day

4. Five-note units:

Sleep   my ba - by   sleep, sleep,   Sleep   my   ba - by   sleep

Any or all of these exercises may, of course, be transposed to various positions:

The use of instruments as aids to pitch-awareness are recommended. Glockenspiels, songbells, and melody instruments are particularly appropriate. One type of glockenspiel featuring removable bars is effective. It is used in the manner shown below to illustrate more concretely the highness and lowness of sounds:

The use of the pentatonic scale in early attempts at note reading and coupled with the inventive possibilities inherent is well founded. If opportunities for music reading are systematically applied, with forethought as to the objectives ultimately desired (preferably over several grades), illiteracy in note reading should soon become a thing of the past.*

THE PENTATONIC SCALE AND PART WRITING

It was stated earlier that any note may follow any particular sound in melody construction using the pentatonic scale. In a general way, it may also be stated that any sound (of the 5) may be played against (at the same time) any other sound. For a second or third part for a given tune, one may proceed almost independently of the first and as though one were constructing another independent melody:

One should avoid parts that lie too close to each other. Notice that Part 2 lies lower than Part 1, and Part 3 lower than Part 2 (except for the last few notes where they cross one another).

Somewhat better distribution is obtained if the bass staff is included:

*See also topics ''Music Reading,'' <u>Growing with Music Series</u>, Books 2, 3, 4, and 5 (Englewood Cliffs, N.J.: Prentice-Hall, 1963).

First part:
Songbells 1:

Second part:
Songbells 2:

Third part:
Alto xylophone: etc.

Fourth part:
'Cello (plucked):

The playing of such ensemble arrangements does not necessitate a complete score from which to read the part. The range for each part may be decided beforehand and the player or singer of a particular part then improvises freely within that range.

The use of simple melodic patterns is also of value. A composition for three melody bells, for example, might begin as follows:

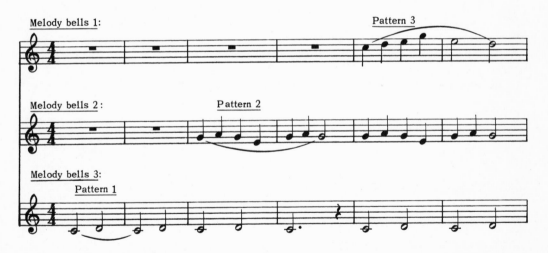

Melody bells 1:   Pattern 3

Melody bells 2:   Pattern 2

Melody bells 3:
    Pattern 1

The adoption of specific patterns eliminates the problem of continuously choosing the next sound. The player is then free to concentrate upon improved rhythmic and interpretive techniques.

A composition for six different instruments featuring distinct patterns for each is shown next.* To complete the selection, as only a portion is given here, it is suggested that each player withdraw or finish in the same manner that he started.

*From Doreen Hall, Music for Children (Teacher's Manual) (New York: Associated Music Publishers, Ltd., 1960), p. 21. Also Toronto: Leeds Music Ltd. Used by permission. (See also Doreen Hall and Arnold Walter, Music for Children, I—Pentatonic [New York: Associated Music Publishers, Ltd., 1960].)

This form of musical activity—the improvisation of musical lines whether singly or in ensembles—may be thought of as a sensed or felt activity, as opposed to the planned or prescored kind suggested with harmonic patterns, pp. 297-301. In the latter, parts or melodies grow out of an analytical situation and then are sounded, whereas in the first they arise from the activity itself, and later perhaps are analyzed and notated.

The improvisational type pertains more to a "child-music" literature and the traditional form more properly to an "adult-music" literature. One is pertinent to music felt "on the spot" as it were, the other to music written and handed down.

Both kinds of composition, both kinds of tonal involvement should be stressed throughout the elementary grades. If some kind of separation is permissible, the emphasis in the Primary grades might be placed more upon the free, improvising kind, and in the intermediate and upper elementary grades more attention devoted to the prescored kind.

Creating Music Using Other Scales

Improvisation need not stop with the use of the pentatonic scale. Similar experiments may be applied to diatonic (major and minor) or other scales. The whole-tone scale, for example, consisting of six different sounds, lends itself to similar free treatment.

The whole-tone scale is different from the major scale in that all half steps are eliminated, and all intervals are whole steps. Beginning on C, the scale would be shown as follows:

These sounds may be used in the same way as the sounds of the pentatonic scale; that is, any sound may follow any other sound in a melodic phrase, and any sound may be sounded against any other sound (with due regard for spacing):

It will be evident that satisfactory results will not be obtained merely by haphazardly inserting certain notes from the particular scale. Each line must reveal a measure of rhythmic interest and unity as well as good voice-leading or "singability." With further experience, a concern for phrase, color, and dynamics will increase. Considerable skill, experience, and training will be needed to achieve any degree of excellence in the final product. However, even the manipulation of sounds "to see what comes out," i.e., tonal "doodling," can be of value. The rules of sound and harmony are discovered not only from textbooks, but from sound itself.

POINTERS AND PRACTICE—
CHAPTER 11

I. A. Using the harmonic pattern shown below, construct three different melodies, each consisting of two phrases. Adopt a certain design or shape for each.

Key of F:

I - I - V I V - V - V - I V I -

Key of D:

Key of C:

B. Construct a waltzlike melody of 16 measures (two phrases each), to the given harmonic outline shown below. Add a few passing notes to vary rhythm.

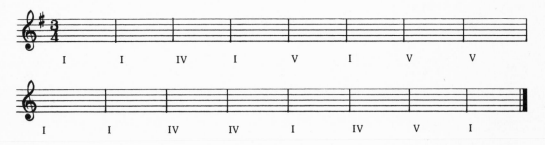

I   I   IV   I   V   I   V   V

I   I   IV   IV   I   IV   V   I

II. The first two phrases of one of Franz Schubert's piano melodies are shown as follows:

What may have been the chord structure from which the tune was created? (See also p. 205.)

III. Mozart, at the age of six years, was reported to have written the "Sonatina," the melody of which is shown below. What chord structure might apply? Indicate below the staff.

Sonatina

Wolfgang Amadeus Mozart

Is the mood light or heavy? Explain.

IV. The first two phrases of the spiritual "Go Down, Moses" begin as follows:

What is the key?

What is the harmonic pattern?

Notate chords for autoharp accompaniment.

On the staff provided below, write a simple harmony part (below the melody) for a two-part arrangement. Try playing it.

V. Construct a melodic phrase consisting only of chord notes to conclude the phrase shown.

Key of C:

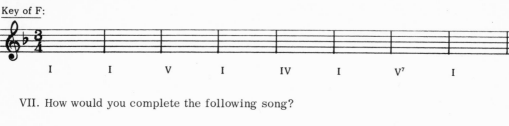

VI. Construct a melody including some passing notes (notes connecting chord notes). Begin and end on the key note.

Key of F:

VII. How would you complete the following song?

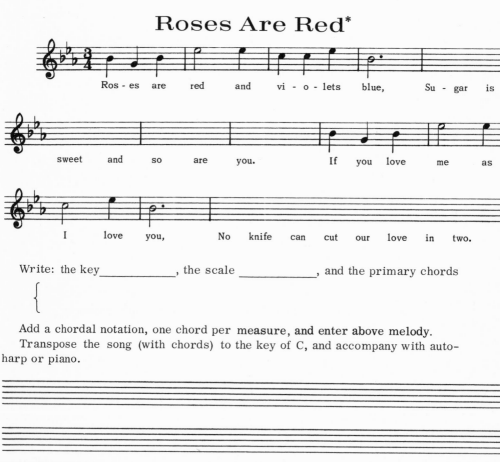

Roses Are Red*

Ros - es are red and vi - o - lets blue, Su - gar is

sweet and so are you. If you love me as

I love you, No knife can cut our love in two.

Write: the key_____, the scale _____, and the primary chords

Add a chordal notation, one chord per measure, and enter above melody.
Transpose the song (with chords) to the key of C, and accompany with auto-harp or piano.

*From Singing and Rhyming of "Our Singing World Series," published by Ginn and Co., owners of the copyright. Used with permission.

VIII. The following song is found in a Grade Three text. How would you complete it?

One, Two, Three, O'Leary*

One,   two,   three O'- Lear - y,   four,   five,   six,   O'- Lear - y,

sev'n,   eight,   nine,   O'- Lear - y,   Ten,   O'- Lear- y   Post - man

Write the key _____, the scale _____, and the primary chords

Add a chordal notation, one or two per measure, and enter above melody.
Under the staff above, write an appropriate rhythm part.
What type of rhythm instrument would be most appropriate? Why?

Add a descant part to the ending—last two measures.

IX. On the staves provided below, write four different but complete pentatonic melodies, with or without bar lines.

X. Compose a set of words to suit the following pentatonic melody and enter below the staff:

Using autoharp or piano, test by ear the chords which seem most appropriate, and enter results above the staff (See also p. 309.)

Write a simpler "patterned" part under the melody notes. (See pp. 315-316).

Is there any advantage in the ability to write melodies or parts of this kind when learning to play the songflute, tonette, flutophone, or recorder? Explain.

XI. Compose a pentatonic melody for the text provided:

Slum - ber now, my darl - ing one; Rest, for now the day is done;

Moth - er sings a lul - la - by; Hush, my darl - ing, do not cry.

Compose a minor melody (key of E$_m$) using the same text, (a) without a harmonic pattern:

and (b) with the following harmonic pattern:

I$_m$ I$_m$ IV$_m$ I$_m$ V^7 V^7 I$_m$ I$_m$ V^7 I$_m$

I$_m$ I$_m$ IV$_m$ V^7 V^7 I$_m$ IV$_m$ V^7 V^7 I$_m$

XII.

The Moon Ship*

From the Japanese

In the o - cean of the sky, Borne on ris - ing waves of cloud, The

moon-ship goes a - glid - ing by Through a for - est of stars.

*From <u>Singing and Rhyming</u> of "Our Singing World Series," published by Ginn and Co., owners of the copyright. Used with permission.

What scale is implied for the melody shown above?

Transpose to the key of G (melody only):

Play the melody on recorder or melody bells.

XIII. Set the following poem to an appropriate melody:

Come sun, come sun, dry up all the rain,
Pitter, patter, pitter, patter,
On my window pane.
It drives me crazy,
Although there is no pain,
Come sun, come sun, dry up all the rain.
Words by Stuart Slind, age 9

XIV.

Frog Went Courtin'

Traditional

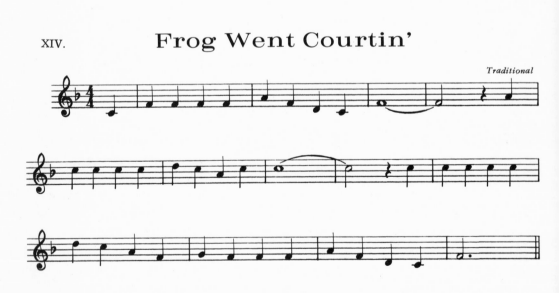

A frog went courtin' he did ride, uh, huh,
A frog went courtin' he did ride, uh, huh,
A frog went courtin' he did ride,
A sword and pistol by his side, uh, huh.

Miss Mousie she came tripping down, uh, huh,
Miss Mousie she came tripping down, uh, huh,
Miss Mousie she came tripping down
In a brand new hat and her Sunday gown, uh, huh.

What scale sounds are used for the melody above?

With two autoharps experiment with a combination of I and VI_m, and II_m and V^7 for accompaniment. Enter results (notation above the melody).

Is it possible to add a free or improvised songbell part along with the melody? If so, what sounds might you use?

12
EVALUATION AND
TESTING–CONCLUSION

In this text, the authors have envisaged a broad-based, multisensory approach to music learning and teaching. The central purpose has been to involve pupils with sound, whether the pupils were skilled or unskilled, talented or untalented. This embraces three aspects of music learning: appreciating, doing, knowing (literature, skills, literacy*).

Evidence of this involvement is reflected in different ways: in the frequency and variety of questions asked by pupils following interesting musical experiences, in the demands made for recess or after-school practice opportunities on instrumental aids such as the autoharp, songbells, etc., in the interest shown in planning and participating in school performing groups and concerts, and in many other ways.

All such learning should be encouraged and carefully noted, and should be included in report-card ratings. Where formal tests or examinations are given they should include aspects of this broad-based involvement as well. To single out any one skill for testing purposes at the expense of other relevant abilities is not a reliable measure of musical growth.

First, such a test is often discriminatory. Pupils tested on a skill in which they have been specially trained outside the classroom (private piano lessons, for example) will normally rank higher than those who have not had this opportunity. Second, if the teaching is as broad-based as has been suggested, the test will not do justice to what has been taught. Finally, such a test, accepted as conclusive, is an inadequate measure of all-round growth in musicianship, or of interest and attitude.

The best tests are representative of the total program, and are of one of the following types:

1. The teacher prepares a test so that each aspect is fairly evenly represented. For example, one third of the test may be devoted to theoretical aspects, a third to skill improvement, and the other third to literature and appreciation.

---

*See Part II, Introduction.

2. As above, but with the addition of a fourth area representing native ability, interest, or specialized training. A progress chart, kept for each pupil, may be constructed and used in the following manner:

Name	Theory	Skill Voc./Inst.		Literature	Ability and Training	Total
	25	25		25	25	100
Jim Brown	22 or A-	7 D	10 B	25 A	18 B-	88 B+
Mary Smith						

3. Dykema and Cundiff* suggest a more comprehensive procedure under the following headings:

Singing.
Listening.
Rhythmic.
Creative.
Theory.
Instrumental.
Home and social activities.

Each is marked on a numerical scale such as: 5 for excellent, 4 for very good, 3 for average, 2 for below average, and 1 for poor. By averaging the total marks for each area, the total for the term may be indicated.

Whatever the system used, the objectives should be clear: (a) to improve upon teaching procedures, and (b) to ensure maximum growth in ability, interest, and participation.

In conclusion, it must be re-emphasized that music is more a feeling than an intellectual state. The momentary completeness or fullness of a genuine musical experience is itself sufficient, and often impossible of testing. The final good is essentially enjoyment nurtured by ability, activity, and understanding.

---

*Peter W. Dykema and Hannah M. Cundiff, School Music Handbook (Boston: C. C. Birchard and Co., MCMLV), pp. 295-296.

APPENDIX A
PLAYING THE RECORDER-
TYPE FLUTES

The wooden, end-blown recorder flute was popular in the Gothic, Renaissance, and Baroque periods (A.D. 1200-1700). Many music educators today are enthusiastic about its classroom use in bringing experiences in playing music to all children.

The recorder flute offers many advantages: It is capable of beautiful, expressive tone. It is easily played. It is inexpensive.* It provides tonal experiences upon which good ear-recognition and music reading can be based. It provides refreshing variety in the music program.** Recorder playing can be continued throughout life, and is satisfying to the trained musician as well as to the occasional player.

Various plastic adaptations of the end-blown flute (not true recorders) are also available under such trade names as "Song Flute," "Tonette," "Flutophone," "Symphonette," etc. The cost is about $1.00, but tone quality and range are usually sacrificed. The fingering is easier, however.

The following procedures apply to either instrument (recorder or plastic flute), with exceptions noted. The emphasis is once again upon music rather than music notation, i.e., "sound before sight." Children should explore and discover musical sound by means of this instrument, and not become too involved in fingering problems.

1. Introduce recorder playing by having children hold the flute in the <u>left</u> hand, covering the top hole with the index finger and the underside hole with the thumb, in a "pinch" position.

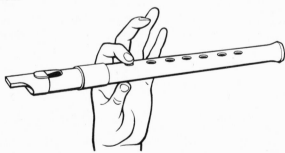

---

*The Japanese export a highly satisfactory plastic recorder, the "Aulos," which costs $2.00 and which excels in quality and utility many $5.00 wooden recorders. One supply $ Empire Music Company. See fn., p. 10.

**It is educationally most important that flute playing become a <u>supplement</u> to the music of listening, singing, moving, and playing of other instruments. and <u>not a substitute</u> for th music activities.

2. Have children experiment in playing as softly as possible without the tone faltering, and as fully as possible without the tone "fracturing." The recorder must be played between these extremes.

3. Have children play familiar <u>fundamental natural rhythms</u>, such as those below, by thinking the word <u>toot</u> or the softer sound <u>dood</u>.

| Walk | walk | walk | walk | run - run- run - run | run - run | run - run |

doo   doo   doo   dood   doo doo doo doo doo doo doo dood

Skip - ty skip - ty skip - ty skip - ty slo - ow   slo - ow

doo do doo do doo do doo do doo ood   doo ood

Then have the children play <u>phrase rhythms</u> involving several kinds of movement:

> Walk walk   walk walk Skip-ty walk   slo-ow
>
> Walk run-run walk run-run run-run run-run slo-ow

Write these phrase rhythms for the children to read and play.

Have child or teacher originate a phrase rhythm by stepping, clapping, or playing; the class plays back the rhythm they heard on this one pitch, and someone comes to the visual rhythm board (see pp. 10, 11) or to the chalkboard and shows the way he believes the notation should appear, e.g.:

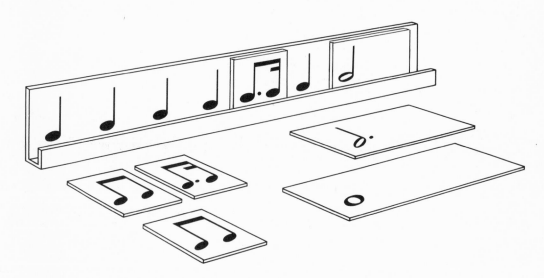

4. Add the middle finger, left hand, over the next-to-top hole and have children listen to the resulting change of pitch, then sing showing the relative pitch levels with hand contouring (see p. 30). Here again, the teacher or a child may improvise rhythm phrases as above, but involving two pitches, and the class or

individual children try to reproduce what they heard on their own flutes, by their voices, or in notation:

5. Add the ring finger, left hand, over the next hole and play three-note patterns with the three finger-positions thus far introduced. Have them notice how this newest tone begins to emerge as "home base" or sound 1. Play "Hot Cross Buns," or other simple three-note tunes. Improvise little rhythm phrases using these three sounds as above. Play the following four tunes on the flute with autoharp or piano chording. Alternate playing with singing the tunes by scale numbers, by letter names, and by rhythm movement, and encourage original words by the children:

Tunes to play, using:

Example 1:
Marchlike

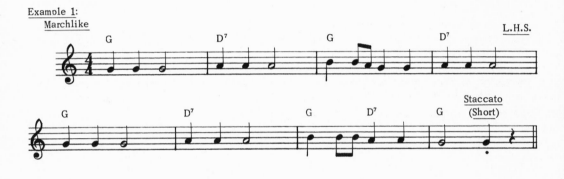

Example 2:
Smoothly

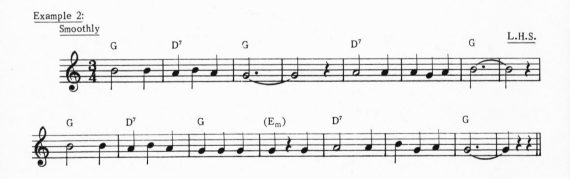

Example 3:
Brightly

Example 4: *

6. Play sounds 1, 2, 3, 4 (by lifting the index finger from the top hole) and 5 (by lifting the thumb from its hole, so that all finger holes are open).

Note: If using plastic flutes this fingering will be correct. If using authentic recorder flutes, sounds 4 and 5 will be sharp in pitch. To correct this follow the fingering in step 6, above, but as sounds 4 and 5 are played, cover the next-to-top finger hole with the middle finger. Help children to listen, and to recognize the need for "shading" these two fingerings to bring them into pitch. (See chart p. 336.)

7. Play by ear, by number notation, by staff notation, the familiar five-note melodies of Chapter 2, pp. 42, 45, 47-49.

8. Help the children to identify these five tones as G, A, B, C, D.

9. To play "Hot Cross Buns" in a new key, let A be sound 3 and play 3 2 1 -. The new sound 1 will be made by adding the right-hand index finger (the little finger of the left hand is not used to cover a hole).

Note: If using the recorder this new sound 1 (F) will be sharp in pitch. To bring it into true pitch see chart:

---

*Help children to understand new rhythms as modifications of the fundamental natural movements they already know. Thus:

New rhythm:

Familiar rhythm:

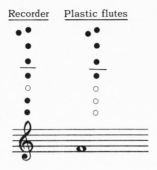

Recorder   Plastic flutes

By using number notation, can you play the four three-note melodies given in step 5, above, using these new sounds 1 (F), 2 (G), and 3 (A)?

10. Continue down the flute using E as sound 3 and play "Hot Cross Buns" in this key (key of C). Notice you must blow more softly to produce these lowest of sounds.

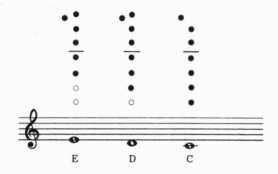

E   D   C

11. In this key of C, play the five-note songs as in step 7. Remember the "shaded" fingering for sound 4 (F) when using the recorder.

12. Play "The First Noel" in the key of C. (Remember the "shaded" fingerings for both F, sound 4, and C, high 1, if playing the recorder):

Play in 3s:

‖: (3 2)| 1 (1̲ 2) (3 4)| 5 - (6 7)| 1̲ 7 6 | 5 -
(6 7)| 1̲ 7   6 | 5 6 7 | 1̲ 5 4 | 3 -:‖
(3 2)| 1 (1̲ 2) (3 4)| 5 - (1̲ 7)| 6 - 6 | 5 -
| 1̲ 7   6 | 5 6 7 | 1̲ 5 4 | 3 - ‖

Note: Repeat the two enclosed ‖:   :‖ phrases.

13. It is feasible to play flutes in the keys of C, G, and F in elementary classrooms.* As we played in these keys on the keyboard we found G and F scales required which black keys? (See pp. 41, 43.)

---

*For more advanced recorder playing in other keys, consult a method book such as: Allen L. Richardson, One and All (New York: M. Witmark and Sons, 1960); Mario Duschenes, Method for Recorder (New York: Associated Music Publishers, Inc., 1957, and Toronto: BMI Canada Ltd., 1957); Hugh Orr, Basic Recorder Technique (New York: Associated Music Publishers, Inc., 1961, and Toronto: BMI Canada Ltd., 1961); Frank Gamble and Campbell Trowsdale, Fundamentals of Recorder Playing (New Westminster, B.C.: Empire Music Publishers, Ltd., 1964).

<u>Note</u>: To play the flute in the key of G we must sharp F, sound 7, any time it occurs. To sharp F, open the F-hole and cover the hole below it. (Recorders will need all three of the bottom holes closed.)

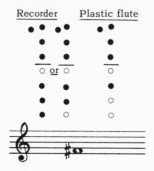

<u>Note</u>: To play in the key of F we must flat B (sound 4) any time it occurs. To play B♭ , make the fingering for B (pinch position) and add the ring finger of the left hand. (Recorders may need one more finger to bring B♭ into tune—the index finger of the right hand.)

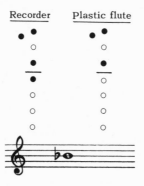

CHART OF BASIC FINGERINGS FOR PLASTIC FLUTE AND RECORDER

<u>Where recorder differs, its separate fingering is shown</u>. Elsewhere the fin-<u>gerings are identical</u>. (For F♯ and B♭, see above.)

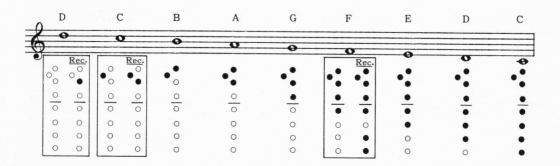

Study the plastic-flute fingerings to see the acoustical principle involved and then note the additional "shadings" required by the authentic recorder flute.

Tunes to play, using:

Chorale

L.H.S.

Au Clair de la Lune

J.B. Lully (17th century)

Au clair de la lu - ne, mon a - mi Pier - rot

Pre - tez - moi ta plu - me, pour é - crire un môt,

Ma chan - delle est mor - te, Je n'ai plus de feu,

ouv - re - moi ta por - te, Pour l'a - mour de Dieu.

From this text or other song texts find similar songs to play.

Tunes to play, using:

Symphony Theme

(from Symphony No. 9)

Ludwig van Beethoven

Flutes 1

Flutes 2

Note: It has become customary to insert the sharp sign (♯) at the beginning of each staff as shown above. Notice that it is placed on the top line and not on the F-space below. This practice is, of course, followed for other key signatures as well.

Norwegian Dance

Traditional

Flutes 1

Flutes 2

The Postman*

Jaan Märtin

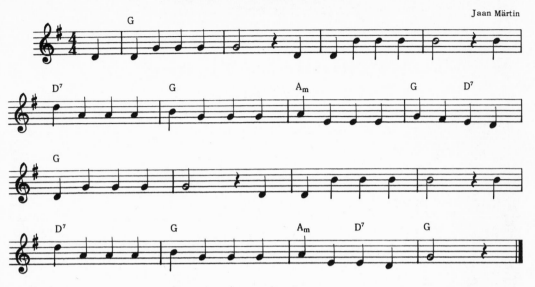

Evening Song

Baltic Folk Song

Sun, sun, gold-en sun at eve-ning, Long days ev'-ry one will wel-come,
Build, build, fires that leap and flick-er, Bright fires crown-ing lof-ty moun-tains,

Come, dance turn the wheel in greet-ing, Bid cold dark-ness to be gone,
Light, light, ra-diance for all peo-ple, Life, warmth, for all liv-ing things.

There's Music in the Air

George Root

There's mu-sic in the air,_____

When the in-fant morn is nigh, And faint its blush is

---

*Reproduced from <u>Recorder Tutor</u>, Book I, by Jaan Märtin, by permission of the publishers, Boosey and Hawkes (Canada) Ltd.

seen, _____ on the bright and laugh - ing sky.

Many - a harp's ec - stat - ic sound thrills us with a joy pro-found,

While we list en - chant - ed there to the mu - sic in the air.

Theme from Eine Kleine Nachtmusik

Wolfgang Amadeus Mozart
Adapted

<u>Related listening</u>: Eine Kleine Nachtmusik by Mozart.

Playing the Flute and Drum*

Henry Berg
Portuguese Folk Tune

Too, too, too, I play up - on my brand new flute,
Ev' - ry time I press an - oth - er fin - ger down,

When I play my tongue helps me to too, too, toot.
Then the tune will change and make an - oth - er sound.

---

*From <u>Singing and Rhyming</u> of "Our Singing World Series," published by Ginn and Co., owners of the copyright. Used with permission.

340

Song of Spring

French Folk Tune

Mary and Martha

Traditional Tune
Arranged by Allen Clingman

Ma - ry and - a Mar - tha's just gone 'long,

Ma - ry and - a Mar - tha's just gone 'long,

Ma - ry and - a Mar - tha's just gone 'long to

ring these charm - ing bells; cry - ing

Free grace ___ un - dy - ing love, Free grace ___ un -
Way o ___ ver Jor - dan, Lord, Way o ___ ver

dy - ing love, Free grace ___ un - dy - ing love, To
Jor - dan, Lord, Way o ___ ver Jor - dan, Lord, To

ring those charm - ing bells. ___ Oh! bells. ___
ring those charm - ing

Our Boys Will Shine

Traditional

Our boys will shine to-night, Our boys will shine,

Autoharp G   C   G

Piano

Piano chording: Once fluency is gained in moving from one chord to another, a more rhythmic accompaniment can be attempted (see pp. 187–189).

Assignment: Transpose the lowest note in the piano accompaniment one octave higher, and play the piano part with recorders. (See also version p. 346.)

O Come, O Come, Emmanuel

Traditional

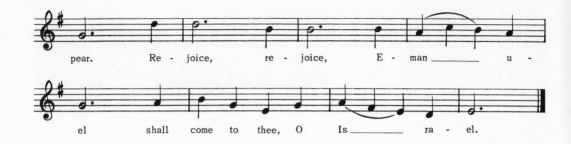

pear. Re - joice, re - joice, E - man_____ u -

el shall come to thee, O Is_____ ra - el.

Good King Wenceslas

Old English Carol

A Christmas Round*

Words: Don Malin
French Tune

The Christ - mas mes - sage comes a - gain to

peo - ple far and near, No - el! No -

el Good - will through all the year.

*From Don Malin, <u>The Symbols of Christmas</u> (1962), p. 21. (A 20-minute Christmas pageant for narrator, simple instruments and voices. Suitable for elementary grades.) Used by permission of the copyright owner, B. F. Wood Music Co., Inc., New York City.

Tallis' Canon

Thomas Tallis (1520-1585)

Ac - cept our praise, O God this night, For all the bles - sings of the light, Keep me, O keep me, King of Kings, be - neath Thy own Al - might - y wings.

Related Listening: Fantasia on a Theme by Tallis by Ralph Vaughan Williams.

Winds Are Blowing

Kunz

Winds are blow - ing, blow - ing, blow - ing,

. Winds are blow - ing,

Win - ter winds are blow - ing so strong.

blow - ing, blow - ing so strong.

Winds are blow - ing

Winds are blow - ing, blow - ing, blow - ing

blow - ing,   blow - ing,   blow - ing so   strong.

Win - ter   winds   are   blow - ing so   strong.

Tunes to play, using:

Our Boys Will Shine

Our boys   will   shine to- night,   Our boys   will   shine.

(Or, try a chord rhythm of:
Our boys   will   shine)

etc.

They'll shine   in   glo - ry bright   All   down   the   line.

Our boys   will   shine to- night,   Our boys   will   shine.   When the

sun goes down and the moon goes up, Our boys will shine.

For this next selection, divide the class into four groups. While one group plays or sings the familiar melody, the three other groups play the chord notes as shown:

Little Brown Jug

Traditional

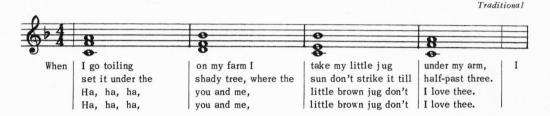

When	I go toiling	on my farm I	take my little jug	under my arm,	I
	set it under the	shady tree, where the	sun don't strike it till	half-past three.	
	Ha, ha, ha,	you and me,	little brown jug don't	I love thee.	
	Ha, ha, ha,	you and me,	little brown jug don't	I love thee.	

Angels We Have Heard on High

Words: Bishop Chadwick
Traditional French Melody

An gels we have heard on high, Sweet-ly sing-ing oer the plain;
And the moun-tains in re-ply Ech-o still their joy-ous strains.

Glo _____ ri - a,

in ex - cel - sis De - o, Glo _____

_____ ri - a, in ex - cel - sis De - o.

Tunes to play, using:

347

Kookaburra

Australian Round

Have three friends join you in this next round ("circle canon"). All four learn the first part. Then play, each beginning when the part ahead has progressed one measure into the tune.

Canon in Four Parts

L.H.S.

The Reaper's Song*

(Excerpt)

Schumann
Album for the Young, Op. 68

*Book 3, Birchard Music Series. Copyright © 1962, Summy-Birchard Co., Evanston, Ill. Used by permission.

Pine Tree Song

Traditional

Lit-tle pines up - on the hill, Sleep-ing in the moon-light still,

Are you dream-ing now of me? Bloomed in - to a Christ-mas tree.

Koom Bah Yah

(Draw Nearer, Lord)

African Folk Song

Some-one's cry-ing / sigh-ing / pray-ing / sing-ing Lord, Koom bah yah, Some-one's

cry-ing / sigh-ing / pray-ing / sing-ing Lord, Koom bah yah, Some-one's cry-ing / sigh-ing / pray-ing / sing-ing Lord,

Koom bah yah, Oh Lord, Koom bah yah.

Susan Blue*

Francis Hilliard

*From <u>Singing Every Day</u> of "Our Singing World Series," published by Ginn and Co., owners of the copyright. Used with permission.

Ballad

Old English Tune

Hark to Me

Haydn

Lament

Traditional French

Slow

You will need soprano recorders to play the following seven selections. Note the fingering for the additional notes:

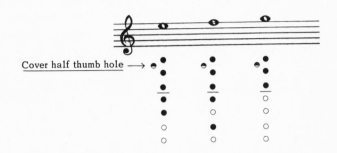

Cover half thumb hole →

Waltz

L.H.S.

Lullaby

J. Whittaker

Andante

Allegro

Ifca's Castle*

(Four-part round)

Czechoslovakian Folk Song

① A - bove the val - ley fresh and green, ② A fig - ure head is plain - ly seen; ③ A hu - ya, hu - ya, hu - ya - ya, tumb - ling goes the riv - er, ④ A hu - ya, hu - ya, hu - ya - ya, tumb - ling goes the riv - er.

Hey, Ho! to the Greenwood

William Byrd (1538-1623)

1. Hey ho, 2. To the green - wood now let us 3. go, sing heave and ho; and there shall we

*See p. 213 for chant arrangement of this song.

find both buck and doe, sing heave – and hoe, The hart and

hind and the lit - tle pret - ty roe, sing heave - and ho.

The Bell Round*

Old English

The Merry Hunter

Wilhelm Bender

*For plastic flutes transpose to key of F.

Triple Flute*

(From the opera Euridice)

Jacopo Peri (1561-1633)

Recorder 1

Recorder 2

Recorder 3

Elizabethan England was noted for two popular musical activities: the singing of madrigals and the playing of recorders. The madrigal was a composition for mixed voices, often in six or eight parts; many instrumental compositions were arranged for a mixed group (family) of recorders. These were in different sizes ranging from the bass recorder to the sopranino. The ranges of the four most common are shown below:

Soprano
(Sounding one octave higher)

Alto

Tenor

Bass recorder
(Written one octave lower)

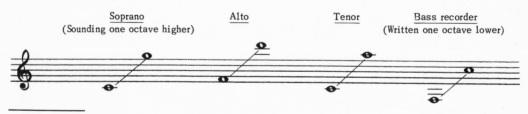

*For plastic flutes, transpose to key of F.

354

The portion of an Elizabethan madrigal by Thomas Weelkes arranged for three recorders is shown below:

Since Robin Hood

Thomas Weelkes (1575-1623)

Since Rob - in Hood, Maid Ma - ri - an and Lit - tle John are gone - a The hob - by horse was quite for - got when Kempe did dance a - lone - a.

Composers of the seventeenth and eighteenth centuries were also prolific in writing for the recorder family. The trio for two soprano recorders and one alto recorder, shown below, was written by an English composer.

Second Terzetto*

(First section)

James Hook (1746-1827)

Soprano recorder 1

Soprano recorder 2

Alto recorder

*James Hook, James Hook Second Terzetto, pub. by Schott and Co. Ltd., London. (Available through Associated Music Publishers, N.Y. and Leeds Music Ltd., Toronto, Canada.)

Many of Bach's chorales may be transcribed for the recorder family as in the following sample:

Chorale 146

Johann Sebastian Bach

The chorale shown next is written in the style of Bach.

Chorale

L.H.S.

The recorder sound is effective also in the modern idiom. Many contemporary composers are showing renewed interest in writing for this family. The following selection is representative of this newer literature.

Dark Interlude*

Allen E. Clingman

*From unpublished manuscript. Used by permission of Allen E. Clingman.

The playing of recorders in the four- to six-voice parts opens up a new area of musical interest for family and social groups. In one year a novice playing several times a week may acquire sufficient reading skills and playing technique to make acceptable music. At such a stage the person is ready to explore the entire treasury of delightful and worthwhile music written for these instruments over the past five centuries. Age-group divisions and other divisive factors are forgotten as players lose themselves in group playing. In the pleasant process, deeper insight, involvement, and interest in music generally is stimulated.

As Socrates concluded in The Republic, "For what should be the end of music if not the love of beauty?" even so might we desire this wide sharing of music experience to be our goal in bringing music to children.

APPENDIX B
TUNING THE AUTOHARP

One of the most frequent complaints to be heard about this instrument is that it gets out of tune very easily. This presents a problem to elementary teachers who do not have a background in music, and yet are responsible for the music in their classrooms. Since they, in many instances, do not feel competent to correct the situation, the instrument is not used.

There are several methods of tuning an autoharp—none of them infallible, each of them having something to be said in its favor.

METHOD 1

Tune with the piano. This means that the piano should be in tune, at least with itself. In many instances older upright pianos used in classrooms have old, "tired" strings, so the piano technician tunes the instrument flat, in order not to break any of the rather brittle strings. If the autoharp is to be used in conjunction with such a piano, it should be tuned to <u>that</u> <u>instrument</u>.

Several general rules might be listed:

    1.   Start with the long, heavy strings.

    2.   Locate the tuning post (left edge), and pick out the correct wire, lining it up with the corresponding piano key.

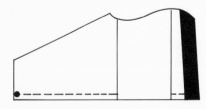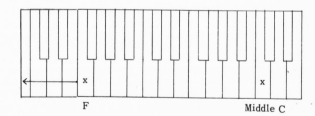

As you match strings and keys, double check by plucking the octaves occasionally, to see if they are in tune.

Caution: It is best to locate the string pitch from the tuning post on the left side of the instrument, rather than depending upon the scale shown under the strings on the right side.

Caution: In using the tuner, "nudge" it rather than turn it abruptly. To raise the pitch (make it higher, sharpen it), move the tuner clockwise (ex. 1). To lower the pitch, ease the tuner counterclockwise (ex. 2).

(ex. 1)   (ex. 2)

No matter which direction, turn very slowly, strumming the string all the time.

METHOD 2

The chordal approach. This method may be used as a check on the "tune-with-the-piano" method, or if no piano is available.

PROCEDURE A. Press the "G" chord bar down firmly. Run the pick slowly along the right-hand end of the instrument. Pay particular attention to the clearly audible sounds. After a tentative strum the length of the instrument (see diagram), start with the heavy strings and repeat this procedure, stopping, or momentarily hesitating, for the audible strings. Try to determine which of the notes are "out," and whether they are too high (turn counter-clockwise) or too low (turn clockwise). See examples above for clarification. After you have tuned up the G chord, proceed to the other chords—D^7, A_m, etc.

PROCEDURE B. This method may be used by persons having a theoretical and aural knowledge of chords. Start with the low string (F) and tune all notes in the F-chord. See diagram below. Check your work by strumming the octaves occasionally.

Always remember to exert very slight pressure on the tuner.

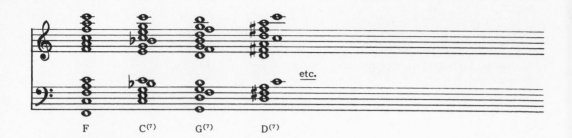

INDEXES

Index of Subjects

Accompaniment, chordal, 167
Art songs, 278
Autoharp, V^7-chord introduced, 62–63
  importance of, 186
  I-chord introduced, 57–58
  transposition, 97
  tuning of, 362

Bells, *see* Pitch instruments

Canons, 234
'Cello, tuning of, 208
Chants, on chord tones, 66–67, 86–91, 106
  single pitch, 28–29
  writing of, 211
Chord accompaniments, autoharp, 186
  finding, 205
  piano, 181, 187–190
Chord endings, 209
Chord instruments, autoharp, 57–59
  bells, chord use of, 59–61, 66
  piano, 65–66, 71–72, 187–190
  recorders, chord use of, 342–343, 346–347
  voices, chord use of, 60–61, 66–67
Chord roots, 91–93, 135, 207, 254
Chords, autoharp, 57–59, 62–65, 97
  V^7-chord, 62–67, 72–73
  IV-chord, 85–87, 89–90
  importance of, 136
  inversions, 89–91
  minor, 105–106, 136
  for minor keys, 138
  I-chord, 57–60, 71
  piano, 65–68, 187–190
  primary chords, 135; importance of, 136
  transposing, 65–66, 97

Chords (Continued)
  what is meant by, 135
    See also Vocal chording
Classroom instruments, 267
Combination songs, 234
Combined vocal-instrumental arrangement, 268
Creating music, from text, 301
  using major scale, 297
  using minor scale, 305
  using other scales, 317
  using pentatonic scale, 307

Descants, 227

Folk dances, 180
Form (design), 140
  minuet and trio, 141
  overture, 142
  rondo, 141
  sonata, 142
  suite, 142
  three-part or ternary, 141
  two-part or binary, 140
  variation, 141
Fugue, 240

Guitar, tuning of, 165, 208

Half-steps, and whole steps, 36–40
  See also Scales
Harmonic patterns, 139
Home study, 140

Instrumental music, 286
Instruments, *see* Chord instruments; Pitch instruments; Rhythm instruments
Intervals, 217

Water glasses, 27
  numbering of, 30–32
  tuning of, 30–32

Word rhythms, 5–9, 12–17, 20–22, 178–179

Index of Songs and Instrumental Selections

Index of Recorded Songs

Index of Related Recordings